Twentieth-Century Polish Avant-Garde Drama

Plays, Scenarios, Critical Documents

Other translations by Daniel Gerould

"The Madman and the Nun" and Other Plays, by Stanisław Ignacy
Witkiewicz, translated and edited by Daniel Gerould and
C. S. Durer.

Avant-Garde Drama between World Wars, edited by Bernard F.
Dukore and Daniel Gerould.

"Tropical Madness": Four Plays, by Stanisław Witkiewicz, translated by Daniel and Eleanor Gerould, with a life of Witkiewicz by Daniel Gerould.

Twentieth-Century Polish Avant-Garde Drama

Plays, Scenarios, Critical Documents

by Stanisław Ignacy Witkiewicz
Andrzej Trzebiński
Konstanty Ildefons Gałczyński
Jerzy Afanasjew
Sławomir Mrożek
Tadeusz Różewicz

Edited, with an Introduction,
by DANIEL GEROULD

Translated by Daniel Gerould
in collaboration with Eleanor Gerould

Cornell University Press   ITHACA AND LONDON

First published 1977 by Cornell University Press.
Published in the United Kingdom by Cornell University Press Ltd.,
2–4 Brook Street, London W1Y 1AA.

International Standard Book Number 0–8014–0952–7
Library of Congress Catalog Card Number 76–13659
Printed in the United States of America by Vail-Ballou Press, Inc.
Librarians: Library of Congress cataloging information appears on the last page of the book.

Acknowledgments

Many friends and colleagues in Poland and America have contributed to the creation of this anthology. Grateful acknowledgment is made to the following for invaluable help and advice in preparing the translations and in obtaining the texts and the photographs: Zofia Trzebińska-Nagabczyńska, Janusz Degler, Lech Sokół, Anna Micińska, Zbigniew Lewicki, Halina and Zdzisław Najder, Grzegorz Sinko, Janusz Warmiński, Bernard Dukore, Stuart Baker, Michael Earley, Rosemary Weiss, Mel Gordon, Louis Iribarne, Donald Doub, and Harold Segel.

For permission to translate *Birth Rate*, the three plays from *Joy in Earnest*, and the selection from *Good Evening, Clown* and "The World Is Not Such a Bad Place . . . ," I am grateful to the Polish Authors' Agency, Warsaw.

Earlier versions of some of the translations have previously been published, as cited in the notes to the plays. Parts of the Introduction appeared in "The Non-Euclidean Drama: Modern Theatre in Poland," *First Stage*, IV (Winter, 1965–1966); "From a Theatre Journal, Paris, Prague, Warsaw: European Influences," in *Break Out*, ed. James Schevill (Chicago: Swallow, 1973); "Bim-Bom and the Afanasjew Family Circus," *The Drama Review*, XVIII, No. 1 (March, 1974); "The Magus Tadeusz Miciński," *yale/theatre*, VII, No. 1 (Fall, 1975); "Tadeusz Różewicz and *Birth Rate*: Playwriting as Collage," *Performing Arts Journal*, I, No. 2 (Fall, 1976).

DANIEL GEROULD

Graduate Center
City University of New York

Contents

8

V   Tadeusz Różewicz

Illustrations

A Note on the Pronunciation of Polish Names

Almost all Polish words and names are stressed on the next to last syllable. The barred l—ł—is pronounced like English w; w like v; c like ts. Cz is like the English ch, whereas sz is like sh. Rz and ż are both the equivalent of the z in the word "azure"; ń is close to gn in the French word "montagne"; ó is pronounced like oo in the English word "root."

The names of the authors in this collection would appear as follows in rough phonetic transcription.

Stanisław Ignacy Witkiewicz	Stan-is-waff Ig-nat-sy Vitkyea-vich
Witkacy	Vit-kat-sy
Andrzej Trzebiński	And-zhea Tshea-bin-ski
Konstanty Ildefons Gałczyński	Kon-stan-ty Il-de-fons Gow-chin-ski
Jerzy Afanasjew	Ye-zhy A-fan-as-yeff
Sławomir Mrożek	Swa-vo-mir Mro-zhek
Tadeusz Różewicz	Ta-dey-oosh Roo-zhey-vich

Twentieth-Century Polish Avant-Garde Drama

Plays, Scenarios, Critical Documents

Introduction: The Avant-Garde In Twentieth-Century Polish Drama

by DANIEL GEROULD

The writers in this collection of modern Polish drama—Witkiewicz, Trzebiński, Gałczyński, Afanasjew, Mrożek, and Różewicz—belong to an unusual tradition of avant-garde theatre quite unlike that of Russia or Western Europe. Although it has always reacted strongly to both East and West and drawn eclectically upon other literatures for new ideas, the Polish tradition of experimental drama is essentially a lonely, private, prophetic one. Initially out of step with its own age, the Polish avant-garde has been a displaced drama waiting for its time to come and for its theatre to be created. It has had to live in the future and feed upon itself.

Centered upon the exceptional individual—intellectual or artist—and his relation to the masses, the Polish avant-garde is pre-eminently a theatre of revolution, social upheaval, and historical crisis, conceived in metaphoric terms. Parables of power that transcend bourgeois theatre and its limited forms, these Polish plays treat of ultimate things—the fate of civilization and the end of the world—seen with amused detachment as tragedies to make you laugh.

Drawing inspiration from Shakespeare, the Polish avant-garde playwrights take Hamlet and his dilemma vis-à-vis the rotten state of Denmark as an accurate model of the world. The figures of the Prince, Fortinbras, and the Gravediggers recur in a hallucinatory drama where the play within the play is constantly being staged according to shifting aesthetic principles. In this world of images and shadows, of the dreamlike and the make-believe, "reality"—theatrical, social, political—is always falling to pieces, and then somehow, out of the ruins, newer realities are constantly being rebuilt. The Polish avant-garde dramatist presides over a graveyard of the past; he jests with fragments of old theatre and culture, bones of dead worlds, out of which he fashions previously nonexistent shapes and images. The destruction of old forms is his province; he carries on a long dialogue with illusion.

Two Traditions of the Avant-Garde

If by "avant-garde" we mean primarily the latest artistic movements that flourish in reaction to those that precede them, then the avant-garde is in constant danger of becoming arrière-garde. Often nothing seems more dated than yesterday's radical experiments, and the history of modern drama is full of obsolete isms and the plays produced according to their formulas. Poland, which until 1918 had not existed as an independent country for almost a century and a half, was at a particular disadvantage in trying to follow the changing fashions in modern dramatic innovation, for it had become isolated and turned inward by its own national obsessions and struggles. Because of Poland's peculiar historical and geographic position, symbolism, expressionism, futurism, dadaism, and surrealism arrived as imports from Russia or Western Europe; and the major twentieth-century avant-garde movements which did take root on Polish soil were derivative and already behind the times before they could hope to establish themselves in the theatre, always the artistic medium most resistant to change.

As a latecomer to nationhood, long subject to more powerful neighbors, Poland could never expect to catch up in being contemporary—or so it seemed—in a field as dominated by successive trends as modern international drama. In the first half of the twentieth century, Moscow, Paris, and Berlin were the important theatrical capitals, not Warsaw. Despite some extremely interesting experiments in staging, chiefly by Leon Schiller, Poland contributed nothing of influence or lasting importance to the various movements and schools that shaped the history of European avant-garde drama from the turn of the century to the end of World War II. As a glance at any of the books on world drama written before the 1960's will show, Poland seemed doomed to be a provincial backwater in the realm of theatre.[1]

In the second half of the twentieth century, however, Polish drama suddenly emerged as one of the leaders of the European avant-garde, and, most surprisingly, Poland has produced a number of major modern playwrights, several important theorists, and a sizable body of plays that are entering the international repertory. Although no one at the time, even in Poland, could perceive the true significance, the roots of the modern Polish avant-garde lie in the period between the wars when its founders were first active. The blossoming of Polish drama in the 1960's is less a new departure than the final fruition of a continuing tradition of isolated, eccentric artists standing outside the mainstream, for whom recognition comes only much later when history and its reverberations in drama have caught up with their highly personal yet prophetic vision of what the theatre can become.

For, if we do not simply equate the new with the currently fashionable, there is another avant-garde that exists outside its own time and apart from contemporary movements of rebellion. Too aware of the impermanence of the present to attempt to build any lasting drama of innovation on the merely up-to-date, the solitary artists of the prophetic, private avant-garde keep their eyes turned inward, imagining what is not yet to be.

Poland has an enduring avant-garde tradition of this second sort, subtly attuned to viewing the new from the perspective of the still newer and to considering the contemporary as already part of the past. The aim of this collection of plays is to trace the development of this line of twentieth-century Polish avant-garde drama from its beginnings with the establishment of Poland as a new nation in 1918 until this tradition itself becomes

---

[1] *The Oxford Companion to the Theatre* (London) is a case in point. The first edition (1951) omits Poland entirely. The second (1957) includes nineteenth-century Polish drama in a supplement. The third (1967) has an article on Poland that mentions Witkacy and Mrożek. The paperback *Concise Oxford Companion* (1972) has a separate entry on Witkacy.

the mainstream in the 1960's. The plays and scenarios chosen represent crucial stages in the history of this evolution. It is significant that none of them was performed until 1955 or after; appropriately, the last work, Różewicz's *Birth Rate*, defies categorization even as drama and is called by the author "The Biography of a Play for the Theatre."

Nearly all the Polish avant-garde plays from the period between the wars were either not performed at all during those years or presented only once or twice under the least favorable conditions. It has taken three or four decades for these plays to find their place in the theatre, and in some cases the process of discovery is still going on today. Such a time gap appears characteristic of Polish avant-garde drama in the twentieth century as well as of its antecedents in the nineteenth century; in fact, being outside its own time and yet ahead of the times is perhaps the most salient trait of this tradition. But even though cut off from its own contemporaneous historical and theatrical reality, the Polish avant-garde has found nourishment in itself, looking back on its own past as well as forward to a day when its dreams could be realized. Polish drama has carried on a long dialogue with itself, with its own ghosts. In this collection the dialogue among the playwrights is represented both by the plays themselves and by the critical documents in which the writers question the premises of existing theatre and cast doubt on the nature of accepted dramatic illusion. Plays and critical documents are closely related; for Gałczyński, playwriting constitutes a critique of the theatre itself, whereas for Różewicz, prolonged reflection on the problems of drama becomes a potential play.

During the long years of partition at the hands of its neighbors, Poland was forced to live on its own illusions; then in 1918 the Polish state reappeared as an independent country for a brief interlude, only to disappear again twenty-one years later. Caught between East and West, between the vicissitudes of existence and nonexistence as a nation, between the constant extinction of an old world and the coming into being of a new one, Poland has quite naturally produced dramatists with a pronounced feeling for the transitory. Faced with the permanence of impermanence, the Polish avant-garde has been concerned, not with immediate novelty, but rather with the process of change itself, with the historical discarding of old forms of society, thought, and art. The peculiar vision of the Polish avant-garde lies in its perception of itself and the world of theatre in relation to time; afflicted with "anachronitis" (acute awareness of chronological displacement), it takes as its province the transitional dilemmas of catching up with history or of being overtaken by it. Waiting for the moment to come, for history to enter onstage, for the curtain to go up or down, the Polish avant-garde playwright dramatizes his apocalyptic expectations in the metaphoric language of a brightly colored theatrical show.

Dissatisfied with all existing dramatic art, the Polish writer in the second avant-garde tradition maintains a high degree of irony and detachment, instead of displaying the usual partisanship characteristic of literary and theatrical movements. He is not part of anything. For this reason, the development of the Polish avant-garde can best be viewed as involving a number of individuals, not a series of movements and schools.

Created largely by poets and painters, the Polish avant-garde in theatre is a drama of metaphor and visual image and at the same time a drama about the nature of such metaphors and images. A victim of its own national and patriotic myths about the future, the Polish dramatic imagination has, from the nineteenth century on, dealt both with the fabrication of illusion and with the converse process of demythification. Reckoning with a multiplicity of illusions and the speed with which one order—theatrical or political—succeeds the other, the Polish avant-garde strives to transcend and transform existing dramatic reality and define it anew. Not content simply to expand the possibilities of the stage, it asks the theatre to do what seems impossible according to inveterate notions of the feasible.

It is little wonder that the Polish avant-garde, operating from such principles of fantasy and imagination, is flamboyantly theatricalist, full of a bewildering profusion of images, often in open defiance of what appear to be the essential conventions

and limitations of the stage. These traits are part of a highly id-
iosyncratic Polish heritage coming from the romantic poets in
the nineteenth century and their successors at the turn of the
century.

The Nineteenth-Century Heritage

Adam   Mickiewicz   (1798–1855),   Zygmunt   Krasiński
(1812–1859), and Juliusz Słowacki (1809–1849), Poland's three
great romantic poet-playwrights, who wrote all their important
plays while in exile in Western Europe, established the pattern
for subsequent Polish avant-garde drama by transcending their
immediate surroundings and ignoring contemporary conditions of the theatre and possibilities of performance. None of
their plays reached the stage in their authors' lifetimes, and it
was only in the twentieth century, with the advent of modern
scenic techniques, that their masterpieces—*Forefathers' Eve*
(1832), *The Un-Divine Comedy (1835)*, and *Kordian (1834)*—have
come into their own in the theatre. By not writing for the
confines of the stage in their own times, Mickiewicz, Krasiński,
and Słowacki helped to expand the dimensions of drama in a
later age.

These poet-playwrights created a prophetic tradition that
was nearly a century ahead of its time in its vast, open forms
and in its use of theatrical metaphor and image in dealing with
political crisis and social revolution. The romantic plays ad-
vocate a revolt against the order of the world and portray an
anguished hero fighting alone in answer to the cry for freedom
and vengeance coming from the country's grave.

The nineteenth-century Polish poet-playwrights, however,
saw an exclusively national mission for drama; the artist's role
was to be that of a charismatic leader and priest of the nation
who must sacrifice himself for the country. The sole theme of
poetry and drama envisaged by the romantics was Poland itself
and its sufferings, to which the individual must be dedicated.
Thus, these visionary dramas remain closely tied to Polish history and call for action to fulfill the national destiny; in other
words, the characters act out the old myths and illusions of past
greatness. Only in Krasiński's *The Un-Divine Comedy* is this strug-

gle transferred to the universal plane of an anonymous class revolution somewhere in an unspecified European setting.[2]

Two Turn-of-the-Century Forerunners

The more immediate precursors of twentieth-century Polish avant-garde drama are the turn-of-the-century writers Stanisław Wyspiański and Tadeusz Miciński, who had direct influence on Witkiewicz and provide a clear link between the romantic poet-playwrights and the postwar generations.

Poet and painter, book illustrator, and maker of stained-glass windows, Stanisław Wyspiański (1869–1907) was also a playwright, stage designer, director, and complete man of the theatre. He made his own costumes, properties, and sets and worked on staging his own and others' plays, including a condensed version of Mickiewicz's *Forefathers' Eve*. In a tragically short life (he died of syphilis at thirty-eight), [3] Wyspiański wrote seventeen original plays, as well as an adaptation of Corneille's *Le Cid*. His two large cycles of dramas, one on classical Greek mythological subjects and the other on national issues and the destiny of the country, re-examined the problems already taken up by the romantics and continued the dialogue which they had begun.

Wyspiański's plays live less in their literary texts, which serve rather as scenarios, than in their theatrical potential for realization on the stage. Taking both ancient Greek theatre and Wagner as his models and making use of folk arts, village customs, popular ceremonies, processions, and Christmas puppet shows, Wyspiański created a total theatre that is all image—shapes, colors, sounds—and that succeeds in uniting many different arts. In these ways Wyspiański fulfilled Mickiewicz's ideas about an ideal theatre of the future that would be native in inspiration and messianic in goals—a sanctuary for celebrating the heroic deeds and spirit of the nation.

[2] For a more extensive treatment of Mickiewicz, Krasiński, and Słowacki, see Harold B. Segel, introduction to *Polish Romantic Drama: Three Plays in English Translation* (Ithaca, N.Y., 1977).

[3] Aniela Łempicka, "Stanisław Wyspiański," in *Literatura okresu Młodej Polski*, ed. Kazimierz Wyka, Artur Hutnikiewicz, and Mirosława Puchalska, II (Warsaw, 1967), 59–60.

In three of his most important plays, all dealing with national subjects—*The Wedding* (1901), *The Deliverance* (1903), and *Acropolis* (1904)—Wyspiański not only made extremely original experiments with theatrical form, utilizing all the scenic means at his disposal, but he also explored and exploded the very nature of illusion. Writing in Gordon Craig's *The Mask* in 1908, the twenty-one-year-old Leon Schiller observed, "Wyspiański crushes and destroys the theatricality of the old theatre" so as to create out of the pieces "the elements of a new theatricality." [4] In his dismantling of old forms Wyspiański prepares the way for the twentieth-century Polish avant-garde.

The Wedding takes place in a small Polish village near Cracow. After the ceremony celebrating the marriage between a peasant girl and a poet from the gentry, designed to unite the two social classes and restore national purpose, the guests—intellectuals and artists as well as peasants—spend the evening talking and drinking. Couples dance in and out like puppets to hypnotic music constantly played offstage. As the night grows longer and deeper, shadowy figures out of dreams appear, and ghosts and spirits from Poland's mighty legends and glorious past mingle with the living until the human characters become engulfed in a phantasmagoric atmosphere halfway between waking and sleeping. The Bridegroom invites the Mulch (a protective covering for the rosebush in the garden) to join the party, and this sinister straw man functions as master of the eerie ceremonies.

Tension mounts as dry leaves fall from the trees and the excited guests imagine that they see signs in the sky of a great conflict to come. A boy is sent to fetch the mythic golden horn of a legendary hero which will give the call to heroic action. The entire group, armed with swords and scythes, looks down the road, waiting for the cock to crow and the great message to arrive. At last they hear the sound of hooves; the boy returns, but he has lost the horn on the way and forgotten the message.

As the blue light of dawn fills the room, the blear-eyed guests, weary of waiting for the revelation that never comes, begin a slow somnambulistic dance to creaking music played on

[4] Leon Schiller, "The New Theatre in Poland: Stanisław Wyspiański," *The Mask*, II (1908–1910; rpt. New York, 1966), 71.

a broken fiddle by the Mulch, who has quietly taken the unused weapons out of their hands. As the play ends, the whole puppet show, as though in a deep sleep, goes through its motions to the trancelike steps of an enchanted dance. The Mulch dance, powerful theatrical image of stagnation, hopelessness, and the vicious circle of death-in-life, is taken up again and again by Polish playwrights and novelists from Witkiewicz and Gombrowicz to Mrożek; it appears in Tadeusz Konwicki's film *Salto* and in Andrzej Wajda's cinema version of the novel *Ashes and Diamonds* (the dreamlike dance in Fellini's *Amarcord* amid the dead leaves is identical in spirit).[5]

The Deliverance is an even more unconventional and daring departure from the normal canons of stagecraft of that time and a prime instance of Polish drama's running dialogue with its own "theatrical" past. The action of *The Deliverance* takes place on the bare stage of a contemporary Cracow theatre, where Conrad, the hero of Mickiewicz's *Forefathers' Eve* (which Wyspiański had staged shortly before), comes to lead the nation by means of strength to deliverance. Conrad first addresses the theatre workmen, then the stage manager and actors who are putting on their costumes, but, he declares, there will be no play today, only a *commedia* improvisation through which the hero hopes to awaken the nation from its paralyzing dreams of the past.

Inspired by Shakespeare's *Hamlet* and its play within a play, Wyspiański creates a remarkable example of "theatre in the theatre" in which the entire drama evolves from Conrad's confrontation with the actors and then with seventeen masks or voices who challenge him and his mission. Conrad is determined to destroy the old theatre and from its ruins build a new one that will represent the nation. He tells the actors, who are ever ready to play their old roles and assume the familiar poses, that he comes to act not "with gesture" but "with deed." Conrad is Hamlet staging "The Mousetrap" to catch the conscience of the Claudius-nation.[6] At the end of the inner play,

---

[5] Stefania Skwarczyńska, " 'Chocholi taniec' jako obraz-symbol w literaturze ostatniego trzydziestolecia," *Dialog*, No. 8 (1969), 99–119.

[6] Schiller, p. 19. In 1905 Wyspiański published his *Study on Hamlet* (Cracow), containing his ideas on staging Shakespeare's play.

when the stage lights go out, the actors come out of their parts and leave, but Conrad persists in his role forever. *The Deliverance* ends with a prophecy in the final stage directions; "TEAR OFF YOUR BONDS" are the final words.

In taking as his hero the principal character of the Polish romantic theatre, Wyspiański attacks the past tradition of Polish history and theatre; instead of action, it has offered only words, bad habits, and a deep sleep. In Wyspiański's reinterpretation, Conrad is conscious and critical of his own role in the national drama in which he has appeared. He must fight with phantoms, with the passivity of society, with himself and his inner doubts—represented by the masks—that assail him. *The Deliverance* is an ironic reckoning with the voices of the past, a settling of accounts with romantic drama, a debate of Polish drama with its own theatrical history. The tradition of "settling accounts" persists. Demythification, dialogue with the past, extensive use of allusion and quotation—all have become characteristic techniques of the modern Polish avant-garde writers, which they turn back on Wyspiański himself.

Acropolis, in contrast, is a hymn of resurrection, a fantastic dream vision in which different epochs and civilizations mingle and specters of the past—both real and imaginary people, all long since dead—come to life in a miraculous allegorical triumph of light over darkness. The play takes place in the cathedral and royal castle of Wawel in Cracow, where Polish kings, heroes, and poets (including Mickiewicz and Słowacki) are buried; all the characters are figures from the sculpture, wall hangings, and architecture who awaken and begin to live again and act out their stories at midnight before Easter, the time of Christ's resurrection.

In Part I, in the interior of the cathedral, as all the bells and clocks resound, the statues of figures from Polish history and legend step down from their niches and enact the joys of human life. By poetic analogy, in Wyspiański's play the royal castle on the hill overlooking the city of Cracow is associated with the Acropolis on the holy hill of Athens. In Part II, which takes place on the walls of the castle—now likened to Troy—as the river Vistula becomes identified with the Scamander, heroes

from Homer come forth from the cathedral tapestries that portray scenes in the *Iliad,* while in Part III, wall hangings depicting scenes in the Book of Genesis become animated and
present a theatrical performance of the story of Jacob and Esau
on the steps of the cathedral. The final part of *Acropolis* sees all
the characters return to their statue alcoves and tapestries at
dawn as a triumphal Christ rides into the cathedral in a golden
chariot drawn by four chargers; identified with both Apollo
and Dionysius, He brings a miraculous victory of life over
death.[7]

Mixing past, present, and future historical eras, juxtaposing
and contrasting different civilizations (Greek, Judaic, Christian), and bringing to life works of art in the form of animated
statues and tapestries that re-enact their stories are among
Wyspiański's most brilliant inventions, which expanded the
conception of theatrical form and opened the way for later
Polish avant-garde dramaturgy. It is hardly surprising that subsequent Polish playwrights and theatre artists in their continuing dialogue with the past return again and again to *The Wedding, The Deliverance,* and *Acropolis,* using them as sources of
allusion and quotation and as points of departure for new
works and reinterpretations. Although at the beginning of his
career Wyspiański created a sensation in the theatrical world
and his early plays were frequently staged, *Acropolis* and many
of his later works were not performed in the dramatist's lifetime. Wyspiański's radical ideas about a new stagecraft were too
advanced for the period and became accepted only in the
1920's.

Tadeusz Miciński (1873–1918), mystical sage, student of the
occult, symbolist poet, and self-appointed madman ("In choos-
ing my destiny I have chosen madness," he declares in one of
his poems), had even more grandiose notions of the function of
theatre than Wyspiański and called for drama to return to its
origins in religious mysteries. Instead of a place of entertainment, Miciński demanded that the theatre be a temple like an-

---

[7] See the detailed discussion of *Acropolis* by Tymon Terlecki in "Polish Historical Antecedents of Surrealism in Drama," *Zagadnienia Rodzajów Literackich,*
XVI, No. 2 (1973), 38–46.

cient Greek theatre, Indian and Persian theatre, and medieval
Christian theatre. A Pan-Slavist himself, Miciński attempted to
write mystery plays that would unite East and West, reconcile
Catholicism and the Orthodox faith, and bring Poland and
Russia together on the basis of gnostic mysticism and esoteric
philosophy. His dramas, which were not understood by his
contemporaries or judged possible to stage, have the weird
structure of a dream, combining by a process of mysterious association the most disparate elements of the everyday, the historical, and the fantastic.[8]

In *The Prince Potemkin* (1906), the 1905 revolt of the Russian
sailors aboard the battleship *Potemkin* in the Black Sea is por-
trayed partly realistically and partly symbolically as a vast struggle between Lucifer and God for the soul of Russia. With the
ship's furnaces blazing like the fires of hell, revolution is seen as
an expression of the Promethean urge that unleashes all the
forces of the natural elements. Both good and evil, Christ and
Satan are necessary for the spiritual development of mankind,
and only a messianic future can resolve the contradictory duali-
ties in the universe.

A vast historical drama about tenth-century Byzantium, *In the
Shades of the Golden Palace, or Basilissa Teophano* (1909) mixes
Christianity, pagan religions and mythologies, and occult sciences. About the meeting of East and West and the beginning
of the decline of the Byzantine Empire and the growing
strength of Russia, *Basilissa Teophano* presents both a spiritual
drama of moral struggle and a savage battle for political power
among characters of superhuman dimensions in opulent settings, full of rich colors, shapes, and lights. The heroine, the
demonic Teophano, daughter of a barmaid, is driven by the
will to power and becomes the wife of two successive emperors,
Romanus and Nicephorus, and the mistress of a third, Zimis-
ces. Written in lush ornate prose of complex rhythms and em-
bellished with an elegant, sensuous vocabulary (including
words from Latin, Greek, Sanskrit, Church Slavonic, Old Ice-
landic, and Old German), *Basilissa Teophano* contains dazzling

---

[8] Tadeusz Kudliński, *Rodowód Polskiego Teatru* (Warsaw, 1972), pp. 300–305.
See also Bożena Danek-Wojnowska and Jan Kłossowicz, "Tadeusz Miciński,"
in *Literatura okresu Młodej Polski*, II, 269–297.

descriptions of palaces and churches in Constantinople and evokes an unearthly atmosphere.

The drama itself is rich and many layered; its fractured reality creates a new kind of dramatic structure based on the inscrutable. Among the huge cast are murderers, monks, and motley crowds. Characters with bizarre names make mysterious and unexplained appearances; their actions are extravagant and without discernible logic; and their language is murky and grandiloquent. Miciński creates an exotic world that operates according to its own internal and self-consistent laws, setting it completely apart from traditional drama of plot and psychology. In this macabre universe, ruled by sex and philosophy, the sun is an object of worship, and a severed head may suddenly appear in the sky.

Sinister imagery and spectacular stage effects characterize Miciński's dramaturgy, as the following excerpt from *Basilissa Teophano* indicates.

NICEPHORUS: You hum the song of the abyss in the caves of your magnetic mountain—reveal to me the secret of your thought.

TEOPHANO: At the feet of my thought hurl down the world with its churches and God.

(*Nicephorus pulls out his sword and—as though resolving on final things—he slits Teophano's robe from the neck to the feet with the tip of his sword. Teophano stands naked, reddening in the dawn like a ripe pomegranate.*)

TEOPHANO: I am the living Sun! I listen and ever more profoundly hear! I am the Chaste Aphrodite, but will you have the knowledge of a Magus—and the ardor of an Eleusian shepherd?

(*Nicephorus seizes her hair and looks through it at the sun.*)

Whereas Wyspiański was recognized by his contemporaries as an important theatrical innovator and at least saw a number of his own plays performed with great success, Miciński, considered obscure and unstageable, is among those writers who have had to wait generations for acceptance. *The Prince Potemkin* was first performed by Leon Schiller in 1925; *Basilissa Teophano* did not reach the stage until 1967. Many of Miciński's other plays still remain unpublished and unknown. A short one-act play that did appear in a small literary magazine in the 1930's gives a further idea of Miciński's farsighted dramaturgy. *The Ballad of the Seven Sleeping Brothers in China* (1905–1910?) takes place in an insane asylum where the madmen, inspired by a new inmate who is a poet, decide to put on a performance in which they will play all the parts.[9] Eventually the poet is confined in a strait jacket for disturbing peace and quiet in the madhouse, but gets an arm free and hangs himself by his suspenders, as the other madmen hide under their blankets and the glow of a dying meteor illumines the sky.

Miciński pursued his studies in Berlin and Leipzig as well as in Cracow and lived for several years in Spain, but from the turn of the century he spent much of his time in Zakopane in the Tatra Mountains, where he frequented the Witkiewicz household and was known as Poet, Master, and Magus. During World War I, Miciński fought in Russia as an officer in the Polish corps. There he became acquainted with the work of Tairov, which he much admired, but he violently opposed Stanislavsky and his system, since for the Magus the actor should have a primarily liturgical function. Miciński died in Russia under mysterious circumstances. According to one account, on his way back to Poland he was mistaken for a similarly bald-headed tsarist general and killed by an angry mob. According to his younger friend and admirer Witkiewicz, Miciński made "the tiger jump into the future of a new drama," [10] but it was the pupil, not the master, who realized the Magus' visionary program for the theatre on a broad scale and became the main force in twentieth-century Polish theatre.

Witkacy

Stanisław Ignacy Witkiewicz (1885–1939)—or Witkacy, the pen name by which he is commonly known—is the classic instance of the avant-garde playwright who stands apart from his own age and is discovered and becomes influential several decades later. Although his career as a playwright exactly spans the interwar years (he wrote his first major play in 1918, his last in 1939), Witkacy did not emerge as the dominating figure in the modern Polish theatre until the post-1956 period. Many of his plays received their premieres in the 1960's and 1970's;

[9] Teresa Wróblewska, "Post Scriptum do 'Romansu siedmiu braci śpiących w Chinach,' " *Dialog,* No. 4 (1968), 151–152.
[10] Stanisław Ignacy Witkiewicz, *Nowe Formy w Malarstwie i inne pisma estetyczne* (Warsaw, 1959), p. 320.

some are still waiting to be performed, while the manuscripts of others, presumed lost, continue to be unearthed. Witkiewicz's "new life" in the theatre twenty years after his death and the resurgence of his plays half a century after their composition is a notable phenomenon that confirms Witkacy's position as the central figure in the history of the Polish avant-garde.

For all his isolation, frustration, and lack of success in his own lifetime, Witkacy always sensed that his time would someday come, and he never lost faith in his vision of a theatre that could not yet exist. He kept on writing plays until a few months before his death. On one of the portraits he painted in the later 1920's, Witkacy put the following inscription: "For the posthumous exhibition in 1955." In this as in his other prophecies Witkacy was remarkably accurate. In 1956 there was a performance of one of his plays for the first time in twenty years, and the triumphal process of Witkacy's rediscovery as writer and artist was under way, leading ultimately to world-wide fame and status as a modern classic.

It appears that from the beginning Witkacy was cast by fate as a writer who chooses not to be contemporary in his lifetime in order to become contemporary after his death. Defying what was for the sake of what might be, he embodies the lonely Polish avant-garde, part of no movement and forming no school, but passing on a tradition of intense individuality and noncapitulation that would serve as the model of the lonely artist-hero for subsequent generations, much as the romantic poet had for a previous century.

Son of the famous-painter and critic Stanisław Witkiewicz, young Witkacy was educated entirely at home by private tutors and encouraged to develop his precocious artistic talents in many directions. By the age of five the boy was painting and playing the piano; at seven he wrote his first plays, under the influence of Shakespeare, Gogol, Maeterlinck, and the Polish comic dramatist Aleksander Fredro, and printed them himself on his own hand press.

His father—humanitarian socialist, follower of Nietzsche's belief in man's need to transcend himself, and severe critic of oppressive regimes and systems, particularly the tsarist rule in Russia and its rigid hold on Poland—was a vehement opponent of all formal schooling on the grounds that it produced only mediocrity and conformity. Accordingly, the creative upbringing which the older Witkiewicz gave his son was highly unconventional, designed to make the child into an exceptional individual and unique artist; yet at the same time it embraced a program of moral instruction imbued with radical democratic principles and the utmost contempt for all existing social orders and the privileges of birth or wealth which they conferred on the lucky few. Young Witkacy was to become, according to his father's plan, one of the elite of the spirit, far above the masses, but dedicated to bringing them good by means of his art—a characteristic Polish idea of the nineteenth century. In letter after letter of idealistic exhortation (over five hundred letters in the period 1900 to 1915), the older Witkiewicz urged his son to go far beyond himself and the age in which he lived.

Look at what is and what will be for a long time yet as at a transitory moment of development. Live in the future. Constantly stand on the heights from where you can see the farthest horizons and spread the wings of thought and action for flight beyond them.

Of the social systems that exist today nothing can remain. These so-called social edifices are nothing but disreputable, foul-smelling hovels, full of dark underground passageways in which crime hatches. We must fight against this with total intransigence.[11]

While seeking to inspire his son with his own enthusiasm for the Revolution of 1905 (which he hoped would destroy Russian autocracy) and urging him to take "the most radical position, that is, the position for absolute social justice," [12] the father grew angry and alarmed when Witkacy—now a twenty-year-old painter—decided that he wanted to enroll in the Cracow Academy of Fine Arts, and study alongside his peers.

If I have understood correctly what you write, you intend to sign up with the herd of piglets led by Professor Stanisławski. Since I cannot regard you as just any mediocre dullard of a boy . . . I thus cannot let you go ahead with this plan without a strenuous effort to convince you that the plan is a bad one.

[11] Stanisław Witkiewicz, *Listy do syna*, ed. Bożena Danek-Wojnowska and Anna Micińska (Warsaw, 1969), pp. 144, 241.
[12] *Ibid.*, p. 241.

You, who as a child were independent and proud of your self-sufficient spirit, now would have to hand over responsibility for your own
art to some lousy school—yes, all schools are lousy!

You won't go along with the herd, you will go alone! [13]

Go alone Witkacy certainly did throughout his entire career,
without the aid of any schooling, mentors, or allies. Few modern artists have been more isolated or deprived of support and
understanding. Given his father's mandates for greatness, it is
not surprising that the young Witkacy felt alienated from the
world around him, yet uneasy that he was not a part of it and
unsure of his supposed superiority to other people. Convinced
of the necessity and inevitability of profound social changes in
the name of justice and equality, Witkacy could not help fear-
ing that revolution and the triumph of the masses would bring
an end to human individuality, which he had been taught to
hold as the highest value.

Witkiewicz the elder had told the boy that he could be whatever he wanted—as long as it was morally uplifting and in accord with his father's ideals. In effect, it had been announced
to the world that he was to be a "serious" artist, but the imma-
ture Witkacy—although desperately anxious to be an artist, or
anything else clearly defined—could not take himself or his art
entirely seriously. His lack of systematic education and speciali-
zation in any field, his haphazard reading in all subjects from
Persian history to modern physics, and his exposure to the new
arts and sciences of the period through contact with the leading
practitioners in Poland, all served to make Witkacy a delicate
register of future trends, a seismographic sensibility. The
actress Helena Modjeska was his godmother; the author
Sholem Asch, the anthropologist Bronisław Malinowski, the
composer Karol Szymanowski, and the pianist Arthur Rubin-
stein were among his friends.

But whereas his gifted contemporaries were already known
for their important accomplishments, Witkacy at twenty-five
was uncertain of his direction in life, without a profession and
materially dependent on his parents, exclusively preoccupied

[13] *Ibid.*, pp. 276, 277, 280.

with who and what he was. Unable to grow up and accept reality, on the verge of madness and despair, the young man underwent a severe mental crisis and was analyzed by a Freudian psychiatrist. After the suicide of his fiancée, for which he felt responsible, Witkacy went with Malinowski on the anthropologist's first expedition to Australia, developing a lasting interest in non-Western cultures and primitive art and religion. Upon the outbreak of World War I, Witkacy volunteered to go to Russia, where he served as a tsarist officer, thereby gravely wounding his father, who still cherished hopes of freedom and justice. Later, during the February revolution, Witkacy was elected political commissar by his regiment and somehow managed to survive all the dramatic and violent events which he witnessed as a spectator.

Upon his return to newly created Poland in 1918, the thirty-three-year-old adventurer and dilettante discovered his calling. Free at last from his devoted, dominating father, who had died in 1915, Witkacy was now to fulfill his father's dream and become an artist. He invented a new identity for himself, regularly signing his most original paintings "Witkacy," to distinguish himself from his father, while continuing to use Witkiewicz for his commercial work. At the same time that he earned his living as a portrait painter, Witkacy wrote prolifically in many genres: plays, criticism, aesthetics, philosophy, and, a little later, fiction and sociology.

An artist who worked at white heat in a state of intoxication and madness, Witkacy painted thousands of portraits and sometimes wrote as many as ten plays in one year. From 1918 to 1926 he produced some forty works for the stage, many unpublished and unperformed in his lifetime, of which fifteen are now lost or preserved only in fragments.

It was his experiences in Russia that brought Witkacy back to playwriting. He had not written plays for twenty-five years, since he first created a child's theatre at the end of the nineteenth century, and he now voiced strong dislike for the stage of the time. However, what Witkacy saw in the streets of Saint Petersburg and the galleries of Moscow led him to drama and to formulating his ideas about theatre. Even before the war, in discussions with his father, a proponent of positivism, Witkacy had started to create a contrary theory of nonrealistic art, which be called Pure Form. In Moscow, together with his friend Miciński, he saw Picasso's works for the first time in the Shchukin Gallery—an event as decisive for the playwright's perception of the world as the Russian Revolution itself. By applying to theatre Picasso's principles of the deformation of reality, Witkacy sought to liberate drama from story-telling and psychology and to give it the formal possibilities of modern art and music. We do not know for certain whether Witkacy saw any of the new experiments in the Russian theatre by Vakhtangov, Tairov, and Meyerhold, but the essay "A Few Words about the Role of the Actor in the Theatre of Pure Form" (1921) shows that he reacted strongly against Stanislavsky and worked out postulates opposing the tenets of realistic acting.

In his critical writing Witkacy argues that theatre arose from the great religious mysteries, but that since the Renaissance European drama has lost its true sacred function and has moved in the false direction of imitating real life. Because religion in the old sense no longer exists, Witkacy sees the only hope for the art of the theatre in the individual and his feelings of the strangeness of existence: what the playwright called "the immediately given loneliness of the individual in the Universe—from which metaphysical fear arises." [14] But because of the growing mechanization of life, producing an anthill civilization, the modern artist—in order to recapture the strangeness—is driven further and further into chaos and madness. Theatre, the most backward of the arts, still has before it a period of feverish experimentation and insanity, its one last moment of greatness before being extinguished forever. For Witkacy, theatre more than any other art could by total fusion of auditory and visual elements of a highly sensuous nature make immediate contact with the spectator's sense of metaphysical wonder. In this way, the philosopher-painter-playwright hoped to create "a pure theatre devoid of lies, strange as a dream, in which, through arbitrary incidents totally unmotivated by life— incidents which are ridiculous, sublime, or monstrous—the

[14] Stanisław Ignacy Witkiewicz, *Pożegnanie jesieni* (Warsaw, 1927), p. 259.

soft, unchanging light of the Eternal Mystery of Existence descends upon us, radiating from Infinity." [15]

In his conception of a magical theatre that would present the mystery of existence directly, Witkacy followed his master Miciński; in striving to join the various arts into one sensuous whole, he subscribed to Wyspiański's idea of total theatre. In fact, in the essay "Pure Form in the Theatre of Wyspiański," Witkacy acknowledges that the example of the author of *The Deliverance,* along with that of Miciński, has been essential to him.[16] But although he found the visual, theatrical aspects of Wyspiański's plays compelling, the younger writer judged their literary quality to be inferior and their poetic pronouncements on national issues irrelevant. For Witkacy as theoretician of Pure Form, such messages were extraneous to drama, which should concern itself only with the composition of images, sounds, colors, and shapes in and of themselves.

Witkacy differs strikingly from his two precursors in dramaturgical style and world view. He is Poland's first important dramatist who is European first and Polish second. Whereas Wyspiański and Miciński are to a large extent cut off from the rest of the world by national themes and bardic language, Witkacy's concerns are universally intelligible and his characters and settings cosmopolitan. Thus, Witkacy's first contribution to the formation of a new avant-garde was to pull Polish drama out of its parochialism and give it an international dramatic idiom by denying an overriding national mission and suggesting an aesthetic one instead.

Undoubtedly, Witkacy's wide-ranging experiences in Australia and Russia as well as his omnivorous reading, penetrating intelligence, and vast intellectual curiosity gave him a perspective on civilization that none of his contemporaries possessed. As a genuine outsider, he was able to see much further and much more clearly. For just these reasons, Witkacy's work seemed, to all but a very few of his contemporaries, in-

[15] Stanisław Ignacy Witkiewicz, "Bliższe wyjaśnienia w kwestii czystej formy na scenie," in *Nowe Formy w Malarstwie: Szkice Estetyczne: Teatr* (Warsaw, 1974), p. 290.
[16] Stanisław Ignacy Witkiewicz, "Czysta forma w teatrze Wyspiańskiego," *Studio,* Nos. 10–12 (1937), 2–7.

comprehensible and marginal. The idea that such a playwright as Witkacy might become the most universal and important Polish artist of the entire period would have struck almost everyone then living as absolute madness. In fact, Witkacy himself was savagely ridiculed by the critics and treated as a madman. The following comments on *Tumor Brainiowicz,* his first play to reach the stage, indicate the degree of hostility that Witkacy constantly encountered.

It seems that we are watching and hearing the ravings of a syphilitic in the last stages of creeping paralysis. . . . Despite the relativity of our ideas about art, despite the experiences of history, which teaches restraint and cautious appraisal of transitional phenomena that at the beginning are embryonic and not fully formed—Witkiewicz's play is a total absurdity from which nothing can ever get a start. For it does not stand on any line of development. It is an unnatural clinical abortion.[17]

In addition to an international dramatic idiom, Witkacy's second legacy to a future Polish avant-garde was a mocking, ironic tone, which particularly disconcerted the critics of the time, but actually corresponded to the jarring postwar world and the sardonic mentality of the 1920's, evident in writers like Brecht and Mayakovsky. Previously the Polish poet-playwright had always been committed to noble ideals, and his language had been elevated. Even at their most grotesque, Wyspiański and Miciński are somber and serious. But Witkacy, starting with his childhood plays and parodies, showed a penchant for clowning and burlesque, and his mature art blends metaphysics with buffoonery, self-ridicule, and a flippant, offhand attitude of detachment that subverts the inflated rhetoric and aggrandizement of emotion characteristic of Polish drama until then.

Witkacy treats hallowed symbols with irreverence. He introduces the peasants from Wyspiański's *The Wedding* into *The Shoemakers* (1934) and has them bring the famous Mulch with them, but Witkacy's Shoemakers settle the peasant question quickly by beating the rustics and throwing them out the door. When the once prophetic Mulch removes his straw, he is re-

---

[17] Marian Szyjkowski, Polish critic and literary historian, quoted in Janusz Degler, *Witkacy w teatrze międzywojennym* (Warsaw, 1973), pp. 21–22.

vealed to be an ordinary Mulch-about-Town in a tuxedo, whose dance is the fashionable tango. In *The New Deliverance* (1920), Witkacy's hero Florestan Snakesnout has an ironic reckoning with past, present, and future as he is first psychically stripped of all his lies and illusions, then tortured on the floor by Six Thugs with pincers and blowtorch. The "deliverance" is indeed new and prophetic, going far beyond the question of Poland to that of the coming holocaust in Europe, as representatives of some yet unknown totalitarian mass movement dispassionately exterminate the cringing pseudo intellectual and bourgeois dilettante.

Although Witkacy makes extensive use of allusion and quotation, as had Wyspiański before him, the younger playwright extends his frame of reference so that, beyond a few gibes at his Polish predecessors, his main source of citation is Western literature in general, ranging from *Robinson Crusoe* and *Treasure Island* to his special favorites, Poe, Conrad, Strindberg, and Shakespeare.[18] Rather than parodying in a clear-cut or systematic fashion, Witkacy takes works by these and other authors as stimuli for the imagination and starting points for his own plays, combining in a highly personal manner fragments, characters, and pieces of plot of diverse origin and making them part of his own obsessive vision.

Characterized by grotesque humor, dreamlike illogicality, vivid color, and spectacular stage effects, Witkacy's theatre springs first of all from feelings of fear and loneliness in the face of an inexplicable universe, and next from the impingement of society on the individual as the concrete embodiment of the dilemma of the self confronted by all that is outside it. Thus Witkacian drama is both metaphysical and social, portraying what the playwright called "the experiences of a group of degenerate ex-people in the face of the growing mechanization of life."[19] The point of view in the plays is that of the class which is going under,—a fact which gives them a tragic

[18] See Lech Sokół, *Groteska w teatrze Stanisława Ignacego Witkiewicza* (Wrocław, 1973), pp. 106–110, 117–118, for extended treatment of Witkacy's use of other authors, especially Strindberg.

[19] Stanisław Ignacy Witkiewicz, "Wstęp teoretyczny," *Tumor Mózgowicz*, in *Dramaty*, I (Warsaw, 1972), 233.

resonance—but this social stratum, to which the author himself belongs, is seen as useless, treated mockingly, and speeded to its well-deserved catastrophe. The supreme value of art and the artist is to perceive for one last moment this ultimate futility. Accordingly, Witkacy's artist-heroes hasten to ignoble and ludicrous self-destruction.

Although his plays show certain affinities to both expressionism and surrealism in themes and techniques, Witkacy lacks the dogmatic and hopeful ideologies of the expressionists and surrealists and avoids their schematic action and dialogue. His "comedies with corpses" and "non-Euclidian dramas"—to use the playwright's own terms—remain unique in their urgently personal and constantly ironic vision of an insane world heading for disaster. The Polish critic Tadeusz Boy-Żeleński, who was virtually alone in his appreciation of Witkacy's genius in the interwar period, described his theatre as "metaphysical buffoonery and supercabaret presenting the sadness, boredom, and despair of modern civilization with a spasmodic laugh." [20]

The Anonymous Work; Four Acts of a Rather Nasty Nightmare, which represents Witkacy in this collection, is one of four prophetic political plays about future revolution (the others are *They* (1920), *Gyubal Wahazar* (1921), and *The Shoemakers*), none of which was published or performed in the author's lifetime. Of all Witkacy's plays, these were the farthest ahead of their times and did not become part of the new Polish theatre until the 1960's and 1970's.

Written in 1921, *The Anonymous Work* was published in Witkacy's collected plays in 1962 and performed for the first time in 1967, for the second in 1972. The play charts the disastrous course of violent social change as it tears down rational pretenses of self-interested control as well as publicly proclaimed but fraudulent ideologies; ultimately everything is swept aside by the irresistible and irreversible tide of destruction. Martin Esslin has observed, *"The Anonymous Work,* with prophetic power, predicts the course of revolutions which, started on the basis of ideology, always tend to be taken over by the brutal

---

[20] Tadeusz Boy-Żeleński, "Le Théâtre de Stanisław Ignacy Witkiewicz," *La Pologne Littéraire,* No. 18 (March 15, 1928), 1.

devotees of power for its own sake." [21] In a startling fashion, Witkacy continues the prophetic tradition of Polish romantic drama, but his forecasts are more sweeping and devastating. He is concerned, not with anything as narrow as the messianic dreams of Poland, but with the destiny of Europe and the collapse of Western civilization.

The Anonymous Work—and almost all of Witkacy's surviving dramas—come from the period immediately after 1918, when Poland's dreams of independence had suddenly been realized by the Treaty of Versailles. However, Witkacy was more impressed by the disintegration of an old empire which he had witnessed in Saint Petersburg than by the emergence of the new nation which he saw upon his return home. At the time of Poland's coming into existence the farsighted playwright perceives only the impermanence of what is and of what will be. For him the myth of Poland had been materialized and was found to be empty. In taking the long view of history, Witkacy set the pattern for the Polish avant-garde as a sensitive register of disintegrating old forms being overtaken by time.

Building *The Anonymous Work* out of these old forms in the shape of obsolescent characters and antiquated plot, the dramatist playfully toys with them until from beneath the surface dark forces erupt and supply totally new explosive content. Lopak, [22] gravedigger and leader of the mob in the black pointed caps, sounds the ominous note, heard at first only as a tremor in the earth, when he warns that the newly established government "won't last long" (Act IV)—which may be regarded as a proletarian paraphrase of the senior Witkiewicz's advice: "Look at what is and what will be for a long time yet as at a transitory moment of development."

In its four acts of "nasty nightmare," *The Anonymous Work* uncovers three layers of society, three political systems, and two revolutions. Initially presented as an ordered structure, the world of *The Anonymous Work* can be viewed vertically. On top is the ruling crew, highly colorful individuals with all the privi-

---

[21] Martin Esslin, "The Search for the Metaphysical Dimension in Drama," unpublished manuscript version of the introduction to Witkiewicz, *Tropical Madness* (New York, 1972).
[22] Girtak in the Polish text, suggesting low social origins.

leges, titles, and leisure to suffer over art and love. This *ancien
régime* is a world of operetta, picturesque in its tinsel costumes,
pageantry, and intrigue, complete with hidden letters, mysterious sums of money, concealed identities, and secrets of parent-
age.[23] Its colors are overbright, like those of a technicolor film
whose gaudy fraudulence strikes the eye.

The next stratum is the shadowy realm of Tzingar (alias
Baron de Buffadero), the pseudoreligious sect of Grizzloviks,
and their prophet and saint, Joachim Grizzelov, the fat old man
with the long white beard who never appears in the play.[24] In
the Grizzloviks, Witkacy explores the theocratic nature of modern totalitarian regimes. When the Grizzloviks seize the reins of
government, the essence of power remains the same, as
Tzingar explains. Despite all the revolutionary rhetoric, it is
only a fascist coup.

However, throughout the play the lowest segment of society,
the semiliterate gravediggers—Lopak and his companion, un-
dertakers of the past—have been excavating and undermining
the already tottering political structure and its degenerate offshoot, the Grizzlovik "revolution." Forces from underground
are coming to the surface. The old gravedigger is Prince Padoval's father, having actually topped the Princess in the cemetery
beside her husband's grave. Schemers like Tzingar, who aspire
to go high, end hanging from the lamppost. With the triumph
of the Lopakian rabble, who sweep all before them, Prince
Padoval, invigorated by awareness of his common blood, picks
up Lopak's black pointed cap which has fallen to the ground
and puts it on his own head. The brilliant, airy hues of the
early acts are overpowered by the stark colors of the prisoners'
uniforms—the blacks, yellows, and reds of servitude. All the
same, aristocratic parasites and bourgeois hangers-on will assume new roles within whatever society comes into being and
successfully adapt.

Only the bewildered painter Plasmonick—an unformed
plasma—is unable to find his place in a world where the past is

[23] Witkacy's interest in operetta as a form for dramatic parody had already
been expressed in *Panna Tutli-Putli,* an operetta libretto, which he wrote in
1920.
[24] Mieduwał in the Polish text, a name which sounds vaguely Russian and
perhaps is related to the Russian word for bear, *miedvied'.*

invalid, the present lacks all fixed principles, and the future remains unknown. For Witkacy as for Wyspiański, Shakespeare's *Hamlet* is a storehouse of images and a mirror for politics. In Witkacy's plays, the would-be artists, confronting a chaotic world, brood on suicide and their own helplessness. Then, most often, the strong man replaces the superfluous man; Fortinbras succeeds Hamlet. *The Anonymous Work* is a version of *Hamlet* in which the Gravediggers supplant the Prince.

Like all Witkacy's dramas, *The Anonymous Work* is also a play about creation and creators. Plasmonick is tormented by the dilemma of the modern artist in a society that no longer has any need or place for his anguish. Since the art of the past is useless, he can create only by destroying himself. Politics has begun to swallow art, the mass is aborbing the individual, and ethics will soon do away with metaphysics. Plasmonick's is a lonely, difficult art with which he must struggle; overwhelmed by doubts and lost in theories, he is finally unable to create at all. His fate is to become an artist kept by the state and to paint a pseudomodern portrait in socialist-realist style of the odious, benign Grizzelov.

Rather than live in such a society, Plasmonick deliberately chooses incarceration for life, declaring, "In our times there are only two places for metaphysical individuals: prison or the insane asylum." In a world of crumbling forms where one mask is substituted for another, prison is a sanctuary in which permanence and a halt to change can be attained. Therefore, Plasmonick murders his demonic love, Rosa van der Blaast, in order to return to jail forever.

Another kind of artist is represented by Lopak, author of "The Anonymous Work"—revolution—a collective creation which comes into being mysteriously apart from the individual and his wishes. Like the poems that write themselves as Lopak digs his graves, this creative work happens all by itself; the only artist who can be thoroughly happy is the unconscious one. Instead of destroying himself, Lopak destroys others and brings down an entire society as part of a vast act of mass creativity.[25]

[25] In this respect, Lopak resembles Pancras, the revolutionary leader in Krasiński's *The Un-Divine Comedy,* whose only law is the destruction of the upper class.

Written in the same year as the publication of Ernst Toller's *Man and the Masses,* which shows the failure of a proletarian revolution led by "The Nameless One" because its materialistic philosophy was false to the individual, Witkacy's *The Anonymous Work* is, on the contrary, about a "nameless" creation which succeeds because it sinks to the lowest level and espouses unconscious mass destructive impulses. Ideology, even ideology as hypocritical as that of the Grizzloviks, is buried by the gravediggers. The art of sardonic violence triumphs. When Toller's idealistic heroine goes to a heroic death in prison in defense of her principles, her nobility effects an awakening of conscience in two thieving fellow prisoners. After Plasmonick slits the throat of his only love with a razor and is locked up once and for all, his father, the great aesthetician Dr. Plasmodeus Blödestaug—recently appointed Minister of Health and Art in the new regime—invites everyone home for coffee and nice fresh rolls.

For all Witkacy's identification with Hamlet-Plasmonick and his plight, his own art has affinities with Lopak's as well as with Plasmonick's. The play's epigraph, "The Grizzloviks yelp at the sight of Black Beatus the Trundler," [26] came to the playwright in a dream before the war and furnished him with the mysterious sect of workers and their priests, such as Tzingar. The unconscious sources of Witkacy's plays were dreams, drug-induced visions full of intense colors and grotesque shapes, and obsessive fears of mass leveling and violence that he had harbored long before his experience of the Russian Revolution and that only later found concrete corroboration there. Like Lopak, Witkacy himself digs deep.

Nonetheless, if the inner impulses of Witkacy's art are Lopakian, from the subterranean regions of the psyche, the playwright as creator of Pure Form insisted on an artistic realization of the work in objectively formal terms. In "A Few Words about the Role of the Actor in the Theatre of Pure Form," Witkacy discusses the need for externalizing a play's inner content in performance through exact shape, movement,

---

[26] This phrase, mysterious in meaning, left a deep impression on Witkacy; he uses it in two other works: his major novel, *Insatiability,* and his most philosophical play, *The Shoemakers.*

and sound, as in painting or music. Picasso and Stravinsky are proper models, not Stanislavsky.

In the composition of a play the same principles hold true. The characters in *The Anonymous Work* are projected less in terms of psychology than through a system of typage, similar to that used later by Sergei Eisenstein in film,[27] by which each figure is immediately and indelibly established on first appearance with hard contours and sharp focus; costume, profile, hair color, shape of beard are noted in precise detail. The technique serves a further purpose of dramatizing the illusory nature of the autonomous self and its inner life. Essentially, Witkacy's characters are nineteenth-century figures who have outlived their epoch and lost their original functions and places. Having lingered on into a new age, they retain their outlines and colors, their features and gestures, while at the same time they shift with the winds of political change, discard identities, and become mere puppets of the times. Like his Russian contemporaries in theatre and film (though with greater ironic perspective provided by distance), Witkacy saw that the already antiquated psychological methods of the Moscow Art Theatre no longer were adequate to portray what had actually been happening in Moscow, Petersburg, and all of revolutionary Russia. For a modern vision of the chaos and disarray of violent social upheaval and the passing of an old order, clowning and *commedia* offered the best theatrical formula because of the tautness, precision, and impersonal daring of their techniques.

Whereas the German expressionist Toller contraposed, in the form of high-flown rhetorical debate, the intellectual's noble vision of a better future for humanity to the soulless philosophy of the enemies of man (whether capitalist or communist), Witkacy perceived history, not as ideological argumentation, but as nasty nightmare played out among *commedia* figures. Witkacy's vision in *The Anonymous Work* is remarkably close to Karl Kraus's summation of the same period, in his preface to *The Last Days of Mankind,* as "a gory dream, those years in which operetta figures enacted the tragedy of mankind." [28] Our lives,

[27] See Sergei Eisenstein, "Through Theatre to Cinema," *Theatre Arts Monthly,* XX, No. 9 (September, 1939), 739–740.
[28] Karl Kraus, *The Last Days of Mankind,* tr. Alexander Code and Sue Ellen Wright (New York, 1974), p. 3.

Witkacy suggests, are run by secret conspiracies directed by clowns and buffoons (hence Buffadero), who are nonetheless dangerous madmen. The grotesque operetta runs its course, turning imperceptibly into the nightmare of modern history. Ultimately irrational forces, unconscious drives, and the lowest elements gain control and drive revolution to extremes. The artist-intellectual—himself weak, confused, internally divided— will be totally superfluous in the coming anthill civilization.

In "A Few Words about the Role of the Actor in the Theatre of Pure Form," the artist-intellectual Witkacy calls on drama to "resist the petrification of everything into a uniform, gray, un-differentiated pulp that is only superficially heteroge-neous"—in other words, the Lopakian ideal of "the uniform, gray, sticky, stinking, monstrous mass" (Act IV). Paradoxically, *The Anonymous Work*, written on the theme of social mechaniza-tion and showing the defeat of color at the hands of the mob, is Witkacy's most brightly colored play. Witkacy's dramatic uni-verse, it would appear, stands between worlds, between the old motley masquerade and the new gray mass, and his drama-turgy, based on the destruction of old forms, is also intermedi-ary between past and future.

Witkacy was opposed to all theatre as it then existed—the traditional, the new realistic, and the fashionably experimental. An early and consistent opponent of Stanislavsky, he also fought against the futurists and dadaists. For, however much he distorted the usual elements of drama and deformed reality, Witkacy believed that a play should have formal unity and beauty, and he argued for the supremacy of the spoken text over stage movement and visual aspects: "The most important thing is the spoken word and the other elements must be adapted to it." [29] In a sense, he was a classic author writing as an avant-gardist.

The result was total isolation and loneliness. In addition to suffering unceasing attacks by the bourgeois critics for outra-geous obscurity, Witkacy was rejected by the artistically radical as too comprehensible and by the political left as too conserva-tive. The futurist Anatol Stern accused Witkacy of being noth-ing but a decadent working in the tradition of the conventional

[29] Stanisław Ignacy Witkiewicz, "O artystycznej grze aktorów," *Przegląd Wieczorny*, No. 127 (June 4, 1927), 3.

psychological theatre, who, in his attempts to destroy the old canon of the stage, pushes its methods and aims to the absurd.[30] For his part, Witkacy criticized the futurists for insufficient interest in creating large, serious forms,[31] and he parodied the dadaists by inventing a movement that he called Pure Blaguism,[32] designed to show the difference between concocting willful nonsense and writing from genuine creative impulses.

By great strength of will and artistic purpose in the face of universal hostility and indifference, Witkacy held to his aim of producing works of aesthetically formal dimensions capable of expressing a philosophical world view. He achieved his goal of restoring the magical and metaphysical functions of theatre through a grotesque distortion of previous dramatic techniques and a prophetic grasp of future social developments. Witkacy wrote a large body of plays, of which the surviving works are perhaps no more than half his total output, and he accomplished all this in the totally unreceptive atmosphere of Poland between the wars.

However, the playwright's life ended in frustration, defeat, and despair. His dream of forming a theatre that could produce his own and other avant-garde plays—first attempted in the mid-1920's—came to nothing in the late 1930's. Dozens of his plays went unperformed, unpublished, unread. He devoted his last years to philosophy, the great passion of his life, as necessary to him as eating or sleeping. In poor health and deeply depressed at the fate of civilization, Witkacy committed suicide on September 18, 1939, after first the Germans and then the Russians invaded Poland. His younger friend and admirer Bolesław Miciński (a distant relation of the playwright Tadeusz Miciński) wrote of Witkacy in 1941:

Witkacy belongs to those creative artists who, despite even considerable popularity during their lifetimes, must be forgotten and discov-

[30] Anatol Stern, quoted in Degler, p. 42.
[31] Stanisław Ignacy Witkiewicz, "Parę zarzutów przeciw futuryzmowi," *Czartak*, No. 1 (1922), 15–17.
[32] Stanisław Ignacy Witkiewicz, *Papierek Lakmusowy* (Zakopane, 1921). This short monograph, which Witkacy had privately printed, contains a number of short parodies, in verse, prose, and play form, making fun of the dadaists, in particular Marcel Duchamp.

ered all over again after many years, because Witkacy's popularity was connected rather with the eccentricities in his life and with what was the least valuable—and not with his enduring achievements in the realm of ideas and artistic creation.[33]

Other Authors of the Interwar Years

Only a few other Polish writers of the interwar years attempted avant-garde drama, and they found the soil no more fertile than did Witkacy. Of the meager handful of plays written by these poets and novelists few were ever produced in the theatre. Like Witkacy, these writers were out of step with their own age and country, and several actually emigrated from Poland, hoping to find more congenial surroundings elsewhere. Their plays had to wait decades for time to catch up with them, and not until after 1956 did they enter the Polish repertory and assume their position as part of the avant-garde tradition.

Two of the most gifted writers of the period, Witold Wandurski and Bruno Jasieński, derived their inspiration from the Soviet Union; because of their political commitment to communism, they left Poland to work in Russia. Their attempts to join a powerful proletarian movement in avant-garde theatre ended in disaster, and offer another illustration of the tragic isolation and failure of Polish playwrights in the interwar years.

A member of the Communist Party of Poland, Witold Wandurski (1891–1937) spent the period from 1913 to 1921 in Russia; in 1919 he led an amateur Russian theatre group in Kharkov.[34] After his return to Poland in 1921, Wandurski worked in Łódź as a social activist and director of a workers' theatre, writing many articles on his theories of proletarian theatre. In 1925 his most famous and important play, *Death in a Pear Tree*, was presented professionally in Cracow at the Słowacki Theatre according to Wandurski's own plans for staging it, with the author himself managing the final rehearsals after a series of disagreements with the director.

[33] Bolesław Miciński, "Stanisław Ignacy Witkiewicz (Witkacy)—Plan Odczytu," in *Pisma* (Cracow, 1970), p. 197.
[34] Helena Karwacka's *Witold Wandurski* (Łódź, 1968) contains extensive information about the playwright's life and work, and Witold Filler's *Na Lewym torze: Teatr Witolda Wandurskiego* (Warsaw, 1967) provides a short introduction to his theatre.

Death in a Pear Tree, an antiwar fable based on an old folk tale about how Death was imprisoned by a crafty peasant, is Wandurski's attempt to create plebeian drama without individual heroes. Inspired by Meyerhold, Tairov, and the new Soviet theatre, it is a minstrel-morality without psychological analysis or plot complexity in which fantasy mixes freely with reality and the actors are allowed to be the creators. With a huge cast of characters, including Death, Saint Peter, and the Archangel Michael as well as a gallery of contemporary figures extending even to the Prompter and the Theatre Audience, *Death in a Pear Tree* strove to be truly popular avant-garde drama by returning to the sources of theatre in homilies and entertainments for the people.

The 1925 production created an uproar; rotten eggs were thrown at the actors, and the play was hissed as communist propaganda. The censor required additional cuts each evening until, after only six performances, the authorities closed the production. A later effort by Wandurski to stage the play in Łódź with his own workers' group was stopped by the police.

In 1928, despite an advanced case of tuberculosis, Wandurski was arrested for communist activity and imprisoned. Released as a result of protests by a group of Polish writers, he escaped from Poland illegally via Danzig before his trial and fled to Berlin. There he established and directed a Polish workers' theatre until his deportation to the Soviet Union in May, 1929. While in Berlin, Wandurski presented his new agitprop play, *In the Hotel Imperialism.*

In the Soviet Union the Polish playwright in exile organized and directed the Polish National Theatre Studio from 1929 until 1931. In 1932 he completed his play *Mêlée,* a documentary drama in newsreel style, with songs and choruses, about a workers' revolt in an industrial community in "Fascist Poland in 1931." It was performed first by the Polish National Theatre in Kiev and then in Russian in Moscow at the MOSPS (later MOSSOVIET), the Theatre of the Workers' Union. In the summer of 1933, Wandurski, along with many other members of the Polish Communist Party, was arrested by the secret police; he died in a concentration camp somewhere in the Soviet Union in 1937 and was rehabilitated in 1956. *Death in a Pear Tree* was performed again in Poland in the 1960's, most notably by Józef Szajna in a brilliant production first given in Nowa Huta in 1964 and repeated in Warsaw in 1966.

Bruno Jasieński (1901–1937) spent the war years from 1914 to 1918 in Moscow studying at a Polish school.[35] There he became acquainted with the work of the Russian futurists, and upon his return to Cracow, where he attended the university, the young poet organized a futurist club and began writing verse and issuing theoretical manifestoes. In 1925, Jasieński emigrated to France, and by 1927 he had organized a Polish workers' theatre made up of immigrants living in Paris. Jasieński was an active member of the French Communist Party; when his truculent novel *I Burn Paris,* predicting the city's downfall, was published in the French communist newspaper, *L'Humanité,* he was deported from France as an undesirable alien.

After a short stay in Germany, Jasieński went to the Soviet Union, where he was enthusiastically received as an international celebrity in 1929. He became chief editor of *Mass Culture,* the magazine of the Polish Section of the International Bureau of Revolutionary Literature, as well as of *The Literature of the World Revolution,* in which his best-known play, *The Ball of the Mannequins,* appeared in French, Russian, English, German, and Chinese. The play was also separately published in a Russian edition with a laudatory introduction by Anatolii Lunacharsky, who defended against possible attacks the dramatist's use of fantasy and other nonrealistic devices to present his revolutionary theme.

The Ball of the Mannequins, which is perhaps Jasieński's first work originally written in Russian, recalls Marcel Duchamp's series of dadaist paintings on glass *Les Machines célibataires* in its bizarre visual imagery of animated dummies (although it is doubtful that the Polish writer knew the French compositions). The play opens at the yearly ball given by Paris tailors' mannequins. When a liberal member of the national assembly intrudes on the party by chance, the mannequins, afraid that their secret activities will become known, try the politician,

---

[35] The futurist poet Anatol Stern gives a personal account of his friend in *Bruno Jasieński* (Warsaw, 1969).

whom they recognize as their oppressor, and condemn him to
death by beheading. Subsequently, one of the mannequins puts
the decapitated head on his own body and attends a political
soiree, where he is accepted as the political leader but cannot
endure the hypocrisy of the liberal bourgeoisie and their
human greed. Outside, in the streets, a strike is gathering force
which threatens to shake the capitalist regime. When the guillo-
tined politician comes to demand his head, the mannequin
gladly gives it back, predicting that soon all the mannequins in
the world will rise and chop off their masters' heads.

MANNEQUIN LEADER: (*With a rapid gesture he removes his head like a hat.*)
Here, please, here is your head! (*Hands the head over to the leader.*)
Take it. Take it quickly! I've had enough of it! I am sorry I was ever
tempted to take it! I had won a head and I thought I was happy. I
thought I had found a treasure. Go to blazes with your head! Now I
know what you need your head for. It was not for nothing that we
had decided to chop it off. (*Points to the leader.*) But what's the use? It
is impossible to cut all your heads off. There won't be enough scis-
sors. Besides, this is not our business. Others will come who shall do
it much better than we can. We thought that it was only us whom
you were torturing. It turns out that there are others who will do
the reckoning. It looks as if they really mean business.[36]

During the interwar years, *The Ball of the Mannequins* was performed only in Japan and Czechoslovakia, where it was
directed by the famous Czech constructivist Emil František
Burian. First published in a Polish translation in 1957, Jasieński's play was staged in the same year in both Katowice and
Warsaw under Jerzy Jarocki's direction, and it has been revived in 1974 by Janusz Warmiński at the Warsaw Ateneum.

As a member of the executive committee of the Soviet
Writers' Union and an established author writing in Russian,
Jasieński survived the purges and growing terror longer than
Wandurski. In the mid-thirties he published, in both Russian
and Polish, *Man Changes His Skin,* a novel about the new man of
communist society, and when he was arrested on charges of na-
tionalist conspiracy in 1937, he was working on another book,
The Conspiracy of the Indifferent, which he never completed and
which was published only posthumously, at the time of Ja-

[36] Bruno Jasieńsky, "The Ball of the Mannequins," *Literature of the World Revolution,* No. 2 (1931), 49.

sieński's rehabilitation in 1956. According to one account, he died of typhus in 1939 while imprisoned in Vladivostok; another version suggests that he committed suicide.[37]

Facing hostility and oppression at home, Wandurski and Jasieński had tried to realize their dreams of an avant-garde workers' theatre, first in Western Europe, then in the Soviet Union. In the West they were harassed by the police for their radical views and deported. In the Soviet Union, where they expected to find receptive ground for their social and political ideals, they met an even harsher fate. Suspect as foreign radicals, Poles, avant-garde writers, and intellectuals, Wandurski and Jasieński were far more ruthlessly repressed in the USSR than in the capitalist world that they had devoted their lives to criticizing.

In comparison to the ambitious plans which they voiced in their theoretical pronouncements, their actual accomplishments in creating a new drama were slight. Wandurski and Jasieński spent much of their careers battling for something that could never be. They and their hopes of creating an avant-garde proletarian drama were utterly crushed. Based upon public, political allegiances rather than personal visions and private obsessions, their few plays lack the resonance and prophetic detachment of Witkacy's and seem rigid and uninventive because of total commitment to an objective case. The authors fell victim to their own illusions when they attempted to eliminate from drama the individual, his inner feelings, and his dreams.

Death in a Pear Tree and *The Ball of the Mannequins* are, however, significant, if minor, moments in the Polish avant-garde tradition of displaced drama. Wandurski and Jasieński sought in fantasy and the grotesque a parable form for a new theatre that would be at one and the same time popular and experimental in its rejection of the canons of realism and its embracing of visual image and poetic metaphor.

The socialist poet Tadeusz Peiper (1891–1969) also made several ventures into playwriting, but was unsuccessful in gain-

[37] James H. Billington, *The Icon and the Axe* (New York, 1966), p. 553. According to Billington, Jasieński committed suicide during the purges. His selected writings, *Izbrannye proizvedeniia*, were published in Moscow in 1957 after Jasieński's rehabilitation.

ing a foothold on the stage.[38] Educated partly in Cracow and partly in Berlin and Paris, Peiper spent the years from 1914 to 1921 in Spain as a journalist. Upon his return to Poland, Peiper edited the avant-garde magazine *Zwrotnica* ("The Switch") in Cracow from 1922 until 1923, when, after only six issues had appeared, it was closed by the police for inciting revolution. Witkacy's *The New Deliverance* was published in the third number and his *Cuttlefish* in the fifth. Peiper revived the magazine in 1926 and 1927.

Peiper's own plays are experiments in the dramatization of time. *Six O'Clock! Six O'Clock!* (1925) contrasts stage time with real time by reversing chronological order and arbitrarily manipulating the conventions of the theatre. For example, a naked woman jumps up from a sofa and dashes offstage only to return instantly fully clothed; an actor leaves from one side of the stage, then enters immediately from the other; and the entire second half of the play precedes the first.

If There Isn't Any Him, Peiper's major work for the stage, written and published in 1933, is based on actual clashes between workers and police that had taken place in Cracow ten years earlier. The play explores the different relationships of the characters to an offstage revolution that is brewing in the streets. Peiper presents a world without continuity in which man's lack of memory makes him a prey to time, an ever changing puppet without character or will.

By simply happening to be at a certain place at a certain time, the hero, In (a name suggesting "intruder" or "interloper"), first leads the workers to revolution, then later betrays them and their cause. Confronted by the theatre of masks and illusions which In constantly presents, the heroine, Stena, says, "You're changing so rapidly that there isn't any you at all." At various times a child of the slums, revolutionary leader, factory owner, and traitor to the people, In himself declares: "I have no memory. My memory doesn't store up anything! I am responsible for only the quarter of an hour which I am experiencing. What I did an hour ago is totally unimportant."

[38] Accounts of Peiper as a playwright are given in Maria Czanerle, *Wycieczki w dwudziestolecie: O dramacie międzywojennym* (Warsaw, 1970), pp. 63–66, and in Józef Ratajczak, "Co jest 'Skoro go nie ma?' " *Dialog*, No. 10 (1970), 79–94.

Such a lack of memory, resulting in loss of duration, destroys individuality; the hero becomes a chameleon, a man without qualities in a kaleidoscopically changing world where history is determined by chance and external events. As in Witkacy, so in Peiper, revolution is the historic moment and setting for the man without qualities who tries and sheds many different roles until he finally becomes lost as an individual in the mass fluctuations of social upheaval. Peiper's most original contribution to Polish drama, *If There Isn't Any Him,* waited forty years to reach the stage; it was performed for the first time in 1973, in Wrocław, and again in 1974, in Warsaw. Fifty years after it first appeared, *Six O'Clock! Six O'Clock!* received its premiere in Gdańsk in 1975.

Witold Gombrowicz (1904-1969), one of the most interesting and important authors to begin his career in Poland between the wars, had similar experiences with the theatre.[39] Best known as a fiction writer—his first collection of stories was published in 1933, his novel *Ferdydurke* in 1937—Gombrowicz wrote only three plays, but they span his life as a writer and serve as yet another illustration of the displacement characteristic of Polish avant-garde drama. Gombrowicz's first play, *Ivona, Princess of Burgundia,* was written in 1935 and published in Poland in 1938; his second, *The Marriage,* was written in 1946 in Argentina (Gombrowicz was on a summer cruise when the war broke out in 1939, and he remained in South America for twenty-five years) and published in Paris in 1953; and his final work for the theatre, *Operetta,* was written and published in France in 1966. *Ivona* reached the stage in Poland in 1957, *The Marriage* in 1972, and *Operetta* in 1975 (in an outstanding production by Kazimierz Dejmek at the New Theatre in Łódź), although it had already been presented in Western Europe and America.

Gombrowicz's plays pit the conflicting images of reality held by the characters one against the other. The tragi-farce *Ivona*

[39] Good introductions to Gombrowicz's theatre are available in English in Czesław Miłosz's *The History of Polish Literature* (New York, 1969), pp. 432–437; in Louis Iribarne's "Revolution in the Theater of Witkacy and Gombrowicz," *The Polish Review,* XVIII, Nos. 1–2 (1973), 58–76; and in Bolesław Taborski's "Gombrowicz," in Michael Anderson et al., *Crowell's Handbook of Contemporary Drama* (New York, 1971), pp. 186–188.

takes place in an absurd fairy-tale kingdom where, bored with
the empty ceremonies of court life, young Prince Philip becomes engaged, as a joke, to the ugly, repellent, and utterly
silent Ivona. As a result of this senseless prank, a ludicrous atmosphere of the incongruous pervades the court, revealing the
nastiness, malice, and asininity of each of the characters. The
courtiers now see themselves rendered ridiculous in the distort-
ing mirror of Ivona's presence. The situation grows more and
more grotesque until they all decide that Ivona must be killed if
the tyranny of nonsense is ever to end. Ivona is served fish for
dinner, and as all the courtiers watch intently, the cause of all
their discomfiture chokes slowly on a bone that gets caught in
her throat.

   Written in both prose and verse and utilizing stylized literary
devices such as a chorus, *The Marriage* is a vast and complex
dream play, rich in allusions to Shakespeare and Wyspiański
and full of the dazzling and ambiguous transformations of
time, place, and identity characteristic of avant-garde Polish
drama. The play is an exploration of the self, its endless possibilities for creation through words and images, and its intricate
poses and diversions. According to Gombrowicz, everything is
created by and among people as they artificially form one another by means of imagination, pretense, and lies.

   Henry, a young soldier returning home from the war, finds
his family, fiancée, and house in a fluid, dreamlike state of near
collapse. All actions, gestures, and words are in imminent
danger of disintegration. In order to restore order and assume
control of the increasingly unruly situation, typified by a noisy
drunk, Henry plans an elaborate marriage ceremony. In "this
world of games and eternal artifices, of eternal imitations and
mystifications," as Gombrowicz calls it in the preface to the
play,[40] the domestic relationships keep expanding into political
ones; father, mother, son, fiancée, and friend become king,
queen, prince, princess, and traitor, ultimately peopling an entire state and playing all the roles, as Gombrowicz tries and in-
dicts the myths of nationhood.

   After Henry has deposed his own father and become king

----

[40] Witold Gombrowicz, *Théâtre* (Paris, 1965), p. 88. Gombrowicz says that the
process of deformation produces what Witkacy calls Pure Form.

himself, he turns into a dictator. Doubt and treason grow as his tyranny spreads, and the wedding ceremony is disrupted by insurrection. The fairy-tale realm turns into a "nasty nightmare." When the prince's friend is forced to kill himself as a traitor, Henry first proclaims his innocence, but then orders himself arrested and imprisoned. Above all "a drama of Form," according to Gombrowicz, *The Marriage* demonstrates the way in which the word creates what is said and what is said creates the one who says it. Deeds spring from the creative power of language; through the imposition of his subjective forms of vision on others, each participant in human intercourse deforms and is deformed.

The tendency toward parody apparent in *The Marriage* finds full expression in Gombrowicz's final play, *Operetta,* in which the playwright tellingly uses the absurd conventions and style of operetta to deal with the equally absurd events of modern history. In the tradition of Witkacy, Gombrowicz charts the course of the decline and fall of Europe from the turn of the century to the present—including two world wars and two revolutions—by means of the preposterously colorful characters and situations of a Viennese operetta.

However, *The Marriage* and *Operetta* do not fall within the interwar period, and Gombrowicz left Poland forever without seeing *Ivona* reach the stage. When in September, 1939, first the Germans and then the Russians invaded Poland—newly independent only twenty-one years before—and divided the country between themselves, it would have appeared that Polish avant-garde drama had died without ever having come to life. Witkacy committed suicide; Wandurski and Jasieński were already dead. There had been no Polish Meyerhold capable of bringing these plays to the attention of the world. Leon Schiller's famous monumental productions were of classics, foreign works, and nothing more recent than Wyspiański and Miciński. In fact, in the period from 1918 to 1939, there was not a single artistically important production of contemporary Polish avant-garde drama worthy of international notice, and not one of the plays produced by the Polish avant-garde playwrights entered either the native or foreign repertory (except for the isolated case of *The Ball of the Mannequins,* performed in Japan and

Czechoslovakia). No word of the existence of a vital Polish avant-garde drama reached the outside world.

Andrzej Trzebiński and the Underground

Most surprisingly, in the face of overwhelming obstacles, dislocated avant-garde theatre refused to die out even during the Nazi occupation, the darkest period in Polish history, when the nation was threatened not only with nonexistence (a state which it had successfully endured for a century and a half), but with systematic annihilation. Previously Polish avant-garde drama had been forced to exist marginally, without a stage or audience; now it literally went underground. All serious Polish theatre came to an end with the German occupation, and most actors chose voluntary retirement, declining to play for the Nazi conquerors. Only a trivial, totally compromised public theatre remained.

However, an underground theatre sprang up, and one of its most interesting productions—never actually presented, although it went into final rehearsals in the apartments of the actors—was Witkacy's *Madman and the Nun,* performed in the spring of 1942 by members of the student theatre at the Clandestine Warsaw University (the university itself was closed by the Nazis).[41] The student actors were all young writers in their very early twenties, led by the poet Wacław Bojarski, founder and editor of the mimeographed underground literary magazine *Art and the Nation.*[42] Bojarski, who played the role of the mad poet Walpurg, composed a special prologue in which Walpurg appears as Witkacy and reads from the playwright's theoretical works on the theatre. Next the madhouse doctors come on stage and attack Witkacy for talking nonsense, using the actual words of the most obtuse critics who had reviewed his plays so viciously. Then the sinister Dr. Walldorff appears and has the madhouse attendants put Walpurg-Witkacy in his strait

[41] Information about this performance is given by the editor of Witkacy's collected plays, Konstanty Puzyna, in Stanisław Ignacy Witkiewicz, *Dramaty,* II (Warsaw, 1972), 753.

[42] The four editors of *Art and the Nation* were: Bronisław Kopczyński (arrested and died in the concentration camp Majdanek at the end of 1942); Wacław Bojarski (shot, May, 1943); Andrzej Trzebiński (shot, November, 1943); and Tadeusz Gajcy (killed in the Warsaw Uprising, August, 1944).

jacket and take him offstage, so that the doctor can be left alone to give his harangue, which soon turns into actual gibberish. The lights go out, then on again, and the play proper begins.

Bojarski, who had recently won a prize for his prose poem "Wounded by a Rose," died in the spring of 1943 from wounds sustained when he was shot by the Nazis as he put flowers on the Copernicus monument in Warsaw; he lived less than two weeks after the shooting, only long enough to marry his fiancée as he lay on his deathbed. Bojarski's younger friend and colleague Andrzej Trzebiński (1922–1943), who became the next editor of *Art and the Nation,* had played the part of one of the madhouse attendants in the clandestine *Madman and the Nun.* Fascinated by Witkacy and his theatre, Trzebiński followed his master's example, and with *To Pick up the Rose* (1942), his one and only play, written when the author was twenty years old, the underground poet carried on the Polish tradition of prophetic drama dealing with revolution.[43]

Long under a cloud because of Trzebiński's right-wing, nationalistic politics (characteristic of *Art and the Nation*), *To Pick up the Rose* was first published in 1955 in a small magazine; the work was given its premiere by Janusz Warmiński at the Warsaw Ateneum, and then issued in book form only in 1970, twenty-eight years after it was written. The play, in fact, deals with the process by which history catches up with individuals who are ahead of their times; it took almost three decades for the world to become contemporary with Trzebiński and for its sensibility to become synchronized with *To Pick up the Rose.*

Like the other young underground writers of his generation, Trzebiński was in a desperate race with time. War, the occupation, and the resistance had revived the nineteenth-century romantic traditions of uprisings and martyrdom; poets once again became national heroes. As a soldier in the underground army and editor of a clandestine patriotic magazine, Trzebiński knew that he was doomed to an early death, and one might expect that a play written under these circumstances would be

---

[43] In a similar fashion, Zygmunt Krasiński wrote his prophetic play about world revolution, *The Un-Divine Comedy,* when he was only twenty-one. Zdzisław Jastrzębski has written about Trzebiński in *Bez wieńca i togi* (Warsaw, 1967), as well as in introductions to the poet's works.

full of passionate rhetoric and noble injunctions to fellow coun-
trymen to "shake off your bonds." In *To Pick up the Rose,* however, the soldier-poet Andrzej Trzebiński—who constantly
risked his life and operated under secret pseudonyms—mocks
death, ridicules conspiratorial intrigue and spy rings, and
renders absurd dictatorship and its arbitrary power.

By a remarkable feat of ironic detachment and rigorous intellectual analysis, the twenty-year-old author views the occupation, the resistance, and his own tragic role in these events from
a great distance. *To Pick up the Rose* does not even deal with the
war or German occupation except metaphorically and is devoid
of national issues and pathos. Instead, its themes are revolution
and political power, illusion and reality, perceived in a universal perspective. In the tradition, not of the romantics, but of
Witkacy, Peiper, and Gombrowicz, Trzebiński views history as
running out of control, determined by blind chance and the
senseless acts of buffoons and lunatics. In 1943, a year after
composing *To Pick up the Rose,* Trzebiński was killed by the
Nazis in a random street execution. Toward the end of the war,
to spread terror the occupiers rounded up and shot thousands
of such victims in Warsaw; Trzebiński died under a pseudonym, without his executioners ever discovering his identity as
an underground conspirator.

Trzebiński's diary, kept from December, 1941, until a few
days before his death on November 12, 1943, contains a record
of the poet-playwright's precocious intellectual growth and
helps to explain how at the age of twenty he was able to write a
first play as mature and self-assured as *To Pick up the Rose.*
Forced to condense his entire creative life into two years,
Trzebiński absorbed experiences, ideas, and influences at
breakneck speed. For the young playwright, Witkacy's example
was crucial, and his name appears frequently in the diary as a
point of reference. Trzebiński voices love and admiration for
the two Witkiewiczes, father and son, taking them as his models
for a certain intellectual attitude toward life and as exemplifica-
tions of the supreme value of the individual and individuality.[44]

[44] Andrzej Trzebiński, *Kwiaty z drzew zakazanych* (Warsaw, 1972), pp. 83–84.
The diary is published in somewhat expurgated form, along with a novel and
miscellaneous prose works.

For, although Trzebiński and his friends were prepared to sacrifice themselves, the age of ideals was over, and they had no illusions that there were any values beyond the self. They believed only in rebellion, not in romantic causes. Ideology was a disguise, a mask useful for acquiring power, and power was nothing but doing business in a world where chance rules over the individual, the country, and all existence.[45] Witkacy and Gombrowicz were the favorite authors among the resistance fighters. Witkacy, particularly, was a hero to the young underground authors; throughout his entire life he had battled against viciously hostile critics and resisted a world that was anxious to declare him insane. His self-chosen death was an act of defiance.

Although it is unlikely that Trzebiński could have known *The Anonymous Work* or any of Witkacy's other political plays—none had been published—the young underground writer instinctively shared a similar vision and quickly learned the lesson of the master in dramaturgical technique. Perhaps Trzebiński knew only Witkacy's theoretical writings on the theatre, the novel *Insatiability*, and *The Madman and the Nun*, in which he appeared as a student actor. That play, however, sufficed to give Trzebiński exactly what he needed: an international idiom and style, cosmopolitan characters and setting, employment of the stage as dramatic image and metaphor, and a method for the analysis of power and its uses. Furthermore, the analogies between Witkacy's madhouse and the one in which Trzebiński and his friends found themselves were not to be missed. For these young men, *The Madman and the Nun* offered a brilliant depiction of confinement and oppression, with bursts of humor and sudden terror, and showed the way in which the artist-intellectual can rise superior to his own death and achieve what Trzebiński called "our power in the world. The power of artists." [46]

Engaged in a life-and-death struggle, the poet was able to transcend its horror by penetrating all the lies and finding them laughable. On January 5, 1942, Trzebiński wrote:

[45] Marta Piwińska, "Przed 'Kartoteką' i 'Tangiem,'" *Dialog*, No. 11 (1967), 81–108.
[46] Trzebiński, *Kwiaty*, p. 209.

Throughout my entire life I have tried to defend the world. I have felt a moral duty to justify it to myself. But now—now that I may not live any longer [I'd like] to rid myself of the mountain of lies which I have called the struggle. To laugh at everything without a shred of pity, to laugh at the whole miserable world and all the lies which I have told on behalf of life. As yet I do not have the poison within me, but in this last half hour or hour, when it is clear that there is no danger of a return and that life will no longer take its revenge, what a relief to burst out in laughter which I have suppressed for twenty years.[47]

This laughter at life from the brink of the grave most naturally takes the form of the grotesque, which Trzebiński announces as his "artistic method." Death he saw everywhere; the romantic myth was being fulfilled to the bitter end: being a Pole meant being condemned to die for one's country. "One more death," Trzebiński wrote at the beginning of 1943; "it will be our permanent motto, refrain, dominant note: Our life is more and more an island flooded by the waters of death. By the silver-green tidal waves, the streams of death." A nihilist, the poet-playwright keeps separate self and country, and although ready to die for the homeland, he places the only true value in the individual. "Yes. I'll read your unwritten drama," Trzebiński wrote in his diary, addressing his friend Bojarski after the latter's death, "that first act you were thinking of then at the foot of the Copernicus monument when you lay wounded." [48]

Against this background of death and desperation, *To Pick up the Rose* unfolds its story of a heavyweight boxing champion, world chess master, professor of sociology, and nudist trapped in the game room of the Hotel Morocco, where they play ping-pong to pass the time as rival dictators wage revolutionary warfare down in the streets. The play is permeated with the sense that history is about to commit an outrage on the characters, merely because they happen to be where they are at that particular moment; and indeed several times they are lined up against the wall to be shot. However, all heroic gestures Trzebiński treats as theatre, "unwritten drama," and the violent process of historical change itself he sees as a game and spectator sport.

[47] *Ibid.*, 87–88.   [48] *Ibid.*, pp. 191, 187, 199.

The theme of the play is immediately identified as "the end of the world," but the cool rationalist hero, Professor Arioni, soon suggests that the end of one world may be the beginning of another. "Finally the world will take a great flying leap or running jump and catch up with all of us," he observes, intrigued by the possibilities of the future. Trzebiński's play begins at precisely the point at which most of Witkacy's plays end—with the crumbling old world in ruins—as, for example, in *The Anonymous Work,* where in the last act the Lopakian mob runs wild through the streets in which the struggle for power has been waged. Revolution for the sake of revolution is a constant throughout *To Pick up the Rose;* catastrophe is the normal way of life.

Witkacy and Trzebiński trace opposite trajectories as they follow the emergence of new political worlds. In *The Anonymous Work* power comes up from below; in *To Pick up the Rose* it goes down from above. Arioni finally descends into the street, which he has been viewing from the window throughout the play, waiting for events to catch up with him. Professor—or is it instructor?—of sociology (his actual position in the hierarchy is unimportant), he studies society and its workings as an objective observer. Aware of the domination of symbol over reality, Arioni does not join in the ping-pong himself, but plays games with the players. Power over life resides not in the boxer's might, the chess master's strategy, or the dictators' empty bombast and violence. Rather, irony and perception of the grotesque enable the intellectual to make the final move, from above to below, while the bloated tyrants play their imaginary game. "Weird, contorted, convulsive, hateful, misshapen, with stiff, shrunken muscles, wrinkles on their faces, the dictators take their places on each side of the table and without a word begin their black, infernal, inhuman game" (Act III).

The powerful image of hypnotized dictators flailing away at the enchanted game that deprives them of all will and purpose is Trzebiński's original version of the Mulch dance, now turned into sport; it anticipates the ending of Antonioni's film *Blow-Up,* with its mysterious tennis match without a ball. In his manipulation of symbols so as to make an illusory game replace a real-life struggle, Arioni becomes in fact director of a theatre in

which the dictators are the actors for whom he creates grotesque parts. Although Deromur—dictator *in potentia*—asserts
that "history is no operetta" (Act II), the two strong men are
"characters out of an operetta" (Act III) and must be so, according to Arioni's comic spirit, if humanity is to progress
beyond such masquerades.

The chief prop in this historical world theatre is an insignificant ping-pong ball, the essence of nothingness, which can assume a variety of weighty meanings: signal for the revolutionary forces to launch their attack; evidence of the
conspiratorial guilt of those accidentally caught in the affair;
and ultimately, by virtue of its nonexistence, symbol of the
triumph of illusion. In his theoretical essay "From the Drama
Laboratory" Trzebiński suggests that the new direction in
drama will be toward showing the relationship of man and
thing, and as Thornton Wilder's *Our Town* had taught the
young Polish playwright, things become most strongly felt by
their very absence. The trifling ping-pong ball, once it ceases to
exist, becomes all-powerful, defining the dictators as marionettes controlled by a vacuum.

The form of *To Pick up the Rose* is stripped bare, at once
highly theatrical and cerebral, reduced to the essentials of an
intricate but severe game. Players in blacks and whites move as
on a chessboard; heads turn mechanically from side to side following the flight of the nonball; dictators and henchmen circle
the table spluttering circular rhetoric. Each deed, gesture, and
word in the game room (itself like a padded cell) is countered,
returned, symmetrically repeated, and tossed back. Whereas
Witkacy's world is richly contradictory in its human complexi-
ties and emotionally charged in its irony, Trzebiński, in *To Pick
up the Rose*, makes an ingeniously logical extension of a metaphoric construct. Applying game theory to politics and viewing
revolution as theatre, the underground author creates an abstract, intellectual drama, akin to Mrożek's early one-act parables of power.

Trzebiński's basic analogy in *To Pick up the Rose*, the linking
of politics to sports, is an ominous forecast of the future. The
only worthy task now, in the universe of Professor Arioni's
higher pragmatism, is to study how games are played. Those

who appear to wield power are only puppets whose paddles and minds are empty; their words are all bluster, and ideology is simply mumbo jumbo. In this post-Witkacian society, in which metaphysics has already died out, the mechanism works all by itself, operating according to certain objective laws. The dispassionate professorial analyst of the system, perceiving that truth is on the side that wins, is the true strong man. The new master is not politician, artist, or genius, but social scientist. The end of the world can be programmed to last forever; the illusory game of power between the two dictators "goes its ghastly way ad infinitum."

Oblivia, the play's only woman—a reputed nudist committed to naked truth and emotion—cannot tolerate sham or survive in the nonsensical world of operetta dictators. Making an absurdly beautiful gesture, she throws herself out of the same window through which she had already hurled the ping-pong ball. When Arioni goes down and picks up the imaginary rose represented by the ribbon that Oblivia had worn in her hair— thereby accepting the necessary sacrifice of human life and decency as a ceremonious prelude—he takes over the role and identity of national dictator. Ahead of his time in his perception of politics as an exercise in deceptive emptiness, will the professor of sociology be a more humane or at least a more efficient tyrant than his old-fashioned, crude, half-witted predecessors? From the implacable, closed relationships of war, occupation, and resistance, Trzebiński drew extreme conclusions about the operations of power in the society to come.

Gałczyński and *The Green Goose:* "The Smallest Theatre in the World"

Trzebiński was a unique product of the war years and the occupation, a member of a condemned generation, producing but one play in a drastically condensed lifetime. The older poet Konstanty Ildefons Gałczyński (1905–1953), on the other hand, brings together prewar and postwar generations, uniting different historical epochs. A contemporary of both Witkacy and Mrożek, he is an important link in the continuous chain of Polish avant-garde drama.

Immediately after World War II Gałczyński was the first

Polish writer to develop a new drama built on nonsensical fantasy, absurd humor, and parody of serious forms of theatre and solemn habits of thought. At a time when there was as yet little or no new drama of any kind, Gałczyński created his own theatre outside the theatre (the ambition of all the Polish avant-gardists from Witkacy to Różewicz), which he named The Little Theatre of *The Green Goose* and which existed solely in the playwright's mind.

Born in Warsaw, the poet spent the war years from 1914 to 1919 with his family in Moscow. After his return to Poland, he studied Latin, German, French, and English poetry. For the English Department of Warsaw University, Gałczyński wrote a brilliant seminar paper on Morris Gordon Cheats, a minor British poet whom he invented, complete with quotations in the original language, genealogy, footnotes, and bibliography.[49] He received the highest grade possible and later a diploma with honors in English literature.

Gałczyński began his own literary career in the mid-twenties, writing humorous verse and fantastic stories, such as the nonsense tale *Porphirion the Donkey, or the Blasphemers' Club.* In 1929 he published a long poem entitled *The End of the World: Visions of Saint Ildefons, or a Satire on the Universe,* which takes place in a hallucinatory European city and suggests the catastrophe to come in *opéra bouffe* form. Ildefons was Gałczyński's own self-created middle name; the poet was infinitely inventive in making something out of nothing.

His particular genius as a writer lay in his ability to combine wit, lyricism, satire, folklore, classical mythology, and everyday language with surrealist imagination and yet remain clear and accessible to the broadest public. Gałczyński was in his own lifetime, and still remains, the most popular of modern Polish poets. His readings of his own poetry were immensely successful. A reveler and merrymaker, Gałczyński was the opposite of the isolated romantic poet; rather, he saw himself as a minstrel and troubadour who felt completely at home with the people.[50]

Mobilized as an ordinary soldier when war came again,

[49] Andrzej Drawicz, *Konstanty Ildefons Gałczyński* (Warsaw, 1968), pp. 27–28.
[50] Miłosz, pp. 409–411.

Gałczyński was taken captive and spent the period from 1939 to 1945 in a German prisoner-of-war camp. After a year of wandering in Western Europe, chiefly in Belgium and France, the poet returned home to resume his literary career in a country that had been shattered by the war and was in the throes of a social upheaval, the results of which were by no means clear. At this uncertain moment in Polish history, with the old world destroyed—Warsaw and much of the country were literally in ruins—and a new one yet to be built, Gałczyński began his work as a playwright, inventing an imaginary nontheatre and cast of performers (animal and human) and contributing a new installment of The Little Theatre of *The Green Goose* each week to *Przekrój* ("Profile"), the Cracow literary magazine for which he wrote several hundred of these short plays in the next four years.

Originally intended for reading only, a theatre of the mind whose plays went unperformed in Gałczyński's lifetime, *The Green Goose* became the most celebrated and controversial work of this period—eagerly awaited each week, laughed over, attacked, and denounced. In *The Green Goose*, Gałczyński mocked everything, but most of all the past and various national follies and intellectual pretensions. By demolishing stereotypes, *The Green Goose* shocked and made enemies: Gałczyński was called a clown who was abusing his talent for unworthy ends and came under fire from both the right and the left, in the Catholic press and in communist publications.

Conceived as a joke, Gałczyński's *Green Goose* is, for all that, an integral part of the Polish avant-garde's movement away from conventional drama and its discarding of old, outworn forms of theatre, including even the theatre itself, at least as a place and experience as we have known it. Whereas most Western experimental theatre has hoped "to extend the limits of the possible," [51] the Polish avant-garde often seems more concerned with expanding the limits of the impossible; it has sought to make drama out of that very impossibility. Witkacy challenged realistic illusion in the name of Pure Form; Trzebiński explored the use of absent objects; Gałczyński now

[51] John A. Henderson, *The First Avant-Garde* (London, 1971), p. 11.

created a totally nonexistent theatre whose theatricality was based on the denial of performance.

Called by its author "the smallest theatre in the world," *The Green Goose* contains plays that range in length from three lines to a few pages. Playing havoc with classical dimensions and proportions, Gałczyński uses contraction (as Różewicz later employed enlargement) to render theatre absurd and make the drama lie in the very limitations of dramatic form. Traditionally, Polish drama had been nothing if not sublime and grandiose; Gałczyński writes his plays on the head of a pin and suddenly reveals the nothingness. In putting all the essentials of drama (including hallowed conventions and time-honored ceremonies) into tiny plays—like putting miniature ships into small glass bottles—the creator of *The Green Goose* invites us to view theatre, not on its accustomed scale in all its impressive surroundings, but as a delightfully preposterous trifle once the vast machinery of the stage is reduced to a diminutive toy.

The Green Goose does indeed have all the necessary paraphernalia of theatre—titles, subtitles, stage directions, a curtain—and its own permanent company (or stable) of actors: a *commedia dell' arte* animal family—a pig, a dog, a donkey, and the green goose herself, as well as a professor of angelology and a young male lead named Aloysius Ptarmigan [52]—all of whom became popular favorites, like the heroes of a comic strip. These character-performers appear in repertory, sometimes as themselves and sometimes making guest appearances and starring in different roles. In addition, other characters, real and fictitious, from past history and literature, as well as contemporary life, come on stage in unexpected circumstances. Among the dramatis personae, we meet Hamlet, Dante, and various Poles ancient and modern, ranging from the seventeenth-century king Jan Sobieski to the pianist Ignace Paderewski and Gałczyński himself, and including even the prompter.

Written during a period of uneasy transition in Polish history, *The Green Goose* dramatizes the clash between the an-

[52] In the original, Gżegżółka, a colloquial word for cuckoo, whose spelling is droll.

achronistic heritage of an old society that still lingers on and the realities of a new order not yet fully instituted; the resulting inconsistencies produce pure nonsense. As often happens in Polish drama, two times, past and future, meet incongruously in an uncertain present. Like Witkacy and Trzebiński, Gałczyński views with an ironic laugh the casualties of history.

Dedicated to the destruction of old forms of thought and art, *The Green Goose* is anti-illusionistic in theme as well as in technique. As one of its plays, "The Burial of a War Criminal," shows, skillful gravediggers can turn the interment of old forms into a continuous variety show; Gałczyński theatricalizes cultural gravedigging. Above all, Gałczyński's target is serious literature and all the false, inflated ideals produced by it. Accordingly, the great majority of plays in *The Green Goose* deal with national and topical issues, ridiculing what is most sacred and overblown in Polish history and culture, with its proclivity for messianic martyrdom and bardic mission. In plays like "An Unknown Manuscript of Wyspiański's" and "A Mickiewicz Matinee," Gałczyński carries on a disrespectful dialogue with the noblest traditions of Polish drama, mocking the high calling of the poet and questioning the importance of art itself.

In his ridicule of illusion, the creator of *The Green Goose* reserves a special place for the great creators of illusions: artists, patriots, professors, ideologists. Myths and mythmakers are the objects of his raillery. Playing with the Polish avant-garde's obsession with the relationship of intelligence to power, the intellectual to the mass, the individual to the state, Gałczyński is sarcastically contemptuous of the sensitive, artistic soul and his poses of superiority. It is no accident that Hamlet—along with the Polish romantics who adored him—appears in a number of the *Green Goose* plays. In "the smallest theatre in the world," Hamlet cannot decide whether to order tea or coffee and dies of an acute attack of hesitation, to the hysterical screams of his female admirers. Gałczyński the gravedigger buries the melancholic Prince in a coffin on which HAMLET-IDIOT is written in large black letters.

Although allusion and quotation in *The Green Goose* are for the most part directed against the solemn grandeur of "Polishness," other sources of sanctified tradition come in for equal abuse—namely, Shakespeare, the Bible, Greek mythology, and above all else, the theatre and its accepted conventions. *The Green Goose* parodies the serious rituals of the stage and uses dramatic forms to undermine dramatic form. Gałczyński provides a concise encyclopedia of theatre in which the various genres—society drama, romantic melodrama, bourgeois tragedy, apocalyptic morality, opera, ballet—appear in caricature. Characters are reduced to marionettes (as a matter of fact, *The Green Goose* was first staged by the Grotesque Puppet Theatre in Cracow in 1955). Titles, settings, and stage directions become elements of absurd humor as important as the dialogue itself. Requiring of the stage overliteral effects foreign to its nature, Gałczyński asks his "audience" to enjoy, not what the theatre can show, but what it cannot.[53]

In his jesting with the traditions of the stage, the author of *The Green Goose* assigns an important role to the curtain. This seemingly inanimate object becomes an indispensable actor—sometimes listed in the cast of characters—which must be able to fall expressively and even speak lines as the need arises. In different plays, the curtain is required to fall "discreetly," "majestically," "eagerly," "jauntily," and even "pedagogically." Several times it comes down by mistake, occasionally rectifying the error by going up again. Once it falls "forever," and another time it falls and kills itself on the spot. Or it may sink with an ominous swish and moan, or come crashing down. Once it is lowered by an anteater; another time it gets caught on a palm tree. At the conclusion of "The End of the World," it falls "optimistically." In all cases the curtain in *The Green Goose* falls on traditional Poland [54] and its remnant of masks and puppets (although it keeps going up again for encores, like the corpse in "The Burial of a War Criminal" so brilliantly stage-managed by the gravediggers).

Based on subversion of conventionality and authority, *The Green Goose* is a joyous act of defiance. No theoretical statement on the theatre by Gałczyński is needed, nor did he ever make one, except for a sarcastic letter to *Przekrój* denying that he was

[53] Jan Błoński, "Pozytywny ekscentryk, czyli o 'Zielonej gęsi,'" *Dialog*, No. 4 (1959), 99–106.
[54] Piwińska, pp. 81–109.

influenced by Witkacy's childhood plays.[55] *The Green Goose* itself is Gałczyński's criticism of the stage as it existed or could ever exist. "The smallest theatre in the world" was by design impossible to stage, or so it seemed according to all known rules of the drama. Certainly, by the laws of theatre that had come to prevail after 1949—those of enforced socialist realism dictated from the Soviet Union—*The Green Goose* became an utter impossibility in the new era of oppression for Poland under Stalinism.

In fact, it was not until the time of the October revolution of 1956, which brought liberalization to Poland and the end of socialist realism, that *The Green Goose* gained a foothold in the theatre and became a force for the creation of the new Polish drama. As long as the Stalinists reigned, fabricating new mythologies and sacred dogmas, there was little chance for a mocker of angelology; by 1950 Gałczyński had been forced to curb his high spirits, and he eventually had to "close" his theatre. The creator of Porphirion the Donkey was accused of being "a petty bourgeois in socialist garb" and received threatening anonymous letters. As early as 1946 the censor had called Gałczyński in for a talk before approving publication of "The Seven Sleeping Brothers," telling the poet that either this play was the most subversive work ever written, or that he, Gałczyński, was mad.

Since 1956, *The Green Goose* has been an invitation to imaginative directors to look at the world of stage convention afresh and find their own ways of revealing the absurdity of the theatre. Gałczyński made an outstanding translation of *A Midsummer Night's Dream* and undoubtedly was an enthusiastic admirer of the artistic ingenuity and mimetic skills of Bottom and his company. In fact, the pedagogic aim of *The Green Goose* was to debunk rigid ways of thinking (too often characteristic of the theatre) and inculcate a taste for the unexpected and surprising.

By the mid-1950's in Poland the time gap for acceptance of the new was narrowing; the historical moment had almost caught up with Polish avant-garde drama. Outside the theatre

[55] Konstanty Ildefons Gałczyński, "Cyrograf Witkacego: Zielona gęś zdemaskowana," *Przekrój*, No. 106 (1947), 5.

Gałczyński was already widely popular during his own life-time, and almost immediately after his death the author of *The Green Goose* became a direct influence on the student cabarets and theatres that sprang up at the first stirrings of liberaliza-tion. Although an established writer of prewar formation, Gałczyński anticipated the irreverent skepticism of the younger generation, and in his use of parody, fantasy, and bizarre juxtaposition, he opened the way for the grotesque works of Mrożek and Różewicz.

Similarities between *The Green Goose* and the theatre of the absurd in the West (introduced and quickly acclimatized in Poland after 1956) are readily noticeable, not only in form and technique, but also in theme. Frustration and defeat threaten man's feeble strivings. Nothing works out as planned by the characters; human beings are continually thwarted and crushed by forces outside their control. But a major difference emerges between the Western absurd and *The Green Goose*. Gałczyński's miniature plays are hardly negative or pessimis-tic; rather they function as dramatized fables that teach an un-foreseen moral lesson. Drawing on an anti-intellectual, practical belief in life and common sense, Gałczyński represents the di-dactic absurd, the fantastic tale with a rational basis and in-structive goal.

In "The Flood That Failed in Winter," Noah, his family, and the animals cannot leave on the ark since it is winter and the waters have frozen over. But as often happens in *The Green Goose* when everything seems impossible, the characters are able to exert ingenuity and find another, unheard-of way out of the dilemma: Noah turns the ark into a sleigh, and they all race off on a sleigh ride to Mount Ararat. Gałczyński admires down-to-earth solutions that ridicule and refute the lost-cause heroics of Polish history. The tragic, romantic view is under-cut, and myths leading to defeat, disaster, and war are ex-ploded. The last word is given everyday human things. Jove scrambles and eats the eggs that would have hatched Helen and the Trojan War. The Seven Sleeping Brothers cannot even wake up to their fated destiny, but snore on and on.

Objects—both present and absent—play a crucial role in *The Green Goose*. The relationship between man and thing, proposed by Trzebiński, comes to live in plays like "The Drama of a Deceived Husband," in which an antique credenza obligingly crushes the unhappy hero. In the very short play "The End of the World," that apocalyptic event—much heralded in the Polish avant-garde, even by Gałczyński himself—fails to take place because of a lost document, a nonexistent piece of paper. In the new Polish state, bureaucratic red tape and inefficiency prevent anything as final and decisive as the end of the world from ever occurring (by a similar irony Witkacy's *The End of the World*, a drama in three acts, could never take place because the play became lost during the war). In "The Atrocious Uncle"—a miniature comic version of the anticlimactic ending of Wyspiański's *The Wedding*—the frustrated hero waits, in destructive boredom and stagnation, for the wonderful event that never happens: the absent man on a white horse does not return, and there is no deliverance.

Bim-Bom and the Afanasjeff Family Circus: Avant-Garde Entertainment in Gdańsk, 1954–1964

The "nasty nightmare" of Stalinism was the last, relatively short period of retardation before avant-garde became mainstream in Poland. Success did not come quickly or easily—and there have been many vicissitudes since—but in the new political and social system under communism, avant-garde drama and theatre have flourished in Poland as never before. In the final struggle, it was collective groups of the young who first succeeded in bringing the new drama to the new society and then were able to make it widely popular.

In 1953 and 1954—toward the end of the Stalinist period—as a reaction against the dreariness and constraint of the official theatre, hamstrung as it was by bureaucracy and the dogmas of socialist realism, there arose quite spontaneously in Warsaw, Cracow, and other large Polish cities a number of amateur student theatres that expressed the rebellious viewpoint of the young and their longing for something other than drabness and conformity in art and in life. More than any other phenomenon of the time, these informal, nonprofessional troupes revitalized the Polish stage, brought it back to its true tradition of poetry and metaphor, and made possible the flowering of Polish avant-garde drama in the late 1950's and early 1960's in the major established theatres.

For the most part, the Polish student theatres of the mid-fifties created their own texts or utilized poetry, songs, and pastiches and parodies of operettas. Some were oriented toward political and social satire, others toward musical cabaret. There were those that presented actual plays, ancient or modern, and those that relied on improvisation. Of all these student theatres, the group that developed in Gdańsk—Bim-Bom and its later offshoot, the Afanasjeff Family Circus—was unique in its emphasis on the visual and in its combination of images from painting and sculpture with traditional forms of entertainment. Bim-Bom was essentially a nonliterary theatre which sought its inspiration both in the fine arts and in the popular arts of circus, carnival, street fair, music hall, and film. And like these popular arts, it had amusement as its prime goal, for all that it was modern and innovative. Bim-Bom was popular avant-garde.

Its location on the Baltic coast, the nature of its company and audience, and the circumstances of its growth serve to explain Bim-Bom's special character as popular visual entertainment in the avant-garde mode. The Gdańsk area had no university; and accordingly the students who created the theatre came, not from literature and the humanities, but from the School of Fine Arts, the Polytechnical Institute, and other technical-training establishments. Jerzy Afanasjew, Bim-Bom's guiding spirit from the start and later its historian and theoretician, was a student of architecture.[56] The rest of the company were painters, sculptors, engineers, film makers, even doctors and chemists, as well as musicians and dancers. The two professional actors in the group, Zbigniew Cybulski and Bogumił Kobiela (soon to be celebrated for their work in film, starting with Wajda's *Ashes and Diamonds* in 1957), directed all the productions and played many of the important roles.

[56] Afanasjew gives the entire history of Bim-Bom and The Afanasjeff Family Circus (spelled in the Russian manner for comical effect and in homage to Russian circus) in his book *Sezon kolorowych chmur: Gdańskie teatry eksperymentalne* (Gdynia, 1968), as well as in his article "Świat nie jest taki zły . . . ," in *Teatry studenckie w Polsce* ed. Jerzy Koenig (Warsaw, 1968), pp. 141–161.

With almost all its performers and spectators in their late teens or early twenties, Bim-Bom was a theatre by and for the young. Its purpose was to bring gaiety and spontaneity to lives that seemed hopelessly ground down. Cybulski explained, "We're actively fighting for the well-being of ordinary gray people who want to enjoy themselves, have fun, and relax." [57] The anonymous mass was starting to stir and ask for color and laughter in a world that had been leveled to uniform drabness.

Bim-Bom, from its inception in 1953, was a performers' theatre in which the creation of different pieces was a collective activity. Unlike professional cabaret with topical skits by various writers, each sketch in Bim-Bom was a group effort at fusing the poetry of the whole range of artistic disciplines into a single idea. Painters and painting offered a model; their theatre, Afanasjew maintained, was "closer to Chagall than to Brecht—to Utrillo than to Piscator." It was a theatre of colors and shapes that always reduced words to a minimum and sometimes dispensed with them altogether. The sketches could never be summarized or paraphrased in any other language. The aim was not to stage texts but poetic images; in Afanasjew's words, "The text was the same kind of material as the lighting, costuming, faces, gestures." [58] The performers' talents were those of improvisation, gesture, and pantomime. The most important influences on the Gdańsk student theatre, in addition to the fine arts, were Chaplin and the new Italian films, especially Vittorio de Sica's *Miracle in Milan,* whose pictorial fantasy and romanticism Bim-Bom wished to capture on the stage. Thus, the sketches were not primarily satirical but lyrical, often taking the form of loving parodies of film scenarios, cabaret skits, and circus acts.

The first full show that evolved from the initial premises and experiments, entitled *Aha* and presented in 1955, contains the germ of all Afanasjew's subsequent parodies of circus: an act with trapeze artists, a horse with two performers inside, a barker, and a ballet dancer (who was played by an unshaven, hairy-legged actor in a wig). Audiences were given presents, and performers played unrehearsed gags on one another. For

[57] Zbigniew Cybulski, quoted in Afanasjew, *Sezon kolorowych chmur,* p. 35.
[58] Afanasjew, "Świat nie jest taki zły . . . ," p. 148.

example, one night the pianist in the pit took off the actors'
shoes and tickled their feet; the following night, when they
retaliated by throwing objects, the musician pulled out a water
pistol and shot them. Audiences were invited, through an ap-
propriate form in the programs, to participate in selecting the
name for the theatre; the ultimate choice, Bim-Bom, comes
from A. A. Milne's *Winnie the Pooh,* in Polish translation, as well
as from a famous pair of clowns in the Russian circus.

In 1955, the company made the first of its many tours and
guest appearances, taking part in the Warsaw Student Theatre
Festival. Wherever they went, they traveled in special trucks,
establishing a carnival atmosphere and playing in the streets to
crowds. The girls wore black tunics and yellow skirts with
painted black flowers. The Bim-Bom song became a popular
hit, as did the theatre's yellow scarf with the picture of a dog
lifting his leg on a cactus. In order to prepare a new program,
the group went for the winter to the Tatra Mountains in the
south of Poland, where they lived and worked together like a
family. Each new sketch was slowly matured in a communal atmosphere. A school for actors was developed from these exer-
cises and improvisations. It was Cybulski who initiated the
training program and who also brought about an exchange of
ideas with cinema. As a result, Afanasjew and others in the
troupe began to work in the medium of film and to write film
scenarios, parts of which later appeared in Bim-Bom. Cybulski
also was able to utilize techniques and ideas from Bim-Bom in
his own films. What most impressed Cybulski was that everyone
in the troupe had to be able to do everything:

Our program is totally "handcrafted" in every sense of the word. We
have gone back a bit to the traditions of the medieval mimes, a profession once practiced by students, and to the rich traditions and origins
of the theatre and *commedia dell' arte*—depending on improvisations on
stage by the actor whose character appeared in each of the numbers.[59]

Bim-Bom reached its high point with the second program,
Joy in Earnest, which was premiered in the spring of 1956.
Based on an ideological commitment to the little man, the
Chaplinesque hero, and proceeding on the assumption that

[59] Zbigniew Cybulski, quoted in Afanasjew, *Sezon kolorowych chmur,* p. 48.

theatre is not just a game but a healer of souls, the "joy" was to
be "in earnest" as an affirmative declaration of belief in youth
and love. Writing of this program, the Polish critic Jan Kott observed: "It is a theatre of poetic and intellectual metaphor, as-
tonishing in the freshness of its visual techniques. . . . Bim-
Bom's playing with modernity is not simply for its own sake. It
is steeped in politics. Its surrealistic metaphor and speeded-up
imagination serve moral indignation and moral revolution." [60]

All the sketches and numbers in *Joy in Earnest* illustrated one
central theme, on which the entire program was based: the
contrast between two human types found everywhere throughout the world—roosters and organ grinders—whose images
were projected on the curtain even before the show began.
Roosters appear as self-important, soulless, overbearing of-
ficials, always crowing or showing their tails, whereas organ
grinders are uncertain dreamers and poets of everyday life,
playing what is in their hearts. In a modification of the older
Polish tradition, the poet hero now becomes everyman, and, to
the plaintive strains of the hurdy-gurdy, battles the crested bureaucrat and merciless functionary of the state. The spectators
were asked to take sides in the struggle and yet were made to
realize that roosters can hatch out of ordinary people, who first
grow beaks, then feathers, before finally turning into "Über-
roosters" like the SS men in the sketch "Snouts."

The primary technique used in all the sketches in *Joy in Earnest* was the application of film principles to the stage. Instead
of using film on the stage, the stage itself was used as film.
There was a montage of all scenic elements, including the stage
itself and its physical parts, whereby the spectator's eyes were
made to travel about through the equivalent of close-ups, full
shots, and shots from a distance. Constantly shifting place and
time, dissolves and blackouts, as well as intersecting planes of
light, all synchronized with a sound track played through loudspeakers and special hidden speakers, permitted the greatest
possible variety and fluidity.

Each skit was terse, running from a few seconds to a few
minutes, and rehearsals were timed with a stopwatch. The

[60] Jan Kott, quoted in Afanasjew, *Sezon kolorowych chmur*, p. 36.

rhythm of the lights continued the rhythm of the music; gestures had to be strictly correlated to both of these. The designers constructed small models to work out the interplay of color, light, and movement, making use of mirrors as in the films of Georges Méliès. Sculptural treatment of space allowed the spectator to view the stage from different angles and perspectives, even in different scales.

"We worked from the premise that the contemporary spectator must be attacked with all possible means," Afanasjew maintained.[61] Through the use of lights and screens, spectators viewing the antiwar skit "Pilots" first saw the crew inside an atomic bomber and next looked up from the earth at a huge, faraway sky, heard the sounds of a distant plane, and watched the same plane approaching. They witnessed the pilots dropping the bombs and the crash of the plane, hit by antiaircraft fire, and then saw small silhouettes of parachutists and bombs falling. After the sudden explosion and mushroom cloud, there was total darkness, an incessant ticking sound, and finally sharp light. A young actress at the front of the stage blew soap bubbles at the audience. The theatre of illusion had vanished; the actors appeared, so close that they were almost among the audience, signaling that the play was a nightmare and the real outcome was in the spectators' hands. At the end of the entire performance, bright lights in the auditorium came as a deliberate jolt. The narrator told the audience the time and then said, "Good night, . . . Comrades," sending the young spectators back into the Republic of Roosters with renewed faith in the struggle.

Bim-Bom was an accurate register of history, in the forefront of the social changes that were sweeping Poland. The workers' revolt in Poznań in June brought on the bloodless revolution of October, 1956, leading to greater political and cultural independence from the Soviet Union. From this point on, Bim-Bom, with its depiction of a dreamed-of utopia in which organ grinders triumph over roosters, played throughout Poland to standing-room-only audiences. After regular performances,

---

[61] Afanasjew, *Sezon kolorowych chmur*, p. 47.

the company added extra pantomimes about the "cult of personality" and ridiculed dictators.

The period from 1956 to 1959 was an exciting new era of artistic freedom and innovation that Bim-Bom had helped to initiate. Now financed by the state and given official support and sanction, Bim-Bom appeared at many festivals, first in Eastern Europe, then in the West. Despite its successes in Moscow, Paris, Amsterdam, and Brussels, Bim-Bom deliberately retained its amateur status and its special flavor of fantasy and pranks. The troupe's travels gave them a chance to observe Western avant-garde. What most struck Afanasjew and his colleagues was that Bim-Bom was closer to film than to theatre and not experimental in the usual sense of the term since its performers strove to communicate directly with the audience. The naive poetry that Afanasjew looked for in the theatre could not exist in the busy and hurried marketplaces of European modern art.

Unwilling and unable to turn professional, Bim-Bom came to an end in 1960, and its principal performers either formed or joined other groups. By this time there had been a great proliferation of student theatres until several hundred existed in the early 1960's. In its six-year existence Bim-Bom had produced 4 complete programs, given a total of 370 performances, maintained a company of 58, appeared in dozens of festivals and won numerous prizes. For all its members who went on to careers in theatre, film, cabaret, television, and the visual arts, Bim-Bom provided the formative experience: a creative collective like a medieval troupe, where each performer had his reason for existence.

In order to pursue his goals on a more intimate scale, Afanasjew in 1958 had already formed his own, smaller group, the Afanasjeff Family Circus (spelling his name in the Russian manner in homage to Soviet circus). He believed that only non-mass-produced amateur theatre could counteract the process of dehumanization by which the actor in modern times becomes a mere piece of machinery. For his inspiration Afanasjew went to the traveling street-fair theatre and the eternal masks of the clown. These seemed to him the central images of the human comedy. In Bim-Bom, the performers often wore their costumes offstage as well as on, and Afanasjew, thoroughly accustomed to his outfit as circus director, paraded about in it, on the streets, at home, even on the beach.

In searching for a Polish equivalent to *commedia dell' arte,* Afanasjew, like Wyspiański before him, went to Polish folklore and folk culture (ridiculed by the literati and in the process of dying out), to fairs and to the primitive Christmas pageants, with their recurring figures of devil, angel, priest, bear, and death, as well as to Chagall's world of miracles and magic. Looking to the past and to the East, he hoped to escape from the standardized, fabricated art culture of modern Europe.

Afanasjew's circus consisted of a family of fixed characters, who appeared as themselves in all the shows. He himself played his role as the circus director, Polichinelle; his wife Alina Ronczewska-Afanasjew, a painter, was Columbine; and his brother-in-law, Ryszard Ronczewski, a professional mime, was the clown. It was, in actual fact, the Afanasjew Circus Family playing themselves. The members of the family had already acquired the necessary staging and directorial skills in their work with Bim-Bom. What Afanasjew now wished to achieve was freedom for the actors. This liberation of the actor's personality, he felt, could best be realized by a circus whose models would be the medieval troupe as well as Toulouse-Lautrec, Picasso, Meyerhold, and Calder. In the Circus, the actor would be the self-sufficient element. Afanasjew declared:

In the theatre, the actor is most important. We wanted our theatre to be a dialogue between actor and director. And for the theatre to arise from this dialogue. Let's let the actor be the coauthor. Let the actor stop being only a duplicating machine and loudspeaker for the director and author of the play. Let the actor attempt to "write it himself" and "have his say about the world." [62]

In 1961, the Circus took part in the Gdańsk City Carnival, presenting its *Comedy of Masks* on a horse-drawn wagon with a large platform like the stage of a street-fair theatre. As the troupe drove through the streets at night, shooting cap pistols and throwing candy to the crowd of children following behind,

[62] *Ibid.,* p. 90.

the audience looked out windows and lined the sidewalks. In 1962, the Circus prepared and premiered its fourth and final program, *Good Evening, Clown,* Afanasjew's fullest realization of parodied street-fair theatre. The subject was the clown and his family and their eternal struggle with the circus director. "Our theatre was a waking dream," Afanasjew wrote, "a dream of pictures never painted by Columbine, a dream inherent in Harlequin's everyday costume."[63] During the intermission huge "carnival heads" gave out candy to the audience, and the actors went among the crowd on stilts.

Afanasjew believed the circus to be the ideal theatre, not only for the actor, but also for the spectator, bored by conventional drama. In order to make sure that their new production had appeal for everyone, as a true circus should, the company tried out *Good Evening, Clown* on varied audiences: children, soldiers, painters, miners, and even the deaf. The aim, Afanasjew insisted, was "to free the theatre from satirical texts, to limit the word to the minimum. The question is: How to make people laugh?" To answer that question, the family found that they had to go to films, their gags and clowns, their rhythm and tempo, their improbable situations and absurdities. In explaining their reliance on cinema, Afanasjew declared: "Everything had to be condensed, rapid-fire, without any breaks. Each joke had to come in hot pursuit of the next one; every second had to be crammed with substance."[64]

Jan Kott described his impressions of *Good Evening, Clown* in these terms:

The Afanasjew Family Circus was fascinating in its total technical perfection. It was a parody of circus trash. But a parody done with incredible finesse, a parody which became poetry. It had the atmosphere of an Italian film. It presented trashy circus people, but circus people who once were great artists. This parody had an underlining of lyricism and bitterness. With respect to its artistic qualities I have seen nothing quite so perfect for a long time.[65]

[63] *Ibid.*
[64] *Ibid.*, p. 94. In 1960 Afanasjew had made a film about their circus, called *White Animals,* portraying a performance given on an island in the Baltic. This film without words is filled with allegorical images of the great events and emotions in man's life in relation to the rhythms of nature.
[65] Jan Kott, quoted in Afanasjew, *Sezon kolorowych chmur,* p. 234.

From both the scenarios and Afanasjew's theoretic state-
ments (themselves virtually scenarios in their poetic evocation
of scene, use of color, and burgeoning metaphor), it is apparent that Bim-Bom and the Family Circus continue the eclectic
Polish tradition of avant-garde drama and, at the same time,
represent a new direction, moving still farther away from conventional theatre—out of the theatre itself to the cabaret and
circus arena and even into the streets. Like Gałczyński (one of
the chief inspirations for the student groups), Afanasjew turns
to *commedia* and clowning and, focusing on a clan of performers and their tricks, takes the audience behind the façade
of theatrical illusion and convention. In scenarios like "Faust"
and *Good Evening, Clown,* the audience sees the stage simulta-
neously from different points of view, from back to front as
well as from front to back, and even turned about before one's
eyes.

Like Witkacy before him, Afanasjew is in quest of pure
theatre as an integrated play of movement, color, shape, and
light, free of psychological realism. The director of Bim-Bom
and the Circus likewise sees the proper model in the nonverbal
arts and demands of the actor the precise timing and control of
the musician and the sureness of hand of the painter. But for
Afanasjew—and here he differs radically from Witkacy and his
other Polish predecessors—the performer is the creator, the
scenario does not exist independently from the production,
and theatre should be purified of literary text rather than subordinated to it.

For inspiration, Afanasjew went both to East and West as
well as to his Polish predecessors. To flee from socialist and
bourgeois realism, he ranges back in time to the old folk
theatre and ahead to the newer art of cinema. As authorities,
he cites Meyerhold and Eisenstein along with Chaplin and the
American silent film. For Afanasjew, the 1920's represented
the last outstanding European avant-garde, which served as his
ideal, along with the Middle Ages, the greatest period of communal artistic endeavor for a cause.

Collective undertakings with loyal followings, Bim-Bom and
the Afanasjeff Family Circus were not the lonely and isolated
voices that the Polish avant-garde dramatists of the interwar

years had been condemned to be. Finding an enthusiastic re-
sponse from large audiences of fellow students and young people, the student theatres were now able to be a part of their
own times. Since history was more receptive to them, Afanasjew and his colleagues could take a shorter view of history, and
like their immediate predecessor Gałczyński, they offered topical comment, lyrical and satirical, on the world in transition
around them. Thus Bim-Bom and the Circus ushered in and
popularized the avant-garde theatre that was soon to become
established in Poland as the norm. Drawing on the popular as
well as the visual arts, and above all on cinema, Afanasjew and
his associates made avant-garde theatre accessible and amusing
as entertainment and enlarged the possibilities of the stage for
total spectacle.

In a break with previous avant-garde tradition, the new hero
in Bim-Bom, the Circus, and the other student theatres is no
longer Witkacy's obsolescent artist-intellectual, but the Chaplinesque little man, the powerless nobody in an alien world, as
much at sea in the modern milieu as the nearly extinct great in-
dividualist, but more humble, guiltless, and guileless. He is simply a lost cog in the machine. In the new mass society, the
anonymous, faceless hero is the victim of the state that crushes
him while claiming to serve him.

Mrożek: Parables of Power

Sławomir Mrożek, who was to become the principal Pol-
lish avant-garde dramatist in the decade after 1956, wrote his
first play, "The Professor," for Bim-Bom's *Joy in Earnest.* Born
in a small town not far from Cracow in 1930, Mrożek, the son
of a mailman, studied architecture, painting, and Oriental art.
He began his career as a cartoonist and writer of humorous
sketches while working on a Cracow newspaper and in the mid-
1950's published numerous satirical and fantastic stories, sly
parables about bureaucratic absurdity and its make-believe
world, such as "The Elephant." As a result of his contribution
to Bim-Bom, Mrożek discovered his bent for playwriting, to
which he has devoted the rest of his career, while still occasionally producing books of cartoons, stories, and sketches.

From his brief association with *Joy in Earnest,* the author of

"The Professor" gained a valuable apprenticeship in theatre and developed characteristic techniques and themes for the series of one-act plays that he was to write in the late 1950's and early 1960's. Bim-Bom taught Mrożek the full range of theatrical means at his disposal. For although "The Professor" is a literary text as well as a scenario, it is above all a tightly organized, precisely structured orchestration of sights and sounds that builds to an inevitable crescendo and barbed coda. From *Joy in Earnest* Mrożek learned the craft of exact timing and calculated effect and a style of performance in which cabaret artist communicates directly with audience.

In composing "The Professor" for Bim-Bom, Mrożek also discovered his own leading motifs of illusion, power, and their victims, as he worked variations on the show's theme of organ grinders and roosters. Mrożek's special province in drama is the entrapment of sacrificial offerings who desperately attempt to justify their own extirpation at the hands of inscrutable forces. His organ grinders do not play what is in their hearts but, terrified, sing the praises of the system that crushes them. Returning, in large part, to the Witkacian tradition that pits the individual against the mass, Mrożek's plays chart the capitulation of intellect to Lopakian power. But the younger playwright creates a new type of hero, an amalgam of the Hamlet-like artist-intellectual and the innocent little man caught in the squeeze of history, who uses his brains to rationalize the hopeless situation from which he cannot escape.

In his analysis of the mechanism of power, its operation and its ensnarement of both the very intelligent and the very helpless (who most often are one and the same), the postwar playwright shows that the old gestures and poses are not yet dead and that past history is still alive. Called a gravedigger of the past, Mrożek, following the established Polish practice, utilizes Shakespeare, Wyspiański, Witkacy, Gombrowicz, and a myriad of other allusions and quotations in his work as undertaker of old forms. Uniting Trzebiński's abstract dissection of power, carried to logically absurd conclusions, with Gałczyński's free-flowing fantasy, cabaret style, and taste for the impossible, Mrożek creates an efficient, economical avant-garde drama that has both clarity of form and the resonance of parable, along with technical mastery of theatrical effect.

Starting from absurd premises, the one-act plays develop a single action to its logical consequences. The protagonists do not define the situation; it defines them. In *Out at Sea* (1960), three men in tuxedos—Big, Medium, and Small—inexplicably find themselves shipwrecked on a raft in the middle of the ocean. Since they are growing desperately hungry, it is perfectly natural that they should decide that two of them must eat the third; given their respective sizes, it is immediately clear who the victim will be. As "civilized men," however, they wish to make the choice democratically, and accordingly they hold political rallies, conduct an election campaign, and invent slogans. No matter what is said, Small's smallness condemns him. As the knife is sharpened, first the victimizers and then the victim give excellent reasons why he should be sacrificed for the common good. The arrival of a postman, who—like a character out of *The Green Goose*—swims up to the raft with a letter for Small, discloses that Small's father was a clerk and that he is therefore a member of the privileged class. Historical justice now demands that Small die for the sake of the less fortunate Big and Medium.

Gradually Small realizes that he wishes to sacrifice himself; only by being eaten can he find fulfillment in society. "Let us think logically," he reasons; "true freedom exists only in a place where there is no freedom." As he washes carefully between his toes so that he will not be gritty and cause his fellow men indigestion, Small experiences a new feeling of liberation. As Big explains, "You must be eliminated from Society, and the best way is for society to eat you." Even though Big and Medium discover a can of pork and beans at the last moment, they conceal the fact; Small is so happy at the prospect of being eaten that they cannot bear to disappoint him.

Eat or be eaten: saving one's own skin means devouring someone else's. Both eater and eaten are impelled to find ideological justifications in history for their participation in society's cannibalism. Mrożek's grotesque vision—at once comic and macabre—portrays victim and victimizers, organ grinders and

roosters as controlled by arbitrary forces beyond their compre-
hension to which they must submit. Preposterous dilemmas are
suddenly imposed from outside, without explanation. Although the characters do not create their own predicaments,
they readily accept them and develop them into a philosophy
of existence. Using simple generic types of humanity in these
one-act plays which require neither individual psychology nor
exposition, Mrożek moves instantly to the essential situation of
impossible choices that become nonchoices. Dialogue, elliptical
and telescopic, moves abruptly; tempo constantly accelerates as
the human puppets succumb to the speeded-up mechanism
that takes away their dignity with implacable matter-of-factness.

In *Strip-Tease* (1961), two respectable gentlemen in business
suits and carrying briefcases suddenly find themselves pushed
into a room by an unknown force. One hopes to resist; the
other is totally passive, maintaining his belief in inner freedom.
A gigantic hand next appears and forces them to remove their
clothes, item by item. The unfathomable power treats both
alike, and despite their different philosophies they both obey in
exactly the same way. In these and other one-act plays, Mrożek
traces the comic growth of terror as victims, confronted with
historical necessity, conform to the grotesque workings of absolute power.

Tango, or the Need for Order and Harmony (1964), a full-length
play and Mrożek's most trenchant work, extends the range of
the playwright's investigation to include social, cultural, and intellectual history as well as the strictly political on which he had
concentrated in his previous plays. In *Tango,* Mrożek treats
family drama as a history of civilization encompassing the decline and fall of liberal Europe from the end of the nineteenth
century through the triumph of totalitarianism. By means of
ludicrous discrepancies in setting, costume, and style, and
glancing allusions to Shakespeare, Wyspiański, and Gombrowicz, *Tango* becomes a many layered work, a museum of modern European art, manners, and morals, and a prism for viewing the relation of culture to power and the intelligentsia's
responsibility for the celebration of force as the only value.

In its outer story, *Tango* traces the collapse of a farcical European family composed of three different generations, each

more disorganized and futile than the one before, each representing a further step in the historical debacle. Arthur, the young son, can find no meaning in the world his elders have created for him; his avant-garde parents—products of the rebellious 1920's who dabble in experimental theatre—have left him nothing to rebel against. Seeing the chaos all about him, Arthur concludes that there has been enough freedom; now convention must be re-established. To clean up the mess at home and to create order, the young hero realizes that he must have a wedding, following the precedents set in plays by Wyspiański and Gombrowicz. Only such a formal ceremony can revive old traditions and disciplines.

As a result of Arthur's domestic *coup d'état*—a minor counter-revolution against the license and anarchy of his parents' generation—everyone is forced to dress neatly in old-fashioned clothes, but the disillusioned young hero soon sees that he is creating form without content and that it is impossible to reinstate the absolutes of tragedy and the values of the past. Abandoning his futile efforts to bring about a spiritual rebirth in his family, Arthur arrives drunk at his ridiculous formal wedding (complete with Mendelssohn's music and posed group photographs). The entire performance, which Arthur has staged, has failed of its desired effect and is as absurd as his father's avant-garde pottering. Ala, Arthur's new bride, with whom he has been sleeping for some time, has been deceiving him with Eddie, the fat semiliterate butler and hanger-on who has been lurking in the background and fraternizing with the hero's mother.

Inspired by alcohol and disgust, Arthur discovers the idea of death-dealing power as the only value that can exist in a world of chaos and nullity, but he is too weak and too much an intellectual to put his own brilliant principle into practice. Instead, it is the gross boor Eddie who pre-empts the idea and suddenly kills its inventor with two sharp blows on the back of the neck with the butt of Arthur's own revolver. Thereupon, the thug assumes power in the crumbling, decadent family. Within Arthur's abortive coup, a second, genuine class revolution along Lopakian lines takes place with surprising speed.

Tango ends with the sort of striking scenic effect, initiated by

Wyspiański and continued by Witkacy, that has become characteristic of Polish avant-garde drama. Asserting that at last there
will be order in the household, Eddie puts on Arthur's coat,
which is too small for his broad shoulders, and Great-Uncle
Eugene, muttering that he submits to brute force although he
despises it in his heart, unlaces his new master's shoes. Then
Eddie plays a recording of a tango—the dance that for Arthur's
parents symbolized liberation and rebellious abandon—on an
old wind-up gramophone with a large horn and forces the
great-uncle, pitiful relic of old Europe, to dance with him. The
compelling music of the tango does not stop even after the curtain falls. Eddie, the new man, is dancing cheek to cheek with
the doddering humane tradition that always capitulates to force
and dances to its tune.

As part of the play's elaborate network of allusion, the tango
is Mrożek's version of the famous Mulch dance of despair,[66]
and Arthur is *Tango*'s Hamlet, replaced by the strong man
without scruples, Eddie-Fortinbras.

Interestingly, "The Professor," Mrożek's first play, contains
in miniature the seeds of *Tango*. The short skit for Bim-Bom
forecasts Mrożek's theatre of empty forms in which various old
theatrical illusions are tried and found inadequate for the shifting realities of power as the past collides with the future in a
discontinuous present. Already in "The Professor" Mrożek
starts to sketch the cultural and social history of Europe and its
art from the time of the Hapsburgs to the present. Three distinct historical times meet and overlap in a cold, bleak lycée
classroom somewhere in a middle-European backwater. There
coexist the bust of Caesar, the Professor in his shabby old-
fashioned clothes, the students in their uniforms, the director
in his business suit, the drab rainy street outside, and the animated, colorful, clamorous world of illusion which the Professor conjures up from out of the past.

"The Professor" is theatre in the theatre carried one additional step, since the illusion which the Professor evokes is an
illusion of an illusion: the world of the Wien Burgtheater. For a
moment it all comes to life: the classroom becomes a theatre;

[66] Mrożek had already used the Mulch dance in his one-act play *Party* (1962).

the scoffing pupils who begin as nonbelievers are converted into performers and celebrants; the Professor as conductor directs his students in the overture to a great drama. The voices of the past that he invokes overpower the apathy, disorder, and boredom of the present; the Professor seems close to imposing the old art of a lost world. But the strains from the past are only a prelude to the arrival of the angry director, the bureaucrat, administrator, man of the future. The wonderful spectacle envisaged by the Professor never takes place.

The nostalgic power of the past cannot compete with the power of power; the dialogue with the voices of an earlier age is abruptly cut short. The Professor now must dance to the tune of the director, not direct an imaginary orchestra in an imaginary Wien Burgtheater. Charming, cultured old Europe is seen as theatre, from the perspective of a dreary classroom in which the relics of civilization are perpetuated and purveyed to bored, unruly students. But they know a good show when they see it. All the audience of young students—played by student actors and watched in the real theatre by an audience of real students—can do is to applaud the Professor's performance. Mrożek uses the double perspective of Bim-Bom's theatre in the theatre (used elsewhere by Afanasjew in "Faust") to present the decline of European civilization as theatrical spectacle, as collapsing illusion.

Mrożek has lived abroad since the early 1960's, and because of his protest against the invasion of Czechoslovakia in 1968, his plays came under a cloud in Poland and ceased to be performed, although his new works continued to be published regularly in the Polish drama magazine *Dialog*. This ban came to an end in 1974, and Mrożek's latest parables of power, such as *Testarium* (1967), *Quartet* (1967), *Second Course* (1968), *Vatzlav* (1970), *Happy Event* (1973), *The Slaughterhouse* (1973), and *Emigrants* (1974), can now be performed and fill the gap caused by their absence from the Polish stage. Although he makes his home permanently in the West and his plays are often performed there first, Mrożek is a Polish playwright writing in Polish in the tradition of Wyspiański, Witkacy, and Gałczyński, not in the style of the international Parisian avant-garde.

Avant-Garde Becomes Mainstream

As a result of the social and political changes brought about
by the events of October, 1956, the achievement of greater
independence from the Soviet Union, the return to an autonomous Polish cultural policy, and the liberalization of con-
trols, the avant-garde in Polish music, painting, sculpture,
dance, theatre, and film flourished and quickly became the
mainstream. History had finally caught up with the Polish
avant-garde and its great moment came. It was at one with its
own time and place, was accepted by the public, the critics, and
even the state (despite innumerable difficulties of political censorship)—and was soon to be recognized by the world at large
for the first time.

Suddenly, in 1956, Polish theatre became wildly receptive to
everything new; all that was experimental, daring, and unexpected was good. There was a massive reaction against realism,
whether bourgeois or socialist, and a return to the native Polish
tradition of metaphor, poetry, parody, and the grotesque.
Western avant-garde drama, previously banned, immediately
struck a responsive chord and was eagerly assimilated. During
the great influx of foreign plays in 1957 and 1958, Brecht,
Beckett, Dürrenmatt, Ionesco, and Frisch were wholeheartedly
accepted and genuinely popular in the theatre; they did not encounter any of the puzzlement and hostility that often greeted
their work in the West. A country that had been waiting a century and a half for the great event that never happened experi-
enced no trouble at all in understanding *Waiting for Godot;* Poland already had its own tradition of plays about futile waiting,
such as Wyspiański's *The Wedding.*

The accumulated and long repressed avant-garde writing
that poured forth made the years from 1956 to 1968 a great
period in Polish theatre. All Polish theatres were avant-garde;
in effect, there was no commercial stage and no complacent,
entertainment-seeking audience. With approximately four
hundred new productions a year, mainly of contemporary
plays, the Polish theatre in this era had perhaps the most interesting and varied repertory in all Europe. Even average Polish
spectators responded favorably to avant-garde plays, native and
foreign; the absurd and grotesque were a natural part of their

past, their tradition, their history. Rather than an acquired taste for a special intellectual elite, the new theatre was part of the sensibility of an entire society, which, in the words of a Polish critic, "has not yet come to terms with itself, or with history, or with daily life and which does not believe in its old traditions or in the future." [67]

There was a sudden explosion of playwriting. Nearly everyone in the literary world—poets like Zbigniew Herbert, Stanisław Grochowiak, Tymoteusz Karpowicz, and Tadeusz Różewicz, as well as philosophers like Leszek Kołakowski—wrote avant-garde plays, not simply because it was fashionable but because it was a natural way for them to express themselves. In all its aspects, Polish theatre felt the impact of modern sensibility even though this theatre did not have a modern subject matter derived from daily life and, because of censorship, could not deal directly with contemporary social or political reality. Rather, it continued to live on its own poetic, metaphoric heritage.

The creative outburst in Polish theatre after 1956 is the final flowering of the tradition that began with Witkacy and is more a culmination than a new start. Significantly, most of the plays that were written during the early phase of the avant-garde movement were now staged for the first time. Witkacy was rediscovered and became the most important older playwright on the Polish stage in the period after the liberalization. Witkacy's posthumous fame was furthered by two outstanding painters turned directors who have devoted much of their careers to presenting his plays in the theatre.

In 1956 Tadeusz Kantor, an experimental visual artist working in Cracow, staged the first postwar production of Witkacy, *The Cuttlefish,* at his Cricot II, a combination art gallery, theatre, and club.[68] Kantor has gone on to produce Witkacy's *The Mad-*

---

[67] Jan Błoński, "Les Nouveaux Auteurs," tr. Gilberte Crépy and Zygmunt Szymański, *Dialog,* Special French-Language Issue, VIII (June, 1963), 133–141.

[68] *The Cuttlefish* had been first performed during Witkacy's lifetime in 1933 at the Cricot, an experimental theatre in Cracow organized by a group of artists. See Jerzy Lau, *Teatr Artystów: Cricot* (Cracow, 1967), pp. 61–63. Kantor, in calling his theatre Cricot II and making his first production *The Cuttlefish,* has stressed his continuation of the avant-garde tradition from the period between the wars.

man and the Nun, In a Small Country House, The Water Hen, and
Dainty Shapes and Hairy Apes; he has also taken the last two
productions abroad to festivals in Venice and Edinburgh and
presented *The Shoemakers* in Paris with French actors.

Józef Szajna, who spent the war years in the death camps at
Auschwitz and Buchenwald, studied to be a painter and scene
designer; all his work for the theatre is shaped by a terrifying
and moving vision of the horror of the extermination camps,
expressed in powerful visual images and through the use of objects. Szajna found Witkacy's portrayal of a world gone mad
perfectly suited to his own intense obsessions. He has designed
and directed *The Madman and the Nun, They, In a Small Country
House,* and *The New Deliverance,* as well as a composite play
called *Witkacy* in which several works are interwoven.[69]

One of the most original theatre artists in Poland, Szajna radically transforms the texts he uses, carrying on a dialogue with
the past, as had his predecessors, Witkacy and Wyspiański. In
the production of Wyspiański's *Acropolis* which Szajna cocreated
with Jerzy Grotowski for the Polish Laboratory Theatre in
1962, the action of the play is transferred from the cathedral of
the royal castle in Cracow to the Nazi concentration camp thirty
miles to the south, at Auschwitz. Wyspiański's allegorical fable
about death and resurrection becomes a modern parable about
human suffering in the death camps. Objects like wheelbarrows
(made by Szajna himself) take on a value higher than man, who
is subordinated to them and reduced to the level of a thing.

In his production of Wandurski's proletarian morality, *Death
in a Pear Tree,* in 1964, Szajna goes one step further in depicting the dehumanizing machinery of war. Utilizing only objects,
Szajna creates a war scene from which all traces of the human
have been banished. Szajna has explained his method thus:

The action is created by metal wheels of various sizes rushing at each
other from different directions and lit up by crossed spotlights. Some-

[69] During the rehearsals of *Witkacy,* Szajna told the actors: "He is our
Ionesco, and that is flattering for Ionesco. In comparison with Witkacy, even
Gombrowicz could be called the son of a great father; Mrożek is the son of
Gombrowicz, but the greatest was the grandfather. Witkacy was like a prophet;
he stood beyond categories and beyond literature. And he became theatre in
which everything is possible" (quoted in Maria Czanerle, *Szajna* [Gdańsk, 1974],
p. 51).

times they pass by each other; now and then, though, they collide and, with a great deal of noise, collapse on the stage. As a result of this "fight" they form a shapeless heap of hardware.[70]

The most famous and influential contemporary Polish theatre artist, Jerzy Grotowski, began his career as a director with Ionesco's *The Chairs* in 1957, when he was twenty-four and part of the first wave of avant-garde rebellion that was then sweeping Poland. Grotowski went on to found his own theatre, first the Theatre of 13 Rows in 1959 in Opole, and subsequently the Laboratory Theatre in 1965 in Wrocław, where it is still located.

In addition to *Acropolis,* Grotowski has chosen other classic plays, both Polish and foreign, and transformed them for his own purposes: Byron's *Cain* (1960), Mickiewicz's *Forefathers' Eve* (1961), Słowacki's *Kordian* (1962), Marlowe's *Doctor Faustus* (1962), and Calderón's *The Constant Prince* (1965). However, Grotowski essentially uses the body of the actor as his text, and the play and playwright disappear. In *Apocalypsis cum figuris* (1969), Grotowski has constructed the scenario himself from the Bible and works by Dostoevsky, T. S. Eliot, and Simone Weil.

Grotowski's method of training actors has become celebrated throughout the world and produced disciples and schools of followers, particularly in the United States, where its anti-Stanislavski techniques were seized upon as an antidote to the still dominant realistic style of acting. In Poland there was a slight time lag in recognizing Grotowski's full importance; at first the Polish cultural establishment in avant-garde drama and theatre—itself virtually routine by the mid-1960's—found little of interest in what seemed to be marginal experiments outside the mainstream. However, Grotowski's fame and influence in Europe and America, which came first, helped to bring him acceptance in Poland, where he has been at least tolerated and ultimately respected, even if he is not as widely known and admired at home as abroad.[71]

[70] Quoted in Andrzej Hausbrandt, "An Interview with Józef Szajna," *Le Théâtre en Pologne/The Theatre in Poland*, Nos. 5–6 (1969), 22.

[71] Jan Błoński, "Grotowski and his Laboratory Theatre," *Dialog*, Special English-Language Issue, 1970, p. 142.

Grotowski clearly carries on the tradition of the Polish avant-
garde in seeking out totally new ways, in rejecting what already
exists, and in radically redefining the nature of theatre, while at
the same time pursuing a dialogue with the past as it appears in
the Polish classics. Grotowski himself has acknowledged continuity with his great predecessor, saying that he preferred to be
considered indebted to Witkacy as playwright-theoretician than
to the French writer Antonin Artaud (who developed ideas
similar to Witkacy's somewhat later). Grotowski declared that '
he owed to Witkacy the essential idea that the theatre can be a
religion without religion.[72]

Różewicz: Playwriting an Assemblage

Of all the post-1956 Polish playwrights, the one most appro-
priate for the final position in a collection of avant-garde
drama is Tadeusz Różewicz. No contemporary Polish writer has
moved further from traditional notions of drama—even avant-
garde drama—than Różewicz. As Grotowski seeks new techniques of acting, Różewicz looks for totally new directions in
playwriting. Since, after fifty years of struggle, the avant-garde
has become the mainstream in Poland, the truly creative playwright must rebel against that avant-garde and go beyond it,
not merely repeat its formulas. Conventional drama no longer
exists, but the conventions of drama persist, even in the avant-
garde. Like his predecessor Gałczyński, Różewicz pits himself
against the very nature of drama.

Born in 1921, of the same war generation as Trzebiński and
ten years older than Mrożek, Różewicz was a soldier in a guer-
rilla unit during the German occupation. His first literary
works, published after the war, were poems that expose literature as a lie and attack all literary convention. Short-story
writer and poet as well as dramatist, Różewicz has sought to destroy all distinctions and limitations of genre and form. Deliberately striving for maximum impurity, Różewicz, antipoet and
antiplaywright, creates "junk art" out of scraps of quotations,
clippings, lists, and documents. Afanasjew's statement that the
poetry of the circus is an old piece of newspaper read as it

[72] Reported in Raymonde Temkine, *Grotowski*, tr. Alex Szogyi (New York,
1972), pp. 144–145.

floats by in the air is an apt description of Różewicz's poetic collage made up of disparate pieces of trash.

In his first play, *The Card File* (1960), Różewicz celebrates the anonymous man.[73] During the entire drama the generic nameless hero lies in bed in his room, through which a street appears to run, and passers-by wander in and question him about his life and commitments. These figures make up the cast of characters of his life: friends, relatives, and acquaintances out of his past, present, and future. Interrogated by these ghosts and voices, the hero tries desperately to resist all pressures by remaining totally passive and irresponsible. Lying in bed, looking at his own hand, and opening and closing his fingers, Różewicz's everyman clutches at his own concrete humanness like a baby and hides from those forces outside himself that seek to fit him into restrictive categories. "I like the little toe on my left foot better than I do all of humanity," the inert protagonist asserts, rejecting all noble sentiments and big emotions. At least one's little toe is real—perhaps the only thing in the world that is.

At the end of *The Card File*, a journalist, pen and notebook in hand, interviews the hero and asks him a series of questions about his goals in life, his political beliefs, his love of mankind, and his desire for world peace—questions which Różewicz's average man is unwilling and unable to answer. He does not know. The play ends with the hero simply keeping quiet.

Throughout Różewicz's works there runs a deep suspicion of abstractions, ideologies, and principles, particularly those forcibly imposed on human beings in the name of humanity. A crucial difference exists between individual humanness and humanity in the abstract. The poet mistrusts all words and seeks truth in nakedness, in the bare biological facts of the human organism and the world of things that surrounds it. The only verities are concrete. A montage of shreds and fragments, misplaced emotions, stray characters, lost in a world of fluid time and space, *The Card File* is without normal dramatic action; it is, rather, a figment of the human memory passing judgment upon itself.[74]

[73] Jacek Łukasiewicz, "The Poetry of Tadeusz Różewicz," *Polish Perspectives*, X (August–September, 1967), 67–68.
[74] Miłosz, p. 469.

As Różewicz continues his attempts to write plays in the face of the impossibility of such an enterprise, stage directions replace dialogue; the author is forced to abandon writing normal plays, even avant-garde ones. Instead of literary texts, he produces arguments with the theatre and scenarios in which playwright and performer must be cocreators.

In *The Interrupted Act* (1964), Różewicz makes a play out of his dissatisfaction with all existing dramatic forms. The conflict in the drama is between the idea of the play and the impossibility of its execution. Continuing the tradition of Gałczyński and the destruction of old dramatic forms, Różewicz writes a play about what cannot be shown in the theatre. Remarks by the author, personal intrusions, theoretical deliberations, and polemics interrupt and subvert the play itself and produce a new kind of narrative script. Scenes in *The Interrupted Act* illustrate various ways in which such a play could be written, as different dramatic conventions are tried out and then discarded, while all the time, the playwright, in stage directions and comments on the role of dialogue, action, gesture, and silence, carries on his debate with Witkacy, Leon Chwistek, and other theorists of the theatre.

Różewicz has moved to ever more extreme positions, striving, by a process of expansion (the opposite of Gałczyński's use of contraction in *The Green Goose*), to burst the bonds of drama and break open its forms. In *The Old Woman Broods* (1968) the poet creates a score, an elastic scenario in which he invites the collaboration of a director and theatre; the playwright himself cannot complete the work. Różewicz's stage directions, which constitute over a third of the printed play, are not descriptive or prescriptive, but offer the director suggestions and ideas that he is free to carry out as he wishes. The author does not tell the director how to produce his play, but once having posed the problems, deliberately leaves the work partly unfinished and open to different kinds of solutions.

The Old Woman Broods is Różewicz's "The End of the World"—one of the most popular Polish themes—showing that, after the end of the world, the world goes on much the same as before. Poland had already endured several such apocalypses, and Gałczyński had hopefully suggested that bureaucratic inefficiency would prevent ultimate catastrophe from becoming official and definitive. In his theoretical writings, Afanasjew proposed that a dump was as good a setting as a palace nowadays. Różewicz builds his play upon such a premise. *The Old Woman Broods* is a series of variations on the theme of rubbish. Rubbish is the all-inclusive metaphor; the play portrays the contemporary world as a giant trash heap and graveyard—a cosmic garbage can for all culture and civilization.

Amid refuse, in a café-necropolis, a grotesque old woman wearing multiple layers of discarded clothing imagines that she is giving birth to new life. She celebrates the abdomen: digestion and gestation. Throughout the play, she is hatching something in all the pollution and filth. While the old woman talks about childbirth, larches, and the most beautiful river in all Europe, refuse and old papers pour through the window. Modern civilization's waste products are its only true art, its impermanent artifacts. The sound of dustbins clanking and the roar of the garbage truck can be heard outside. The characters' conversation is also junk, old scraps from the newspaper and radio—about the weather, the new world crisis, the possibility of war. Human beings are fighting a losing battle with rubbish and ugliness; they are garbage themselves. The old woman realizes that she has no time to lose; she must give birth. As the first scene ends, she calls for water and sheets. The curtain falls; it is a huge, white, blood-stained sheet.

Like Gałczyński before him, Różewicz uses both the curtain and the stage directions to comment on the play itself and on the nature of drama, challenging and pushing beyond normal limits the conventions and resources of the stage. In the second scene, the war has taken place and now trash, particularly paper, engulfs the entire world. There is no ground, no water, no air—nothing but garbage. "A rubbish dump like the sea from shore to shore. A rubbish dump right up to the horizon. . . . Perhaps a battlefield. A colossal rubbish dump. A polygon. A necropolis. And yet a beach."[75]

Proliferating people and things engulf the stage and the

[75] Tadeusz Różewicz, *The Old Woman Broods*, tr. Adam Czerniawski, *Dialog*, Special English-Language Issue, 1970, p. 50.

play. Różewicz portrays the apocalypse as a recurring phenomenon: human beings go on reproducing and accumulating
things on the surface of the earth. Even after its destruction it
is a world of prosperity, the "sticky, stinking, monstrous mass"
civilization that Witkacy foresaw, made up of mannequins,
puppets, robots, automata, and multiplying matter.[76]

In this anthill garbage culture, people copulate, buy things,
and get rich. Trenches are dug, and war is waged; young girls
sun-bathe and gossip; a gentleman gets his hair cut, and the old
woman has a pedicure at the beauty parlor; hands come up out
of the rubble; and the young waiter appears covered with dirty
bandages from the "third war." The old woman announces that
she has given birth to one boy and three girls and is sitting on
the boy. The road sweepers keep dumping and shoveling "old
newspapers, books, encyclopedias, illustrated magazines, rags,
machines, bottles, animals and people" [77]—some real, some
dummies. This is the cemetery of the soul, where people are
collected like garbage, yet where waiters and hairdressers and
the business of living survive the holocaust and persist. The
end of the world seems a fraud—paper continues to pile up.

Now the beach, the cafe, the field of battle all turn into one huge rubbish heap. However, life continues as normal. All institutions, including the church and health service, operate with comparative efficiency.
There are meetings, conferences, banquets and visits. People enjoy
themselves, tell jokes and gossip. At times we hear lively voices and
even songs. The liveliness and the general mess continue for a few
minutes. Everyone says the first thing that comes into his head. This
may include the singing of old hit songs, the reading of newspaper ad-
vertisements, reports and outdated philosophy and history handbooks.[78]

Then suddenly the curtain falls, like a sword, cutting the
actors off from the audience and the auditorium off from the
performance. Różewicz suggests that the curtain may be made
of heavy metal—a heritage of the "iron" curtain that falls like
lightning at the end of Witkacy's *The Shoemakers* after the final
revolution.

Birth Rate, the biography of a play about biological prolifer-

---

[76] Piwińska, p. 92.   [77] *The Old Woman Broods*, p. 52.   [78] *Ibid.*, p. 54.

ation that overflows the stage and the possibilities of drama, is the logical continuation of all the previous tendencies in Różewicz's art. The process of enlargement has now been carried so far that the play cannot fit into normal theatrical molds, and the playwright must leave his theatre piece unwritten, asking some future director and theatre to compose it in a way that Różewicz cannot yet imagine. As in conceptual art, the author's inability to write the play becomes the drama. Play and critical document are one and the same. Whereas *The Interrupted Act* and *The Old Woman Broods* have both been successfully performed on the Polish stage, *Birth Rate* still awaits a daring realization.

The key to *Birth Rate* lies in the author, who is the hero of his own unwritten lyric drama. In *The Old Woman Broods,* all that remained from *Hamlet* were the gravediggers, automatons shoveling under the corpses of civilization, composing the "anonymous work" itself. But in *Birth Rate* the author himself is Hamlet, meditating in the graveyard of civilization, hero of the greatest necropolis in history. Różewicz dramatizes his own hesitations in trying to write the play, his struggles with the "living mass" out of which he had hoped to form a drama, but in the face of so much death, he wonders if he can write at all. In a long inner drama, the poet carries on a debate with the voices of his predecessors and masters: Witkacy and Gombrowicz, already classics from the past; Beckett, the turning point in modern theatre; and finally his three models for interior drama— all novelists and story writers, all Slavic—Dostoevsky, Chekhov, and Conrad.

If at first the essential drama contained in *Birth Rate* seems highly external in its attempted depiction of expanding population, the work soon becomes internal as the author battles with swarming images and living masses of matter, is increasingly overcome by them, and finally holds his "dialogue" with past writers and dramatists about how to present the very growth of life in the theatre, letting these artists speak through quotations and excerpts.

Birth Rate is also an interior drama of silence in that the processes which it explores occur deep within the human organism. The Lopakian mass is perceived biologically, not as a body politic, but as a physiological entity; the important revolution is one of population, not regimes; dramatic action occurs in organs and wombs. The body is the ultimate concern for Różewicz, and the drama of *Birth Rate* lies in the artist-intellectual's confrontation of the body and his inability to write his play about "the living mass"; in other words, *Birth Rate* describes the playwright's own inability to give birth. In his recent play *White Marriage* (1974), Różewicz, in startling and shocking fashion, dramatizes all the bodily functions and focuses on the biological nature of sex.[79]

Whether the lonely Polish avant-garde tradition in drama can survive its own success is a still unanswered question. Zbigniew Cybulski remarked that Bim-Bom was handcrafted, and this observation can be applied to the entire body of drama in the line from Witkacy to Różewicz. This kind of theatre was made at home, slowly, privately, and at great cost to the maker. It was created long before there was any demand for the product, solely out of an inner need. A genuine personal underground, not a follower of fashion, the Polish avant-garde sprang from deep sources and inner obsessions. Therefore, it worked outside the mainstream and apart from the marketplace of isms, where styles in drama, like fashions in dress, are rapidly expended and soon outmoded.

Now that Polish avant-garde drama is officially sanctioned, publicly accepted, state-financed and -fostered, and as it were mass-produced, can this unique expression of creativity continue to develop? Already the Polish avant-garde has joined hands with the Western experimental movements, and now the grotesque and absurd have become the new neoclassicism in drama, acceptable for mass consumption around the world. This international avant-garde drama is no longer handmade or native but consists of a series of facile, readily available clichés and formulas—the inevitable fate of all successful movements in theatre.

In the late 1950's, Afanasjew already saw the danger and wanted to go in another direction, backward to folklore, the individual actor, and indigenous material. Mrożek and Grotowski

---

[79] Tadeusz Różewicz, *Białe Małżeństwo, Dialog,* No. 2 (1974), 5–33.

have been zealous in maintaining their privacy and individuality and in refusing to go along with the avant-garde herds. Różewicz likewise offers evidence that the Polish avant-garde can survive its own success—the gravest danger for any avant-garde—by going its own way. In endeavoring to write plays that cannot be written and by proposing performances of the unperformable, Różewicz carries on the tradition of the Polish avant-garde, urging it to go beyond playwriting and beyond theatre into the impossible that lies only in the mind of the creator.

I

Stanisław Ignacy Witkiewicz

The Anonymous Work

Four Acts of a Rather Nasty Nightmare (1921)

Motto:
"The Grizzloviks yelp at the sight of
Black Beatus the Trundler."
—From a dream in 1912.

Dedicated to
Bronisław Malinowski

Translated by Daniel and Eleanor Gerould from Stanisław Ignacy Witkiewicz, *Bezimienne dzieło*, in *Dramaty*, II (Warsaw: PIW, 1972). An earlier version of this translation appeared in *Drama & Theatre* (© 1974 by Daniel and Eleanor Gerould), XII, No. 1 (Fall, 1974).

CHARACTERS

DR. PLASMODEUS BLÖDESTAUG, gray, rather short gentleman, with a huge head of hair and a mustache. No beard. Gold glasses. Sixty-two years old.

PLASMONICK BLÖDESTAUG, his son. Dark, handsome, brown-haired with delicate features. A painter. Consumptive.

ROSA VAN DER BLAAST, twenty-eight years old. A famous composer. A reddish blonde, very beautiful.

CLAUDESTINA DE MONTREUIL, twenty-two years old. A light blonde, with short hair. A painter. Very soulful and pretty.

TZINGAR (called Joseph), nearly forty. Broad-shouldered, dark-haired. Short mustache. Thick, somewhat curly hair. A very handsome "lomofam." * A social activist.

COLONEL MANFRED, COUNT GIERS, fifty-six years old. Medium height. Graying brown hair. President of the military tribunal.

Two gravediggers:

GRAVEDIGGER I, old, gray, somewhat decrepit. Clean-shaven.

GRAVEDIGGER II, young, beardless, dark-haired. Twenty-six years old. His name is Joseph Leon Lopak.

Two officers on the military tribunal:

I   An old major with a mustache but no beard. Glasses. Major Daybell.

II   A young lieutenant with a mustache and a small Vandyke beard. Dark-haired. Lieutenant Flowers.

PRINCE PADOVAL DE GRIFUELLHES, twenty-seven years old. Blond hair, beardless.

THE OLD PRINCESS BARBARA, his mother. Descended from the royal house of Stewart. Née Countess Bambord of Clever-haaz.

LYDIA, BARONESS RAGNOCK, the Princess' *dame de compagnie.* Fifty-six years old.

PRISON GUARD, navy-blue uniform with large silver buttons.

SOPHIE, Rosa van der Blaast's ten-year-old daughter.

Rosa van der Blaast's MAID, very beautiful. Dressed in bright green.

* Lomofam: l'homme aux femmes (author's note).

CROWD OF PRISONERS, gray prison suits with large yellow circles on the front; red numbers in the circles.

SOLDIERS OF THE GUARD, green uniforms with white facings and tricornered hats.

GENDARMES, navy-blue uniforms with red facings. Tricornered hats with red plumes.

Eight GRIZZLOVIKS, dressed like workers. Disciples of Joachim Grizzelov, the founder of a religious and social society. Grizzelov is an immensely fat old man with very long hair and a milk-white beard. His face is ruddy and florid. (He is known only through Plasmonick's portrait of him.)

OFFICER OF THE GUARD, dressed like the guards, but with gold epaulettes edged in red.

CROWD, motley in the extreme. In the clothes worn by the crowd there is a total absence of the colors yellow and red in those shades (cadmium lemon and Chinese red) which the prisoners have on their chests. Green, violet, and crimson predominate, and, less frequently, sky-blue.

Act I: A field in the vicinity of the capital of Centuria.
Act II: Rosa van der Blaast's apartment.
Act III: A prison.
Act IV: A square in front of the prison.

ACT I

(*An almost entirely flat field in the vicinity of the capital of Centuria. Day begins to break. In the rear the glow of the distant city. Beyond the horizon are seen distant spires and smoking chimneys. The field is covered by bushes with dark-green leaves and fluffy, light-blue flowers. In addition, high yellowish-greenish grass with bronze sprays is growing everywhere. There are no trees. In places the earth shows through, cherry-red in color. Several large rocks here and there (rose-colored granite). To the right, two gravediggers in gray-blue blouses and trousers of the same color are working, waist-deep in a freshly dug grave. They toss out dirt of the color referred to above. They wear small, round, black caps on their heads. In the middle of the stage, near one of the rocks, stands Manfred, Count Giers. He has long hair and quite a long beard and mustache. No hat. He is wearing the same kind of blouse as the gravediggers, fastened around the waist by a black belt with a large gold buckle. Wide crimson pants, but in color a bit more brick-red than the earth. Black patent-leather shoes with violet pompons. His face is turned toward the audience. He is leaning upon a tall black cane with a gold knob.*)

GRAVEDIGGER I: (*Stops digging.*) Look here, sir. Tell the truth now; what's this grave all about?

GIERS: I'm paying you twice as much as you usually get for cemetery work, aren't I? What's the rest of it to you?

GRAVEDIGGER I: All right—but what about this land? Is it yours or isn't it? Just so we don't get no trouble about it later on.

GIERS: I can tell you who I am, my fine conscientious fellow. The land is mine, and so is most of the land on the outskirts of the city.

GRAVEDIGGER I: Hold on there, sir! You're an honest-to-goodness madman. Maybe you're even the prince himself, our gracious sovereign?

GIERS: Stop bothering me and just dig.

(*Gravedigger II keeps on digging, not paying any attention to this conversation.*)

GRAVEDIGGER I: Listen, the times are over now when even a genuine great lord can get a common man to stop bothering him so easily. Tell us, or we don't dig no more.

GIERS: (*Grudgingly pulls a piece of paper from under his blouse, goes over to the grave and hands it to the gravedigger to read.*) Here, you—take this! Read it, if you know how.

GRAVEDIGGER I: (*Puts on circular glasses and has difficulty reading in the dusk.*) "Manfred, Count Giers, Colonel, chief military judge." (*Gives the paper back to Giers indifferently.*) Since it's like you say, O.K. (*He goes back to his digging.*)

GRAVEDIGGER II (LOPAK): (*Digging*) I understand you, Colonel, sir. I write poems. Actually they write themselves. (*Stops digging.*) You know, it's strange, but I'm totally unable to figure out how my poems pop into my head. ·Take this one for example. (*Recites*)

> Oh you, imperceptibly little facts,
> In the Infinity of black desire,
> Oh, how paltry are all the acts,
> Of those who swagger, their necks in the mire . . .

GIERS: Keep on digging! Nobody asked you for any of your poems! (*Violently*) Dig! Dig faster! It's going to be dawn any minute now, and that'll be the end of it anyhow.

LOPAK: All right, all right. Just tell me; what do you want this grave for, Colonel, sir?

GIERS: (*Impatiently*) I've told you a thousand times: I'm an old man with one foot in the grave. I want to have a grave so I can put one foot in it and meditate. That's all.

LOPAK: Yes, but . . .

GIERS: (*Menacingly, hitting the rock with his cane*) That's enough stupid questions! I said: dig, and quit shooting off your mouth. Leave me alone.

GRAVEDIGGER I: Leave him alone. There's nothing you can do with him. He's a madman and that's that.

LOPAK: Or he's pretending to be a madman, so as to get his own way easier. I know the type.

GRAVEDIGGER I: Quiet! I tell you . . .

(*They both dig. A pause. From the left two Soldiers of the guard carry in Plasmonick Blödestaug on a stretcher; he's wearing a long yellowish-gray coat.*)

PLASMONICK: Good morning, Colonel. Any new developments? (*The Soldiers set the stretcher on the ground to the left and stand at attention. They have their rifles slung over their shoulders.*)

I. A scene from Stanisław Ignacy Witkiewicz's *The Anonymous Work,* Act I. Presented at the Słowacki Theatre, Cracow, in 1967. Directed by Bronisław Dąbrowski. Plasmonick is carried in on a stretcher. (Photograph by Wojciech Plewiński.)

GIERS: At ease!

(*The Soldiers go limp.*)

PLASMONICK: Colonel, why don't you answer? Why do you torment an innocent human being?

GIERS: (*Ironically*) Human being! You are an officer in the reserves and on top of that you're suspected of spying. That's called a human being! Ha!

PLASMONICK: I'm an ex-officer in the Guards. I'm a true nobleman exempted from military service because of consumption. I'm going to die soon. And you still keep on torturing me so in the last hours of my life!

GIERS: If you've got TB, stay home, and don't have them cart you around the countryside at night.

PLASMONICK: I can't, I can't stay home doing nothing. I have visions and I'm not able to work. You won't even let me finish my last paintings before I die!

GIERS: (*Ironically*) What a great pity! I should say so! So much the better; there'll be less of that garbage.

PLASMONICK: It's subjecting an innocent person to cruel and inhuman treatment. That letter can be explained in a totally different way . . .

GIERS: Shut up! Or I'll lock you up tight till the end of the investigation! No exercise or workshop—a dank hole—understand?

(*A pause. Plasmonick sighs. The gravediggers dig in silence.*)

PLASMONICK: If that were my only misfortune! But I'm also involved in an unhappy love affair, I've got TB, I'm suspected of spying, and I can't complete my latest paintings. Oh—it's all too much!

GIERS: (*Tapping with his cane*) Are you going to keep on whining?

(*He stands silently and looks threateningly at Plasmonick. From the right, between the grave and the footlights, enter Claudestina de Montreuil, wearing a gray suit and a little gray cap. A paint box in her hand.*)

CLAUDESTINA: (*To Gravedigger II*) Is this where it is, Mr. Lopak? It really is a lovely place.

LOPAK: This way, Miss. The only bright spot in this cursed boring landscape of ours.

GIERS: Who are you?

CLAUDESTINA: I am Claudestina de Montreuil. I'm a painter. (*Plasmonick raises himself up a little on the stretcher, with interest.*) I was looking for a place to paint the dew on cobwebs. You see, I stylize it a little metaphysically, and then . . .

GIERS: (*Impatiently*) All right, all right—paint anything you want. I don't give a hoot about that. Only don't say anything to anyone about this grave or about any of this. (*Makes a circular motion with his hand.*) I don't want all the idiots and good-for-nothings in town spreading gossip about my supposed mental derangement. Do you understand?

CLAUDESTINA: Yes—I think I do. Oh—those pale blue flowers are wonderful! Oh—this earth, the color of clotted blood

. . . (*She spreads out her paint box on the rock to the right.*)
GIERS: (*In the direction of the Gravediggers*) Lopak, I told you not to tell anyone, but that fool still couldn't keep his big mouth shut.
LOPAK: Won't happen again. Now I know who you are, and I won't breathe a word to nobody.
GIERS: (*With a smile*) In love with that paint slinger, I'll bet? Huh?
(*Lopak starts digging again, without answering. Giers sits down and looks at his watch.*)
CLAUDESTINA: (*To Plasmonick*) And what do you do?
PLASMONICK: I'm a painter like you. The only difference is that I'm incapable of doing anything. They're torturing me in the last moments of my life with some hideous business about spying.
GIERS: Aow—now that whining's going to start again! (*To Claudestina*) Do all these weak-kneed artists always carry on like this?
CLAUDESTINA: (*To Plasmonick*) Go on. Talking doesn't disturb me at all.
(*She begins to paint a bush with light-blue flowers which is growing between Plasmonick and her. It becomes lighter and lighter. The glow over the city dies out.*)
PLASMONICK: Just imagine: I wrote to my friend, Rosa van der Blaast—you know? the composer—and I've got to confess to you that I've been in love with her for two years, and unhappily at that—as I was saying, I wrote a letter thanking her for the money she gave me for doing certain sketches. I didn't think that for artists there was anything at all wrong in accepting such a slight amount, some ten thousand gryblers . . .
GIERS: That's hideous! I can't listen to this! Spy money! Ha!
CLAUDESTINA: (*To Plasmonick*) Go on—I'm listening.
PLASMONICK: But—just imagine, Rosa is suspected of spying. My letter was intercepted—I didn't leave the house, I was sick . . .
GIERS: At least if he were healthy! But he's sick!! I can't stand sick people. If I could, I'd tear down every hospital. Let the bastards all die off!

CLAUDESTINA: (*To Giers*) Don't interrupt. (*To Plasmonick*) Well, what happened then?

PLASMONICK: So now I'm suspected of belonging to a spy ring, and what's more, they say Rosa's lover is the chief spy . . .

GIERS: (*Jumping up*) Shut up! Or off to the hole with you!

(*A pause.*)

CLAUDESTINA: (*Pointing at Giers*) Who is that gentleman?

PLASMONICK: (*In a weak voice*) That's Colonel Giers—president of the military tribunal.

CLAUDESTINA: Aha—well, let's talk about something else. I'm very sorry for you. And what about your paintings?

PLASMONICK: They were sketches. You know—I created a certain theory; actually I didn't, my father did. But I'm the one who's putting it into practice . . .

GIERS: (*Keeps pulling at his beard.*) A little discussion about art is about to begin. Oh—to hell with you and your art! (*To the Soldiers*) You can sit down.

(*The Soldiers sit down on the left. Giers lights his pipe.*)

PLASMONICK: You see, it's a question of expressing the metaphysical strangeness of Existence in purely formal constructions directly through the harmony of colors which are put into certain compositions . . .

CLAUDESTINA: (*Jumping up*) So you're Blödestaug! Plasmonick Blödestaug! I know your father's theory. It's brilliant in its own way. But *I* don't agree with it.

PLASMONICK: And what are you trying to accomplish?

CLAUDESTINA: I paint the wonders of nature, from the point of view of insects, frogs, and other little creatures. Still, I don't paint them as they really are, but in the light of my metaphysical spiritual outlook. For me, *form*, in your father's sense of the word, doesn't exist.

PLASMONICK: It's strange I haven't heard anything about you. Let's talk some more. Then I can forget the frightful situation I'm in, if just for a minute. Physical pain and theoretical discussions are my only pleasures—then I don't think about the reality of my life . . .

GIERS: Stop that whining! I can't stand it . . .

CLAUDESTINA: You see, I understand it, but it's impossible in actual practice. I don't believe that metaphysical feelings can be expressed in pure constructions. That would only be another kind of sensual enjoyment. I'm concerned with the spirit . . .

PLASMONICK: Just how do you bring it out? I don't see any place for the spirit in a painting. In a painting conceived formally.

CLAUDESTINA: It's *there!* It's there when you consider things from a special standpoint. It comes out in an absolutely down-to-earth way.

PLASMONICK: Why, for instance, should the point of view of a field bug give it? Besides, they're such tiny little creatures, we don't know how they see nature.

CLAUDESTINA: You don't understand me. You can paint anything this way, even a spider web from the fly's point of view, a purely hypothetical point of view. What counts is the inner approach whereby everything becomes transformed and I bring out this transformation in the finished painting.

PLASMONICK: So it's a kind of trance? A kind of metaphysical ecstasy?

CLAUDESTINA: Yes—something like that. Now I have to stop talking; I feel *it* coming on. (*She starts to paint.*)

GIERS: (*Gets up and stretches.*) Oh, how boring all this is—how deadly boring!

PLASMONICK: That's not true, Colonel! Basically it's over these things, and not just over trade and industry, that people chop one another to pieces. At the bottom of everything there are only two values: art and religion, which for us nowadays means philosophy.

GIERS: (*Shaking the ash out of his pipe*) Don't get excited. That's a lot of bunk. (*Listens intently.*) I think someone's coming on horseback. Who in hell can it be now?

(*The sound of a horse's hooves. Claudestina paints in a trance. The Gravediggers keep on working furiously. It grows lighter and lighter.*)

PLASMONICK: Oh! When will my tortures end!

(*Giers motions to him impatiently to be quiet. Enter from the left Prince Padoval de Grifuellhes. He is dressed in a riding costume, a long coat, and a sports cap. He has a whip in his hand. Giers turns his back to him.*)

GRIFUELLHES: Hullo! What a large gathering. Aha—the gravediggers are here. Fine. You're the famous Plasmonick, aren't you? Very glad to meet you, but for the moment let's keep our distance. That lady's in a trance—I won't disturb her. But that one! Who can that be? Hey! My good man, turn around!

(*Giers turns around.*)

GIERS: Yes, Your Highness.

GRIFUELLHES: What's this? Then it's true, Colonel, you're the one they're digging this grave for way out here?

GIERS: That's right, Your Highness.

GRIFUELLHES: You picked a fine spot. I've been wandering around in circles for an hour and couldn't find it.

GIERS: But who told you it was here, Prince?

GRIFUELLHES: Who but your former love, Baroness Ragnock? And I found out something else even more interesting from her.

GIERS: Could that be it?

(*He points to the old gravedigger.*)

GRIFUELLHES: It could indeed.

(*He goes over to Gravedigger I.*)

GIERS: (*Raising both fists on high. A pipe clenched in his right hand.*) Oh, these women, these women! Accursed busybodies! (*Sits down helplessly.*) The last place for significant reflections on death has been defiled once and for all.

GRIFUELLHES: (*To Gravedigger I, in a totally indifferent tone of voice*) Listen, my good man: do you know who you are?

GRAVEDIGGER I: Are you kidding! I've been a gravedigger for forty years, and my name is Virieux.

GRIFUELLHES: Well, of course, that's who you are and who you've always been. Still, sometimes events in life all fall together in such a way that without even changing in the least, you can become someone else entirely different. It happened to me two hours ago. I did a small service for a certain elderly lady. She wanted to return the favor. "I'm bored, hellishly bored"—I told her—"I'd like to be someone else entirely different." "You really want to?" she asked me. "Yes." "Swear it." "Fine"—I say—"just as long as it's quick." Then, imagine, she told me that one of these men who are digging the grave for that gentleman (*points to Giers*) is my father.

GRAVEDIGGER I: Well, so what? Think I don't have more than

my share of sons like that all over the world? I got no way of even knowing for sure if they *are* mine.

GRIFUELLHES: (*With a certain impatience*) Well, all right, but for me it's a very important event. It radically changes my attitude toward life: it's exactly what I was waiting for.

GRAVEDIGGER I: And just who are you, sir, that it's changed you so much, my son? Most likely you sit behind the counter in a shop somewhere or in some branch post office. What of it?

GIERS: He's sized him up, him and his fine breeding. A shrewd customer. (*To Gravedigger I*) You don't know who you're talking to, pop. If the crown prince dies, he's next in line for the throne: that's Prince Padoval himself.

GRAVEDIGGER I: Well, what of it? I'm asking. He can be my son if he wants to so bad. He won't make me king. A cabinet minister's probably the most I'll be.

GIERS: It's a waste of breath talking with people like that. Nothing makes any impression on that kind of scum, not even if they found out they were descended from the Titans or gave birth to all the stars in the Milky Way.

(*Gravedigger I crawls out of the grave.*)

GRIFUELLHES: (*Who has been standing biting the knob of his whip*) You know what, Colonel, I'm really furious at that old hag for telling me that. Last night I thought it was amusing, but now it's completely spoiled my good humor.

GRAVEDIGGER I: Well, Mr. Jeers—our work's done for today. Crawl out, Lopak; we're going to go get some sleep. The sun's going to rise any minute.

(*Gravedigger II crawls out of the grave.*)

GRIFUELLHES: Listen, old boy: did you know that the woman you treated so nicely at the cemetery then was my mother? You know—by my father's grave. My father hadn't had any children for twelve years, and then . . .

GRAVEDIGGER I: (*Angrily*) Will you quit pestering me, Prince! I don't know, I don't remember . . .

GRIFUELLHES: But I was told so by that woman who heard it all herself from behind the wall. Only she was so frightened she fainted and . . .

GRAVEDIGGER I: I'm telling you, Highness: don't lower yourself just for the fun of it. The time will come for all of us at the last judgment or even down here. But for the time being, Prince, if you want to, well, give me something, like maybe a little, you know, a little money. But why mess around now with what happened once a long time ago. Right?

GRIFUELLHES: (*Embarrassed*) But I don't have any money with me.

GRAVEDIGGER I: When someone sets out on an expedition to find his long-lost father, he at least ought to have thought about giving him something.

GIERS: How much, Your Highness? I'll lend it to you.

GRIFUELLHES: Well, about ten thousand gryblers.

PLASMONICK: The exact amount I'm atoning for with my whole life . . .

GIERS: (*Motions impatiently to him to be quiet.*) Quiet! Someone's coming. (*On the horizon, which is slightly elevated in a gentle slope, the silhouette of an approaching carriage drawn by two black horses is seen. The carriage passes from right to left.*) Here, Prince. (*Gives the Prince a roll of bills.*) Who in holy hell could be coming here now? A regular human avalanche is crashing down on my poor grave.

(*Grifuellhes takes the bills and gives them to the Gravedigger.*)

GRIFUELLHES: Here, my good man, and now let's forget about this unfortunate incident. (*To Giers*) All this has left me feeling horribly disgusted.

GIERS: But, my Prince, I've known about this for years and years but I didn't say anything, since I knew nothing good could come of it. You've got to forget about it.

(*They listen intently. The carriage turns and goes behind the mound. The creaking of wheels grows louder and louder.*)

GRIFUELLHES: My former direction in life has been destroyed, but I haven't been given a new one. I don't know how to start all over again.

GRAVEDIGGER I: My son, I'm going to give you a bit of advice: get to work starting right now. Think I'm going to stop digging graves? (*The sun rises from the left and bathes the stage in orange light. Claudestina awakes from her trance and stops painting. She sits totally still.*) No—I'll be what I am till the end of my days. You won't get away from yourself, even if you found out you're the son of Beelzebub himself.

GRIFUELLHES: (*Lost in thought, bites the knob of his whip. The creaking of the carriage wheels can be heard nearby, to the left.*) Yes—that's what's really disastrous. I found that out today. (*Shakes hands with the Gravedigger.*) Thanks, father, and we won't see each other anymore.

GRAVEDIGGER I: That's not necessary. Why don't we get drunk together today—and to hell with everything.

(*From the left the following characters dash in: the Princess, wearing black, with a lace scarf over her gray hair, and the Baroness, wearing violet, in a black hat.*)

PRINCESS: My Padoval! At last! Oh, that awful Baroness! This is terrible! Those awful rumors! (*Points to the Gravedigger.*) He's the one! He's the one!!

(*Gravedigger I goes out to the right without saying a word. First he tries to pull Lopak by the sleeve, but Lopak resists and stays where he is.*)

GRIFUELLHES: Well, what of it, mother? No need to get carried away. Nothing bad's happened. I must say, all in all, I'm even glad. Sometimes something happens that seems completely nonsensical at the time, but then afterward, years later, we see that it all had a hidden meaning, and that it's all very deep.

PRINCESS: (*Calmed down*) Is that really so, my son? You haven't suffered a nervous shock, have you?

GRIFUELLHES: (*Gloomily*) When you're the son of a tough old bird like my father, it's not so easy to have your nerves shocked. He's old as a boot, and just look at that hole he's dug. And at night too. At *night!* It's incredible!

BARONESS: (*To the Princess*) He was bored, Your Highness, bored to death. I had to think up something to entertain him.

PRINCESS: It's all right now, my dear. So long as Padoval is happy, I don't ask for anything more. (*To her son*) But you won't think badly of me?

GRIFUELLHES: Oh, you know me, mother: "Never let anything surprise you"—that's my motto. Although I was a bit surprised today. Oh—now I see that if I ever go crazy, it'll come from your side of the family, mother. (*He hugs and kisses her.*)

II. Another scene from the Cracow production of *The Anonymous Work*, Act I. The arrival of the Princess and Baroness. (Photograph by Wojciech Plewiński.)

PRINCESS: Oh, that Giers—what a character. Still thinking about death, Colonel?

GIERS: Yes, Your Highness. I'm an old man with one foot in the grave; please don't forget that.

PRINCESS: Yes, yes. I know about your obsession and I respect it.

GIERS: I'm attempting to become so familiar with death that the thought of it won't prevent me from carrying out the last things at the end of my life.

PRINCESS: (*Doesn't listen to him.*) And just who is that young lady? (*Points to Claudestina; to Plasmonick*) I've heard about you. It's your fault that my poor Rosa is suspected of spying.

PLASMONICK: (*Suddenly jumping up from the stretcher*) Yes, yes— dear Rosa. So dear that Your Highness refused to give her a modest grant for the construction of her new instruments. The devil knows how she was supposed to get the money to do it, and now she's suspected of spying, because she can't explain her source of income. And *I'm* suspected too, since I took that stupid ten thousand from her.

GIERS: That's just the point. Not another word! (*Trying to change the subject*) That young girl is a painter. She creates metaphysical mysteries, from the point of view of field bugs. (*They all go over to Claudestina, who gets up. The Princess and the Baroness look through their* face-à-mains.)

PRINCESS: Everyone has his little faults. I know I'm stingy, but . . . (*Glances at Claudestina's picture.*) Why, that's just marvelous . . .

(*Two Grizzloviks appear from the right. Lopak motions to them to sit down. They sit down on the grass.*)

GIERS: (*Looking at the picture*) It certainly is. I don't know much about painting, but that's just magnificent.

BARONESS: Oh—that spider web! And those drops of morning dew! It's lovely!

PLASMONICK: (*Coming over*) It's an absolutely worthless senti-mental interpretation of nature.

GRIFUELLHES: I don't agree with you. Of course, you're the product of your father's theory: metaphysical construction of forms or something of that sort. Ha! Ha!

CLAUDESTINA: Don't laugh, Prince. Doctor Blödestaug is right, too, but in a completely different dimension.

GRIFUELLHES: Forget about all those Blödestaugs! Perhaps you'd like to come back with us in our carriage and have breakfast at the palace? I think mother is going to make you court painter. (*To the Princess*) Isn't that right, mother?

PRINCESS: Yes—it's lovely. But don't you see: we've got to con-sider the expenses. But please come along with us.

(*Three more Grizzloviks appear at the left. Lopak motions to them. They sit down on the grass.*)

PLASMONICK: Lucky people! They ride, walk, paint. But me? All because of that accursed letter! (*To Padoval*) Prince, I hope Your Highness believes me: I am innocent. Please in-tercede for me.

GRIFUELLHES: (*Reluctantly*) Possibly. Possibly. I'm not commit-ting myself to anything. The investigation will clear it up. (*To the ladies*) Well, let's go. Nothing else significant is going to

III. Another scene from the Cracow production of *The Anonymous Work*, Act I. Prince Padoval admires Claudestina's painting. (Photograph by Wojciech Plewiński.)

happen here now. (*Notices the Grizzloviks.*) And just who are these people?

LOPAK: They're workers laying pipes to drain the swamps, Your Highness.

GRIFUELLHES: Aha. (*To Giers*) Well, what are you planning to do, Colonel?

GIERS: I'm staying. A moment for meditation, and then I'm going to walk home.

PRINCESS: The ghosts of those he has condemned to death are tormenting him, the way they did Richard III. Right, Colonel? Good-bye, good-bye!

(*The Baroness offers her arm to the Princess; Grifuellhes offers his to*

Claudestina. They go out to the left. Plasmonick gets on the stretcher; the soldiers carry him out, following the others.)

GIERS: *Dis donc,* Lopak: what are those people sitting here for? Get rid of them for me.

(*Lopak comes quickly over to him.*)

LOPAK: (*Mysteriously*) Colonel, sir: *they're Grizzloviks.* I arranged to meet them in secret, here by the grave, since it's the only clearly marked spot in this wasteland. I thought everyone would have gone off home before the sun came up.

GIERS: (*Amazed*) Grizzloviks?! So you're one too?! . . .

LOPAK: That's right. Colonel, pretend to be somebody else. I'm taking a chance, but I believe that you'll come over to our side, Colonel.

GIERS: Oh—this is interesting! You want to convert me? I don't know if I'll stay, but thanks anyhow. (*Grasps him by the shoulder.*) This is a very significant moment in my life. Now I can stop meditating on death. But I'm not guaranteeing anything. I might become your real enemy.

LOPAK: For the time being, pretend to be somebody else. The situation's very complicated. We'll clear it up later on. Oh— here comes our president, Baron Buffadero.

(*From the left enter Tzingar, disguised as a worker, with three Grizzloviks. Tzingar stops.*)

TZINGAR: (*Pointing to Giers*) Who's that?

LOPAK: A new member, Baron. A candidate for conversion.

(*Five other Grizzloviks encircle them as they talk, and close in on them.*)

TZINGAR: Fine. (*To Giers*) Do you know what our goals are? But—but where do I know you from? I have the impression I've seen you somewhere before in uniform.

GIERS: It's possible we met somewhere. But I don't think I was in uniform. You've got it mixed up.

TZINGAR: Quite possibly. It doesn't matter. Our goal is the replacement of temporal power by ecclesiastical power. *We'll* be the priests, in keeping with the system of beliefs devised by Joachim Grizzelov, our prophet. The only difference is that he believed in some kind of cryptopantheism, whereas we won't believe in anything. A certain form of mealy-mouthed democracy under the guise of worship. Something along the line of the Egyptian priests. The people howl for a new re-

ligion—the fact that theosophical nonsense has so many followers proves it. We've got to get it all under our control and
spread it throughout society. Understand?

GIERS: Yes, but what's the new system of government going to
be? The form of worship itself doesn't much concern me,
even though in a certain sense of the word I'm a mystic.

TZINGAR: The system of government? What the present brand
of pseudo, mealy-mouthed democracy does unwittingly, we'll
do systematically and thoroughly, in full consciousness, without getting carried away, and the trial-and-error method will
show us what further stages of development there should be.
Point number one: no extrapolations. The only thing that's
needed is to create a new type of state ruled by priests. What
other churches weren't successful in doing because of their
real faith and the concessions they had to make for the sake
of that faith, we'll be able to do quite consciously as a prag-
matic, systematic swindle. . . .

GIERS: Well, all right, but what about the system of government?

TZINGAR: What a thick skull you've got, Mr. Unknown. I keep
telling you: a pseudodemocratic system of government, but
without any parliamentary bluffing. We've got to give the
unions a true fictitious religion, not a substitute like the myth
about a general strike. Believe me, people today are far more
inclined to adopt any old belief than the totem worshipers in
New Guinea. There must be belief—even if we have to make
use of spiritualism and table-tipping.

GIERS: I think I'm beginning to understand.

TZINGAR: Well—heaven be praised. Sit down. (*To the others*)
You too, gentlemen! In the name of Joachim Grizzelov, *we
are about to begin.* I declare the meeting open.

ACT II

(*Rosa van der Blaast's salon. Dim, spectrally pure green light from
above. A grand piano in the left-hand corner. A harp next to it. Lots of
musical instruments on the walls. Portraits of great musicians. Sofas to
the left and right. A single small sofa in the middle of the stage. Lots of
pillows. The prevailing colors are ultramarine blue and black. Oc-*

*casional patches of violet and dark red. Doors to the left and center, the
latter hung with an emerald-green curtain. To the right, next to the
sofa, a black cabinet. In the right-hand corner a green canopy over a
large black sofa. Near the small sofa in the middle of the room a little
table with equipment for tea. Rosa, wearing a light green dress, sits on
the small sofa in the middle of the room holding Sophie in her arms;
Sophie is wearing a blue dress with dark-violet sashes. A pause. From
the left enter a Maid, dressed in green.*)

MAID: The Baron de Buffadero.

ROSA: (*Jumping up*) Show him in. (*To Sophie*) Sophie, go and
play in the Cave of Evil. (*Sophie runs over to the sofa to the right
and plays with her dolls there, not paying attention to anything until
further notice. Enter Tzingar wearing a black frock coat.*) Why are
you so late? Don't you realize I can't live without you? (*She
throws herself into his arms.*)

TZINGAR: Now, don't get so excited, my dear.

ROSA: I got so upset I tore my last prelude into pieces out of
   sheer nervousness—you know, the one in A-sharp that I dedicated to you. I'll have to write it all over again. And on top
   of that, that accusation about spying! That conspiracy!
   Couldn't you at least take those papers away? I'm so afraid.

TZINGAR: I'll take it all away today. But first sit down and listen
   to me carefully. This is the ultimate test of your attachment
   to me. In the first place: I had a talk with Giers yesterday;
   he's joined the Grizzloviks.

ROSA: How did you persuade him?

(*They sit down at the little table in the middle of the room.*)

TZINGAR: Only because I didn't know who I was talking to. It
   all came out later. The next piece of news is worse. The suspicions about your belonging to a spy ring are all the more
   justified since I'm the chief spy for the land of the Macerbators. I had to do it to get money for higher goals.

(*Rosa listens to him stupefied; then she covers her face with her hands
and bends her head down to her knees.*)

ROSA: You're cruel to wait till now to tell me. Now that you've
   got me so completely in your clutches that I'm ready to commit any crime for you. Oh, you horrid man!

TZINGAR: That means you haven't stopped loving me?

ROSA: No—even if it means damnation, I'll be yours till death.

You and music. Oh—and those new instruments of mine, and the possibility of having my Fifth Symphony performed—does it all come from the same source?

TZINGAR: Yes, it does. That's the way it is. Do you love me or don't you?

ROSA: Yes, yes—only now I'm so terribly torn . . . I don't know anything anymore . . . Oh—what a terrible man you are, Joseph! But maybe that's why I love you so.

(*Tzingar strokes her head.*)

TZINGAR: I'll tell you something to console you: I sold documents that are practically worthless, but in hopes of getting better things in the future, they paid me handsomely. From now on—now that Giers has come over to our side and I'm more sure of myself—I want to stop being a spy. That's why I'm telling you this. I couldn't bear to have this lie constantly between us. Understand: there's swinishness and swinishness. Telling lies to you all my life isn't the sort I could commit.

(*The Maid runs in.*)

MAID: Her Highness has arrived, ma'am. The whole house is surrounded by the police. They're not letting anyone out. You can get in, but not out.

(*Tzingar gets up suddenly, but doesn't lose his presence of mind. The maid goes out.*)

ROSA: Oh, God, God! What'll we do?

(*Tzingar runs quickly toward the center door. Voices are heard to the left.*)

TZINGAR: (*At the door, halfway through the green curtain*) Where are those papers?

ROSA: I just put them in that cabinet today. (*Points to the right. Tzingar looks out from behind the curtain and nods toward the cabinet; Rosa does likewise. The Princess, the Baroness, and Giers appear at the door to the left.*) Too late!!

(*Tzingar disappears behind the curtain without being seen. Giers has his beard shaved off and his hair cut. A dark-blue uniform with red facings.*)

PRINCESS: (*Who has heard the last exclamation*) What's too late, my child?

ROSA: Oh—it's nothing . . . I'm so nervous. Excuse me, Your Highness. (*She greets them all.*)

PRINCESS: Don't be afraid, my dearest. I succeeded in persuading Giers to search your house today. Everything will be brought out into the open and finished with once and for all. (*To Giers*) Colonel, I always told you that Rosa's secret lover was just a myth. (*To Rosa*) He didn't want to search your house now, "to give the trap a bigger snap," as he put it. Today he finally decided to act like a human being.

GIERS: Still, I managed to find out that someone came in here and he hasn't left yet. We'll see, we'll see! It's not known what he looks like, since his face was hidden by his coat collar. Quite tall, with broad shoulders. Heh, heh!

ROSA: But, Colonel . . .

GIERS: All right, we'll see.

(*The Princess sits down at the little table with her right profile to the audience.*)

PRINCESS: Please, sit down, all of you. I'm so sure of my Rosa that I'm not afraid of anything. I came along for the search to make you feel more secure, dearest.

(*They sit down.*)

ROSA: (*Vaguely*) Yes . . . That is . . . I thank you with all my heart, Your Highness. (*To Sophie at the right*) Sophie! Come here and kiss her Highness' hand. (*Sophie runs over quickly, kisses the Princess' hand, and immediately goes back to her toys.*) Your Highness will excuse me, I've got to take care of something over here. (*She goes to the right, toward the cabinet.*)

GIERS: (*Getting up*) Perhaps her Highness will excuse you, but I—won't. You'll be so kind as to take a seat.

ROSA: Sophie, get those things out of that cabinet and take them into the bedroom.

(*Sophie abandons her toys reluctantly.*)

GIERS: Sophie! Keep on playing! (*Sophie goes back to her dolls.*) Ho! Ho! Suspicious things are starting to happen here! You'll be so kind as to sit down. Mr. Plasmonick will be here right away for the confrontation. (*He rings. The Maid runs in.*) Ask Lieutenant Flowers and the two gendarmes to come in here.

(*The Maid goes out. Rosa sits down at the little table, showing signs of extreme nervousness.*)

PRINCESS: (*Sipping her tea*) Don't be afraid, dear. Nothing bad's going to happen. Everything's still going to turn out all right.

GIERS: We'll see, we'll see. (*Enter Flowers and the two gendarmes, their hats on. Flowers in the same uniform as Giers. Only their epaulettes are different. They are followed by two guards who lead in Plasmonick.*) Make a search of all the rooms.

(*The Lieutenant and the gendarmes begin their search in the living room.*)

ROSA: (*Getting up*) Look what's happening, Mr. Plasmonick; isn't this just horrible—they're searching *my* house.

PLASMONICK: (*Coldly, ironically*) I don't see anything strange about that. We're both very suspicious characters. But what about your secret lover? Has he been found yet? (*To Giers*) I assume I can talk about everything now?

GIERS: Why, go ahead. Talk all you want. (*He lights a cigarette and looks at the men conducting the search.*)

ROSA: (*To Plasmonick, while watching the men searching, out of the corner of her eye, with terrible anxiety*) So you're against me too! Everyone and everything has conspired against me! (*She falls into the armchair.*)

PLASMONICK: (*Speaks coldly and ironically, still standing between the two guards to the left.*) Unhappy love either changes to mild affection or grows more and more violent until it finally turns to hatred. The latter case applies to me. I don't know what will happen—I don't have the slightest inkling—but I feel such terrible tension in my unconscious will that I think I could blow this house sky-high.

GIERS: Don't be ridiculous, Mr. Blödestaug. This isn't the right moment.

ROSA: Oh, God, God!

(*The Princess starts to watch with cold curiosity, without a trace of her former sympathetic attitude.*)

PRINCESS: This is beginning to get interesting—indeed.

PLASMONICK: I feel the denouement's about to take place. I'm going to act the way the secret voice of higher consciousness tells me to.

(*At this moment Lieutenant Flowers breaks open the black cabinet on the right and pulls out a bundle of papers.*)

FLOWERS: Ça y est, mon Colonel. I found them. The secret documents of the Grizzlovik conspiracy.

(Giers goes over to him.)

GIERS: *(Taking the papers)* This is interesting. *(Skims through them.)* Signed Baron de Buffadero. *(To Flowers)* Is that all?

FLOWERS: *(Rummaging in the cabinet)* Oh—here's another packet. *(He gives it to Giers, who feverishly undoes the packet and becomes deeply engrossed in reading.)*

ROSA: *(Jumping up)* Colonel! Those are my love letters! You can't look at them.

GIERS: Stay where you are. *(A gendarme goes over to Rosa.)* Nice love letters! Between you and the northern fortress of Centuria? *(Waving a map at her)* Between you and the fortress in Croissantia on the Kamur Delta? At last! Flowers, you keep this, and give me the Grizzlovites' papers to look over.

(They exchange papers. Rosa sits listlessly on the couch. Sophie keeps on playing. The Princess observes the situation through her face-à-main. Plasmonick suddenly changes into a completely different person. With a firm step, his head held high, he goes over to the colonel and stands at attention, even though he's dressed as a civilian, in a gray suit.)

PLASMONICK: Colonel, sir, reporting for duty: Reserve Lieutenant Blödestaug, of the grenadiers bodyguard to His Highness, Prince Peter. Conclusive evidence, but on one condition.

(Without realizing it, Giers stands at attention too.)

GIERS: What is it?

PLASMONICK: When you put us in prison, me and her *(he points to Rosa)*, I must have a guarantee that we'll be put in the same cell.

(A pause. The Princess bursts out in screeches of laughter. The Baroness accompanies her with a high-pitched squeal.)

GIERS: What a wild idea! And how can that be arranged?

PLASMONICK: Colonel, I'm warning you, although all weapons have been taken away from me, I still have this *(takes a small object out of his vest pocket)*, a nicely mounted razor blade. Colonel, if you don't promise me this minute, I'll slit my throat on the spot and you won't find out a thing. *Ever!* The thread that could unravel this mystery snaps with me. Come to a quick decision.

GIERS: *(Hesitating)* All right—I agree. As long as it doesn't involve your personal freedom.

PLASMONICK: It doesn't. Your word as an officer?

GIERS: My word as an officer.

PLASMONICK: All right. (*Solemnly*) *I* am the chief spy for the land of the Macerbators. Those papers belong to me. Rosa van der Blaast is my accomplice.

(*Rosa sits dumbfounded on the couch.*)

GIERS: Hullo! Oh, that's marvelous! Now I understand! But why didn't you do this earlier?

PLASMONICK: (*Breathing heavily*) I couldn't make up my mind to. Now it's all over. I'm on the other side.

GIERS: (*To Flowers*) Lieutenant, telephone Major Daybell immediately!

FLOWERS: At your orders, sir.

(*He goes out to the left.*)

ROSA: (*Who until now has been sitting as if turned to stone, staring wide-eyed straight ahead, jumps up and cries out*) That's not true!

GIERS: (*Coldly*) You'll be so kind as to keep calm. The principal defendant has admitted his guilt.

(*Rosa goes limp again in a terrible struggle with herself and falls on the couch. The curtain over the center door is raised, and Tzingar comes out from behind it, completely self-possessed.*)

GIERS: (*Turning around. The others turn around too.*) Hullo! Still more surprises! Baron de Buffadero. What are *you* doing here?

(*Heading for the colonel, Tzingar squeezes Rosa's arm as he passes by her. Rosa cries out in pain.*)

ROSA: Oh!!!

TZINGAR: (*Hypnotizing her by looking her directly in the face*) Shut up, you wretch!! You don't have the right to breathe a single word. I didn't know what kind of house I'd been visiting. My good name was jeopardized at every moment. (*Goes over to the colonel; Plasmonick stands absolutely numb.*) Good evening, Colonel.

(*He offers Giers his hand; Giers shakes it mechanically. Rosa sits, completely reduced to jelly.*)

GIERS: But how did you get in here, Mr. Buffadero?

TZINGAR: I came in the back way.

GIERS: But why the back way?

TZINGAR: Because I felt like it.

GIERS: That's no answer. We're conducting a search here in this nest of spies. Please be more *précis* in your testimony. I'm here in my official capacity.

PLASMONICK: He's the one! She had a lover! She's been deceiving me for two years, for two long years! But now I've got her. Oh—now she'll be mine, only mine. In hell or in prison—what does it matter? You will keep your word, won't you, Colonel?

GIERS: (*Impatiently, turning toward him*) I will, I will. (*To Tzingar*) All right—go on, Baron. Your life is at stake—and something else too, you know? Heh, heh!

TZINGAR: (*Turns toward Rosa and looks at her for a moment.*) Oh—you slut! (*To the Colonel*) I still can't get hold of myself. I was here—Colonel, I can't bring myself to say it. Who is this lady?

(*He points at the Princess, who has been observing the situation continually through her glasses. Completely shattered, Rosa goes over to Giers and speaks.*)

ROSA: Colonel, he fell in love with my maid. Such a great man to fall so low. She is the personification of everything that's perverse. It's horrible.

GIERS: (*To Tzingar*) Is that true?

TZINGAR: (*Lugubriously*) Unfortunately—yes, it is. (*He bows his head low.*)

PLASMONICK: (*Falling on his knees before Rosa*) Then he wasn't your lover? Rosa! This is the most beautiful day of my life. When we're together—you'll have to love me. I'm different now. I have tremendous strength within me. I'll even get the best of my sickness.

ROSA: (*Utterly distracted*) Maybe, maybe. I don't know anything now.

(*She sits down and covers her face with her hands. Kneeling, Plasmonick kisses her limp hand. Tzingar talks in a whisper with the colonel. Enter old Blödestaug, accompanied by Major Daybell.*)

BLÖDESTAUG: Plazy, what are you doing here? I've been looking for you all week. I didn't know you were acquainted with this lady. They just told me now. I've been looking for you at all your friends'.

(*Plasmonick gets up and rushes over to his father.*)

PLASMONICK: Father! Don't judge me. Awful things have been happening. But someday you'll understand me and then you'll forgive me. Someday I'll be completely vindicated.

BLÖDESTAUG: (*Hugging him*) But what is it? What really happened?

PLASMONICK: I'm a spy. I was a suspect. Now I've confessed. My life is over. Now I'll work exclusively on putting your theory into practice.

BLÖDESTAUG: Oh, God! How horrible!

PLASMONICK: Father, greet Her Highness.

(*Blödestaug turns around, goes over to the Princess and kisses her hand.*)

PRINCESS: (*Stroking his head*) God is sending you a difficult trial, Mr. Blödestaug. And me as well. My darling Rosa is a spy, an espionagette. That's right—it's frightful!

PLASMONICK: And now everybody listen to me: an artist's life is pure chance. Up until now in acting as I have, I have followed the voice of my artistic intuition. There are artists who by creating, create positive values in life, and there are those who create most significantly by destroying their own lives and even those of others.

PRINCESS: What a cynical attitude! I'll help you live through this, Mr. Blödestaug.

(*Blödestaug sinks down at her knees. She clasps his head in her hands.*)

PLASMONICK: Listen! I've been living in a dreadful state of anguish, but I haven't been able to find any artistic justification for it, I couldn't change it into significant values. Now it's all over. My father's theory will truly be put into practice and that's how I'll make amends to him for this horrible wrong I've committed. If they locked me up all alone, I'd go mad and I wouldn't create anything.With her (*points to Rosa*) I'll accomplish simply diabolical things. So will she. I'll metaphysicalize her music. I know I have the strength for it now. I owe it all to Colonel Giers.

GIERS: Maybe something will come of that. I don't know about those things. For me you're a loathesome reserve officer and a spy—a combination that physically I just can't stand. The very thought of it makes me sick. (*To Rosa*) What have you got to say about that?

Rosa: Oh, Colonel, art before everything. If he accomplishes what he says he's going to, then even prison holds no terrors for me. But by the way, will I be allowed to have a piano?

Giers: Oh—certainly not. Absolutely no racket. Any kind of noise in prison is out of the question. Besides, can't you compose without a piano?

Rosa: I can, but I'd always rather . . .

Giers: (*Suddenly tapping his finger against his head*) But, but—Mr. Plasmonick, why did you write to this lady for money? As a spy you must have had piles of it.

Plasmonick: That particular day I absolutely had to have ten thousand gryblers. My contact told me that if I didn't get it that very day—he'd squeal on me. And the package from the Macerbators was late.

Giers: Perhaps you'd be willing to squeal on your accomplices that way too? Huh?

Plasmonick: Don't force me to go to new heights of swinishness. Haven't I done enough as it is?

Giers: Just one thing more: the papers are signed by a certain Tzingar. What does that mean?

Plasmonick: Oh, God! How he tortures me! My pseudonym, Tzingar—that's me.

Giers: Fine—nothing more is needed now. This one thread will permit us to unravel the whole mystery. (*To Daybell*) Major, let's get to work.

Plasmonick: Don't despair, father—I'm going to do wonderful things. I feel healthy as a bull. (*To Giers*) By the way, Colonel, how many years will I get?

Giers: At least fifteen.

Plasmonick: That's plenty.

Giers: Well, yes—but as a reward for your quick confession I'll see that you get equipment for Swedish gymnastics, even though the regulations make absolutely no provision for it. Still . . .

(*Grifuellhes rushes in, accompanied by Claudestina de Montreuil and the two gravediggers. He is wearing a guard's uniform, green with white facings. Except for Claudestina, they are all very drunk.*)

Giers: Attention!! (*All the military stand at attention; Giers goes*) *over to the Prince.*) Your Highness, the spies have been caught. I've saved the state from infamous treason. Plasmonick Blödestaug has confessed his guilt himself.

GRIFUELLHES: Very good, very good, old boy. At ease!

GIERS: At ease!!

(*The military go limp.*)

GRIFUELLHES: (*To the Princess, who does not let go of Blödestaug*) Mother! Mother! Forget that old puppet. Have you fallen in love with that old fogey in your old age, mother? But you know what, mother? Knowing the true facts about one's birth still does count for something. I wonder what kind of look our aristocrats would have on their faces if they knew all the secrets about their ancestors. As for me—I've started a New Life. My father's a wonderful man. He's a sage! Maybe I'll become a gravedigger too. It'd be worth being one to have such a philosophy of life.

GRAVEDIGGER I: You're getting carried away, my son. I'm an ordinary drunken bum—that's all I am. To you that's a novelty.

GRIFUELLHES: And what's more I've fallen head over heels in love with that lady. (*He points to Claudestina.*) Mother, she's got to be our court painter and be given a title. Then—I'll marry her.

PRINCESS: Fine, fine, dear boy. Just as long as you're not bored.

(*Blödestaug gets up.*)

CLAUDESTINA: (*To Blödestaug*) You're worried about your son's behavior, aren't you? Professor, I paint too, a little differently perhaps than you'd like, but still there's something to it. Don't lose heart. I'll be a daughter to you.

BLÖDESTAUG: Fifteen years!! Oh, God, God! And besides, it's all so hideous. He'll be locked up with *her!* (*He points to Rosa.*)

CLAUDESTINA: Fifteen years is nothing. When he gets out, he'll be forty-five. An ideal age. In the meantime, consider me your daughter, professor. And anyhow it'll be better for him with her. (*Blödestaug embraces her.*)

PLASMONICK: You can all rest assured that I won't waste that time.

ROSA: But Sophie! I completely forgot about her.

CLAUDESTINA: Your little girl? I'm taking her home with me. I'll have an artificial father and an artificial daughter. I've been so alone the last few years!

GRIFUELLHES: And take me as your artificial husband, Miss Claudestina. I can't live without you.

CLAUDESTINA: I don't know yet. You have too violent a nature, Prince.

GRIFUELLHES: I'll tone it down. Still, I'm very grateful to the Baroness for these revelations. Would it ever have occurred to me before to marry a lady painter? Freedom! What a wonderful thing!! Lopak, old pal, you'll forgive me for taking your love away from you. That's the way it is—you'll find somebody else more suitable.

LOPAK: Right now I'm not concerned with those problems. I have something more important on my mind, Your Highness.

GRIFUELLHES: Most likely poetic nonsense. Well, my friends, let's go—everyone to his proper place.

GIERS: Yes—take the defendants. The trial will take place tomorrow. (*To the officers*) Since there's been a confession, it'll be a mere formality. Let's go.

TZINGAR: Colonel, one more favor, please. I want to say a couple of words of farewell to Miss van der Blaast.

GIERS: Certainly. (*Laughs.*) Just don't break any of her bones during the conversation. (*To the others*) All right—let's get out of this den of horrors.

CLAUDESTINA: Sophie, you're coming with me. Mama's very busy today.

(*Sophie runs over to her. Claudestina takes her by the hand. The Princess leads out Blödestaug, who is unsteady on his feet. They are followed by Claudestina with Sophie, and then by Plasmonick between the two guards.*)

PLASMONICK: (*On his way out, to Rosa*) We begin, starting tomorrow night.

(*Rosa is silent. Tzingar stands next to her. Both betray frantic impatience. Giers goes out last with the officers and gendarmes. The door closes. Rosa and Tzingar talk hurriedly in choked whispers.*)

ROSA: Do you love me? Do you understand what I've done for you?

Tzingar: (*Embraces her and kisses her on the lips.*) I know. You are truly great. Besides, this won't last long. I'll get you out in no time. Once our conspiracy has proved successful.

Rosa: I'll never be his. Don't you believe me?

Tzingar: I'd like to believe you. Anyhow, we've got to sacrifice everything for things on a higher plane.

Rosa: I love you. I'll torture him to death in that prison. The abject reptile.

Tzingar: I enjoy this kind of life. Just think how everything hung by a thread. If I hadn't met Giers yesterday, and if he hadn't joined the Grizzloviks, and if that idiot didn't love you—we'd both rot away in prison. What a series of coincidences! Two weeks ago the death penalty was abolished. Ugh—I could have been hanged. And if the death penalty still existed, that blockhead never would have taken the blame on himself. You know, life is ruled by chance far more than we think it is under normal conditions.

Rosa: But not the life of artists. You'll see what diabolical things I'm going to compose *there*. But it seems to me you're not upset enough by the fact that they're locking me up with him. You don't love me. Remember, if I didn't love you as much as I do, you wouldn't have gotten out of this either. You don't take that into account at all.

Tzingar: Yes, I do—believe me, I do. I resign myself to the inevitable—what else can I do? Once our conspiracy has proved successful, the world will be groveling at your feet: new instruments, new music, everything! (*He kisses her*).

Giers's Voice: (*From behind the door*) Come on—hurry up, Baron. (*Opens the door halfway—that is, Giers, not his voice.*)

Tzingar: (*Grabs Rosa by the arm.*) Get going! You goddam dirty swine! Rot in a dank cell!! (*Shoves her brutally toward the door, which Giers opens.*) Because of you I almost lost my good name!

ACT III

(*A large prison cell. Gray walls. A window, with bars, facing the audience. Through it can be seen flowering fruit trees, bathed in sunlight, outlined against the blue sky. In the corners two beds covered with gray blankets with yellow stripes. A bolted door to the left. Three plain wooden chairs. To the right an easel with a picture on it, the back turned toward the audience. Plasmonick, in a gray prison uniform, sits at the easel. On his chest he has a large yellow circle with the number 117 in red. To the right, nearer the audience, about ten canvases turned with their faces to the wall, and still nearer the audience an iron wash basin, over which hangs a huge tank. Beneath the window a table piled high with papers and books. To the left, between the footlights and the door, a small table, at which Rosa sits, also in a prison uniform. She has the number 118 in red on a yellow circle. She hums something, then writes it down on music paper. Plasmonick paints. A pause.*)

PLASMONICK: (*Putting away his painting materials and going away from the easel*) Rosa, it can't go on like this any longer. It's three in the afternoon—Tuesday. A week's gone by, and you haven't said a single word to me. Don't you realize I've got enough misfortunes as it is? I've got to do this cursed portrait of Grizzelov, or else I won't earn enough for extra food for the two of us. Do you understand what it means for me to have to paint from a photograph, when I want to do something entirely different: finish that composition with those intersecting lines. (*Rosa remains silent.*) Rosa, I beg you, just say one little word. Don't torture me any more. (*Silence.*) Well, damn it all to hell, this has got to stop once and for all! When will you finally realize that I love you to distraction, to the point of utter madness? I've metaphysicalized your music, haven't I? If it hadn't been for me and my theory of art, or rather my father's theory of art, if I hadn't explained it to you—since you've got to admit you didn't understand a single phrase in my father's books with that poor little bird brain of yours—you'd still be wallowing in that disgusting shallow sentimentality. New instruments and new scales wouldn't help you—it wouldn't amount to anything but a simple question of musical notation. (*Rosa remains silent and hums.*) Will you say something, or won't you?

ROSA: Do you want the guards to pour cold water on us again the way they did in March? (*Points to a scar on her forehead.*) Look at that and shut up. Keep on slinging paint at your stupid pictures. Painting is not art. (*She goes on writing.*)

PLASMONICK: Rosa, don't start discussing theories of art, when you know it's really about something totally different.

ROSA: (*Cynically*) I know—for you what it's really all about is tonight, and after that, all the other nights to come.

PLASMONICK: What a horrible cynic you are, Rosa! You absolutely fail to understand what dimension my attachment to you assumes . . .

ROSA: The third undoubtedly. At any rate not the second or fourth. Ha! Ha! Ha! (*She hums and writes.*)

PLASMONICK: I beg you, this has to end here and now. I can't stand having those secrets come between us any longer. They're poisoning our life.

ROSA: (*Gets up, after having drawn two perpendicular lines.*) Remember what we swore to each other: never to speak about that. Only on that condition can our life together somehow be possible.

PLASMONICK: I can't go on living this way—I simply *can't.*

ROSA: Remember what I told you—that resolving certain things will turn our life into pure hell and we'll have to live apart.

PLASMONICK: But I'm suffering. I can't live without you. The more I'm with you, the more attached I become to you. You're like Cleopatra: one can never tire of you or get enough of you.

ROSA: Then just be glad you have me. Remember, if they locked you up for fifteen years without me, you'd undoubtedly go mad and wouldn't even paint half those blobs. In fourteen years you'll leave here, the greatest painter in the country, maybe even in the world. Oh, what a low art painting is! If it weren't for the publicity you're getting about all this imprisonment, you wouldn't even be what you are now.

PLASMONICK: Rosa, please, don't insult my profession. I don't meddle in music at all, except for having metaphysicalized *your* music. Theoretically I recognize that music has a right to exist.

ROSA: (*Mimicking him*) "Metaphysicalized," "theoretically!" I can't stand those expressions of yours. There's something about you that reminds me of a pedantic German professor. I'd have come to the same conclusions myself even without

you. You know what Beethoven said? "Musik ist höhere Of-
fenbarung als jede Religion und Philosophie."

PLASMONICK: Read the introduction to Cennini's treatise on
painting, and you'll learn something totally different.

ROSA: No wonder—it was a painter who wrote that.

PLASMONICK: And it was a musician who said that.

ROSA: Oh—it's impossible to reach any kind of understanding
with you. No matter what anyone says, at best painting will
never be anything but nature deformed—that's all. All those
attempts to musicalize painting are nothing but a big lie—you
painters will never free yourselves from the objects you
paint.

PLASMONICK: Just as music, even the most abstract music, will
never free itself from human emotions. But neither music
nor painting is important—the only important thing is Pure
Form . . .

ROSA: "Pure Form!" If you mention that Pure Form of yours
one more time, I'll go stark raving mad. I can't stand hearing
that expression anymore.

PLASMONICK: But you yourself are concerned with form in
music.

ROSA: No—all that's just a means for expressing metaphysical
feelings. Music creates feelings which don't exist in real life.

PLASMONICK: That's a delusion—all feelings can be reduced to a
combination of simple qualities.

ROSA: Oh—"qualities!" Another word I hate. You keep repeating your father's drivel like a parrot. He's got an answer for
everything—like an automaton.

PLASMONICK: You don't like to discuss things purely dialec-
tically, just like women in general and unintelligent
men . . .

ROSA: You're not in the least intelligent; you have clever little
formulas for everything. You say something, and then you
start to think it's really so. That's "dried-up drivel," as the old
Princess called it.

PLASMONICK: Yes—your drivel is moist. Some Greek sage
claimed that moisture is the essence of Existence. You can
use that as your starting point and create a new wet theory.
Bergson and other mythomaniacs will help you.

ROSA: Say whatever you like—I know, because I can feel it myself: I can feel how what I compose, but don't actually hear, creates another world within me, and that's without even having the work played.

PLASMONICK: You don't have any self-knowledge. That's just unsound introspection.

ROSA: Will you drop that pseudoscientific jargon of yours once and for all? You can paint one of your blobs and at least you get more or less what you had in mind, but I can only put little circles and dots down on paper. You don't know what torture it is not to be able to hear one's own works.

PLASMONICK: (*Going over to her*) I know you're wretched. Rosa, don't get so upset. You know how I love you. I took the whole blame myself . . .

ROSA: Don't say it, don't say anything! That's all petty, hideous, disgusting. Don't come near me. You got me by a trick.

PLASMONICK: But did I really get you? I don't know. Sometimes I think I did, but other times I'm monstrously tortured. Rosa—it *can't* go on like this any longer. We quarrel about art, but really an abyss is growing between us because of those secrets. We've got to put an end to that.

ROSA: If you want to end everything with me, then go ahead—just ask me about it!

PLASMONICK: It's not quite so easy to end everything with me. The court sentenced us to prison together. It's not just a question of moving to another room, like in a hotel. It would take a retrial. But what if I go back on my previous testimony? Then your secrets will have to come out in the open.

ROSA: I implore you, keep quiet! You torture me more than the executioner could. I want to forget about it. It won't be long now . . . (*She gets hold of herself.*)

PLASMONICK: (*Suddenly uneasy*) Are you planning to kill yourself?

ROSA: Kill myself? Ha, ha, ha! Why, you idiot . . . (*Gets hold of herself.*) Let's not talk about it.

PLASMONICK: I'd *prefer* not to talk about it. But don't you see it's always there, lurking at the back of all our conversations, of everything that happens to us? It's monstrous!

ROSA: Yes—it *is* monstrous.

PLASMONICK: I keep asking myself the same hellish questions: Why didn't you defend yourself after I confessed, who was the chief spy, and were you his mistress?

ROSA: I implore you once more, for God's sake: keep quiet and don't ask anything more.

PLASMONICK: I've got to tell you something: sometimes—this is comical—I think it was that damned Buffadero, or whatever his name was. That thought haunts me too. (*Rosa remains silent.*) Do you know, the fact that you might have been an espionagette yourself doesn't make you any less attractive to me?

ROSA: All of this is so revolting, so disgusting, so petty, that I'm simply suffocated by it all! If you could see how loathesome you are! If you were at least a musician! But a painter! *A painter!* That word alone is capable of poisoning everything.

PLASMONICK: (*Speaks morosely, sitting down in the chair in the center.*) If that's the case, then my position is really getting terrible. Those secrets have created a hatred in you which didn't exist before.

ROSA: There wasn't any, because I wasn't your mistress. I even had a favorable opinion of you, before we became close. Now I hate you, hate you, hate you. Understand? Forever and ever.

PLASMONICK: Then it's all over between us?

ROSA: Why, no, not at all. I can still be your mistress. Your *mistress!* Or even your wife. We can have a wedding if you like. I don't care. Just so you know I hate you. Worse still, I despise you.

PLASMONICK: (*Jumping up*) No—that I can't bear. I've got to know everything!

ROSA: (*Laughing*) And the fourteen years that are still ahead of us? Doesn't that terrify you? Will you still be able to endure living with me after what I'm going to tell you?

PLASMONICK: (*Hissing*) Now I've got to know. If you don't tell me, I'll strangle you. You've got to. Understand?

ROSA: Remember today is visiting day. Someone may come at any moment. Wouldn't it be better if we didn't get so excited?

PLASMONICK: No, no, no! Answer these questions! Why did you

follow me here and not even try to save yourself? Quickly! Answer me!!

ROSA: Because I loved a *certain person* and I still love him and only him, and I wanted to save him.

PLASMONICK: (*Through clenched teeth*) Who is he?!

ROSA: Joseph Tzingar, the chief spy for the Macerbators.

PLASMONICK: (*Insanely curious*) Which one was it? Was it the one who . . . ?

ROSA: The one who came out of my bedroom then: he was acting as a Grizzlovik, under the name of Buffadero.

PLASMONICK: That slob! That bastard! And it was for him . . . ! Oh—this has got to come to an end once and for all! It was for him that I went to prison, for that scoundrel!

ROSA: Not for him, but for me. You got what you wanted: I was your mistress.

PLASMONICK: (*Hissing*) So he was the one you were getting the money from and *I* was in *his* debt for that ten thousand? Oh—how hideous!

ROSA: Never accept anything from women, remember that and then you won't get involved in such messy situations.

PLASMONICK: Aaaaah! What monstrous swinishness! I've plunged down from the loftiest heights to the very bottom. I'm completely destroyed.

ROSA: You never were on any heights. He painted a couple of pictures and thinks he can be low-down on account of that. You are a miserable, weak little wet noodle. He thought he was a hero!

PLASMONICK: So you never loved me the least little bit? So you didn't even like me? Oh, you . . . !

ROSA: Don't get into too great a state of despair. I liked you well enough to be your mistress when he wasn't around.

PLASMONICK: Oh—then if I wasn't around, you'd be capable of being the mistress of the guard there who's keeping an eye on us. What kind of a morass have I sunk into!

ROSA: A morass of your own making. You brought it all on yourself.

PLASMONICK: Now for the first time I see who you are: a hideous espionagette, a scoundrel's mistress. Now I see.

ROSA: Only now? But just a minute ago you said it didn't make

me any less attractive to you—the first of those things, not
the second. He wasn't a scoundrel—he had to have money
for higher goals. He brought the great principles of Joachim
Grizzelov back to life—the man whose portrait you're smear-
ing away at there.

PLASMONICK: So that's what such a lofty cause is based on? A
new religion, made a reality by an ordinary scoundrel and
rastaquouère! I'm sinking lower and lower. It's horrible!

ROSA: He is strong, he is truly *great*. From that day on he
stopped being a spy.

PLASMONICK: Stopped being a spy! Do you understand what
you're saying? It's not the same as stopping drinking or playing cards. An out-and-out rogue from start to finish, right
down to the innermost fiber of his being—that's what he was
and still is. He stopped being a spy—that's preposterous.

ROSA: He's a strong man. I prefer evil to a jellyfish like you. A
painter—an artist! Ugh.

PLASMONICK: Shut up! For the sake of art one has the right to
do even swinish things. But even for the sake of art, *I* didn't
do anything wrong . . .

ROSA: Because you don't have either the strength or the
courage. If you were stronger, you'd be a hundred times
worse than he is. Maybe I'd fall in love with you then.

PLASMONICK: Oh—don't talk about us! There's an abyss between us. Now you're as repulsive to me as a bedbug.

ROSA: (*Coquettishly*) Now—but in six hours it may be a bit different. Just think . . .

PLASMONICK: (*Inwardly shaken*) Don't talk that way . . . I'm not
reproaching you because you took spy money for your
music, only because you could love *him* so much that to save
him you'd go to prison and deceive me for such a long time.
When I loved you so . . .

ROSA: That wasn't love; that was just weakness.

PLASMONICK: I can't begin to understand how lying can make a
social prophet seem great to you. He's got to personify his
cause in his own life, or else he won't create anything. You're
judging it by standards you'd apply to art, not to life. You'll
see that that Tzingar of yours . . .

Rosa: Don't talk about him. You've said enough already. What happened, happened.

Plasmonick: But how are we going to go on living? Fourteen years! No—I've got to get out of here. I simply can't—I can't love you anymore. Oh, God, God! There has to be a retrial. It's all a stupid, hideous dream. It's got to come to an end.

Rosa: Just stop and think, Plazy, what proof have you got? They'll take you for a madman and that's all. The court isn't a tool for psychophysiological experiments—the court has got to have evidence.

Plasmonick: Aha—so you're afraid of staying here, are you? I'll persuade them by the power of the truth itself. By the power of suggestion which enabled me to persuade them when I was lying, plus the fact that in this case it'll be the truth.

Rosa: Don't you dare! You may ruin everything and simply go from here straight into the insane asylum. And this time without me! Ha, ha!

Plasmonick: (*Undecided*) Then what are we to do?

Rosa: I'll tell you: Tzingar's organizing the great Grizzlovik revolution. It's going to start any day now and then we'll get out of here for sure. I'll ask him to let you out too, after all you're *someone* . . . I got a letter from him. (*Pulls a piece of paper from her bosom and reads.*) "Dearest Rosa: The day when we'll meet is near. It seems likely that now I'll be able to run the risk of visiting you. I'm already far enough along in my work so I don't have to be afraid of arousing suspicions. But what will your victim, poor Plazy, say about it . . ."

Plasmonick: (*Rushing at her*) Stop it! . . . I can't stand any more . . . How vile you are, Rosa!

(*Knocking at the door to the left.*)

Rosa: Quiet! Someone's coming. Don't you dare let on by as much as a wink that there's been anything between us. (*In the direction of the door*) Come in!

(*The doors are unbolted. Enter Lopak in a black shirt, red tie, black pointed cap, and Giers's pants from Act I.*)

Lopak: (*Without removing his cap*) Morning. Got the portrait ready?

PLASMONICK: It will be soon. Tomorrow perhaps.

LOPAK: Let's see!

(*Plasmonick turns the easel around so that it faces the audience, and we see the portrait of an old man, done completely naturalistically, with a certain stylization in which the contours are "hard." Pseudocubism. The old man is fat; both his hair and beard are fabulously long and milk-white.*)

PLASMONICK: Here it is. That's sinking as low as an artist possibly can in order to make money.

LOPAK: Terrific. You got that monkey just right. He won't be running things for long—not even in that portrait. Ho, ho! You don't know what's brewing. But here in this hole, what do you care? Strange, strange things are going on. (*Recites*)

    Cattle, grown human, have begun to integrate
    Their lack of power into monstrous might.
    With stealth these cattle thoughts set out to wind
    The ribbon of louse feelings in a spring coiled tight.
    Leaven of Marx's works, poured into cattle skulls,
    Creates a most strange mixture with the brain.
    Some thug jams all this in a fire hose
    To squirt it on the world out through the drain.
    Someday in a picture the little man of the future
    Will look at these events and whine with rapture,
    History in shiny helmet of pure gold
    Will portray the splendid moment beyond recapture.
    But once again *that* moment will never return—
    It's passed, and after it the abyss gapes still.
    With the boredom of waiting it sates the dark force
    Of the masses who never once gulped down their fill.

(*Knocking to the left.*) Ssh—not a word about what I said just now.

(*The door is unbolted. Enter Giers, the Princess, and Padoval de Grifuellhes. All of them are dressed as in Act II. Lydia Ragnock follows them.*)

PRINCESS: Good morning, dearest. I can come here only if the colonel escorts me. They're afraid that I'll become an espionagette too. (*Rosa kisses her hand. The men behave quite coldly and don't greet anyone.*) For me you're first and foremost a great artist.

PLASMONICK: To the extent that it's possible for a woman to be an artist at all. A woman's feelings always get the upper hand to the detriment of form—that is, of Pure Form.

PRINCESS: (*Coldly*) I didn't come here to visit *him,* only Rosa. *Allez-vous* out of my way, *per favore.* (*She talks with Rosa.*)

GIERS: Yes—you'd better pretend you're not here. (*Notices the picture.*) Oh! Grizzelov! He came out perfectly. Perfectly.

PLASMONICK: Someday you'll find out the truth, Colonel. I don't have any proof, but I *am* innocent.

GIERS: Yes, yes. But doesn't your official confession count for anything? Just as if it didn't exist? You're starting to get hard to handle, Mr. Plasmonick. Control yourself, or there'll be trouble.

(*Knocking.*)

ROSA: Come in.

(*The door is unbolted. Enter Dr. Blödestaug with Claudestina.*)

BLÖDESTAUG: Your Highness will excuse me, but he is my son after all. And besides, Miss Claudestina wanted to look at his paintings. (*To Plasmonick*) How are you feeling, Plazy?

PLASMONICK: I'm in a state of great inner transformation, Father. For me the world has turned round a hundred and eighty degrees at least.

(*Claudestina silently points to the pictures to the right. Plasmonick shows her the canvases covered with incredibly pure Pure Form, leaning them against the easel with the Grizzelov.*)

GIERS: It will turn even more, but in dead earnest. Since Prince Padoval is on our side, I'll tell you frankly: I have become a Grizzlovik. Under other circumstances I would have stuck with the old system to the very end. But present circumstances have convinced me. We're changing the form of power, but not its real nature.

LOPAK: Ha, ha, ha, ha, ha, ha!!!

(*The men all look at the paintings in silence.*)

GIERS: What's that poetnik laughing at? Power will continue to be power. I was always something of a mystic, but I didn't know how to relate it to my guiding principle about the supremacy of the state. He's the one (*points to the portrait*) who showed me how. I'm a Grizzlovik *faute de mieux.* No telling what will come of it later on.

LOPAK: I know, but I'm not going to tell. Anyhow, it's got to be put to the test.

BLÖDESTAUG: I have my own set of beliefs too. The Mystery of Existence is unfathomable, regardless of what system of ideas we're operating with. The calculated nationalization of this mystery, while preserving diversity for the expression of different ideas, is the sole principle which can save mankind from a total decline and fall.

LOPAK: That's utter rubbish, professor, but even so the post of minister of health and art in the new government is yours. Ha! Ha!

(*Knocking to the left.*)

ROSA: Come in.

(*The door is unbolted. Enter Tzingar in a white flannel suit. He has a blue necktie, and on his head a white, soft hat, which he immediately takes off.*)

PRINCESS: Greetings, Mr. Buffadero.

(*Tzingar greets the other ladies and Rosa, who jumps right out of her skin. Every muscle tensed, Plasmonick comes out into the middle of the stage, leaving Claudestina with the paintings.*)

PLASMONICK: I never asked that man to visit *us*.

TZINGAR: I didn't need your permission, young fellow. Keep still and behave yourself. (*To all of them*) Today is the decisive day: the *coup d'état* takes place tonight. (*To Giers*) General— since I can call you that now—you'll see to it that our garrison is put on the alert for ten tonight. I had to speed up events. (*To Plasmonick*) And as for you, young man, don't you get too fresh, since it's in my power to keep you in this hole for fourteen years or let you go free tomorrow.

GIERS: Mr. President! A spy can't be set free, even in a new state based on Joachim Grizzelov's principles. The state remains the state.

TZINGAR: Don't forget that you are *my* minister of war and that's all you are—*my* minister of war! You're being watched by *my* agents. Your function is only to execute *my* will.

(*Rosa looks at him adoringly.*)

GIERS: I've become involved in some hideous moral compromise. Making certain kinds of concessions exacts its own vengeance. Remember I can always refuse at the last minute.

TZINGAR: You're forgetting that the propaganda among the officers has been carried out quite effectively. At the most, maybe two or three people from the Prince's immediate entourage support you. Let's not talk about that. I have certain obligations to that gentleman. (*He points to Plasmonick.*)

GIERS: The President has obligations to a spy. A fine state of affairs!

TZINGAR: From my earliest youth. It's a family secret.

GIERS: Your origins are quite suspicious. At a certain point the thread breaks off and from there on absolutely nothing is known.

TZINGAR: (*Emphatically*) *General,* I don't advise you to become too absorbed in investigating those secrets before ten o'clock tonight. You could easily find yourself in that gentleman's place. (*He points to Plasmonick.*)

GIERS: That's how it is: "Trust a slob," as someone once said. The moral compromise I made is exacting its vengeance on me with fatal consequences. What's done is done—I can only sink in deeper.

TZINGAR: That's the best thing for you to do. You'll find yourself on heights you never even dreamed of.

ROSA: Talk all you want; although I refuse to acknowledge painting as an art, Plazy *is* our only painter. He must be saved.

(*Tzingar bows.*)

GIERS: There's something suspicious going on here. (*To Tzingar*) What did you actually come here for?

TZINGAR: (*Insolently*) To meet you and give you your final orders. That's what. Ha, ha!

(*Giers shrivels up.*)

CLAUDESTINA: (*Moving away from the paintings*) Excuse me everyone, but *I'll* take care of Mr. Plasmonick. I'm clairvoyant: (*To Rosa*) you want to destroy him by playing on his lowest level, on his instinct for life. I'll protect him from you. I know that now, together, we're going to create something significant in painting.

ROSA: I don't want to destroy him or to put him on a pedestal either. I want to get him out of here and never see him again.

GIERS: To make matters worse, they're starting to rave about art. Shall we go, Your Highnesses?

GRIFUELLHES: (*Who until now has been standing like a mummy behind the Princess' chair*) Miss Claudestina, you're forgetting that I'm your fiancé.

CLAUDESTINA: I'm breaking off my relations with you from this moment on, Prince. I must keep his spirit from giving way to despair. That's the truly significant task in my life. Prince, you can find consolation with anyone, even with women of that person's ilk.

(*She points to Rosa. The Prince draws back toward his mother, very displeased.*)

PLASMONICK: Do you really believe in me? I'm at the very bottom.

CLAUDESTINA: You wanted to destroy yourself violently and systematically. You wanted to speed it up, the way Mr. Buffadero wants to speed up his revolution. I'll destroy you too, but in a far more creative way. I won't let you sink to the bottom of life. You're going to play yourself out in Pure Form, without sinking to swinishness in reality.

(*Plasmonick shakes his head incredulously. The Princess gets ready to leave.*)

GIERS: That's enough of all that nonsense. Let's go. What awaits me is the simply hellish task of overcoming my own nature.

ROSA: Yes. That's quite enough. Couldn't all of you deal with those matters tomorrow—in the outside world?

(*Claudestina silently crosses over to the left and without saying good-bye to anyone [even to Plasmonick] leaves at the same time as the Princess, Giers, and Padoval.*)

BLÖDESTAUG: Take care of yourself, Plazy. Tomorrow you'll be free. I'm minister of art and public health. On the day of the *coup d'état* I don't imagine I'll be very busy—we'll have a chance to talk about everything. (*He leaves. Lopak follows him.*)

TZINGAR: (*Toward the door*) Don't close the door there! I'm just about to leave. (*The door closes, but is left unbolted.*) All right— now we can talk frankly. Only let's not have any long faces, my friends. Mr. Plasmonick, I turned your love for Rosa to my own advantage and I owe my life to you. From the looks on your faces I realized that Rosa wasn't able to keep it to herself and blurted out everything.

PLASMONICK: You're forgetting that I can tell all and it'll be quite a comedown for you to go from the presidency to a gray uniform with a yellow circle on it.

TZINGAR: Nobody will believe you now. My technique for covering my tracks is infallible. None of my accomplices is alive anymore. What happened to them—the devil himself couldn't find out. Contagious diseases—do you see what I mean? We'd better try to reach an understanding and you'll be director of the Academy of Fine Arts. We don't need those naturalistic old fogeys anymore.

PLASMONICK: Never! I don't believe that any remaking of society, based on individuals like you, can ever succeed. If Joachim Grizzelov could see the kind of people who are carrying out what he felt was the mission of the priesthood—he'd die a second death out of shame and despair. I am alone and that's the way I'll stay.

TZINGAR: As you like. Tomorrow you'll be free or we'll all die. Still, you've got to admit that I was discreet: I didn't see my Rosa for almost a year. I didn't want to bother the two of you until I was sure of victory.

PLASMONICK: I'd prefer that it never got started than to have it end like *this*. Still, I've got to admit you're a monstrous scoundrel, Mr. Tzingar.

TZINGAR: You're wrong. The position I now occupy has ennobled me. Napoleon was an ordinary crook at the start of his career. But leading France to glory made him truly great—the way he was at Waterloo. Now I would be utterly incapable of being a spy.

PLASMONICK: What megalomania! Rosa, can't you see he's a disgusting clown, that darling Tzingar of yours?

ROSA: Can't *you* see what a clown *you* are? No, Plazy, he has true greatness in him. We can't begin to evaluate him properly; we're seeing him too close up. Only history can judge him.

TZINGAR: All right—that's enough of all that babbling. Rosa—a great future lies ahead of us. With your kind permission, Mr. Plasmonick, I must kiss the future Mrs. President just once. (*He kisses her.*)

PLASMONICK: (*Rushing at him*) Don't you dare! You—low come-
dian! You *scoundrel!*

(*Tzingar slips off quickly to the left. Plasmonick stands still, breathing
heavily. His fists are tightly clenched. The guard appears at the door.*)

GUARD: Hey, you—number hundred and seventeen! Gonna be
quiet? Want to go back to solitary again, like when you beat
up number hundred and eighteen?

(*He glares threateningly for a moment. Plasmonick goes limp. The
guard withdraws and bolts the door.*)

PLASMONICK: Oh! If only I could get out of here right now.
(*Suddenly changes his tone.*) Rosa! The last day. That scoundrel
is capable of not letting me out. It was a mistake for me to
lose my temper. Rosa! Try to love me the way you used to.
Maybe I can convince you that I'm the only one who really
loves you.

ROSA: You'll find consolation with your Claudestina in any case.
She'll destroy you in an incredibly subtle way. Ha, ha!

PLASMONICK: Rosa, stop joking. This may be the last day of my
life.

ROSA: All right, my darling. After all, I am indebted to you for
saving Joseph Tzingar's life and for the fact that I'm going to
be the President's wife. Come here! Kiss me.

PLASMONICK: You don't know how monstrously you're torturing me . . .

ROSA: I do know—I know perfectly well. (*They kiss.*) Torture is
the absolute essence of love . . .

ACT IV
IN THE SHAPE OF AN EPILOGUE

(*A square in front of the prison. The prison wall, a pale ochre color
with white stripes, goes at a sharp angle to a line parallel to the line of
the footlights, in the right corner of the stage. Gate with bars. To the
left the corner of a house, in the shadows right next to the footlights.
Dawn. The sky cannot be seen. It is only reflected in the prison windows. Distant bursts of machine-gun fire and the very distant but con-
tinual rumble of artillery are heard. To the left a crowd is waiting in
front of the prison. To the right there are also a few people. The most
diverse clothes, all mixed together. Very bright colors. Green, carmine*

red, and violet predominate. Less frequently, sky blue. A complete ab-
sence of yellow and light red—colors that indicate the prisoners. In the
middle of the square there stands a lamppost and lantern, which burns
with a yellowish-greenish glow. At the gates two members of the guard
push back those who come too close. In the first row of the crowd to the
left: the Princess, the Baroness, Blödestaug, Claudestina and Sophie,
Rosa's Maid, Gravedigger I, and Lopak, who is dressed as in Act III.)

FIRST WOMAN: Oh, God! When will they let them out!

FIRST MAN: They say the palace's already been captured by
   the Grizzlovites. Giers led the attack himself.

SECOND WOMAN: The palace has been taken, and even Prince
   Padoval was put in prison for Grizzlovism. Look—you can
   see old Princess Barbara—over there. (*Points to the left.*) She's
   waiting for her son, just like us.

SECOND MAN: He just got put in the clink yesterday. They say
   the papers still haven't come yet.

FIRST WOMAN: Always the same old story in this country. The
   papers come very slowly, sometimes slower than a person's
   life.

(*The Officer of the guard comes through the prison gates.*)

OFFICER: The papers have come. The prisoners will be coming
   out in two or three minutes. I can inform you that the palace
   has been taken. Our army is fighting victoriously beyond the
   eastern gate to the city against the forces of Count Münsterberg who came to relieve the Prince. Victory is certain. Long
   live the memory of Joachim Grizzelov! Long live the New
   Theocracy!! Hurrah!!!!!

(*Rather feeble cheers from the crowd.*)

BLÖDESTAUG: I'm terribly alarmed. As minister of health and
   art, I don't have anything to do today—which is usually the
   case with people in this profession during a *coup d'état,* but I
   have the worst sort of forebodings.

LOPAK: You ought to have, Professor—there's a tiny little cloud
   on the horizon. You're going to see some strange things yet.

BLÖDESTAUG: I don't like the way the lowest elements are behaving. That's the basic material for a revolution.

LOPAK: And I'm just delighted with how they're behaving. The
   Grizzlovites won't last long.

BLÖDESTAUG: Not so loud! Just who are you, anyhow?

(*The crowd listens closely to what they are saying.*)

LOPAK: (*In a loud voice*) Ho, ho, Professor! Things like this can't be settled "among ourselves," just in passing. I am the creator of *The Anonymous Work!*

BLÖDESTAUG: Just don't go too far, Mr. Lopak. You could easily find yourself hanging *there.*

(*He points to the lantern, which at this very moment goes out. The light of dawn can be seen more distinctly on the wall of the prison.*)

LOPAK: No telling yet who's going to be hanging there today, me or Mr. Tzingar.

BLÖDESTAUG: Tzingar was the pseudonym my son used as a spy. Plazy will be free today—Buffadero promised.

LOPAK: Oh, that's just it—Buffadero! I was talking about a completely different Tzingar, not about your Plazy. He's about as much of a spy as I am, or even still less.

BLÖDESTAUG: What's that you're saying? Then he was imprisoned for almost a year even though he was innocent? That's horrible!

LOPAK: A lot of other horrible things are going to come out in the open. As soon as *my* little trick works.

BLÖDESTAUG: You're devilishly sure of yourself, Mr. Lopak.

LOPAK: Just don't you be too sure of yourself. Oh—look: here come the prisoners.

(*The crowd of prisoners starts to come out through the gates. All of them are dressed like Rosa and Plasmonick; only they have small, round, gray caps without visors.*)

OFFICER: (*From the window*) From now on, the prison dress will become the uniform of the Grizzlovik guards. All prisoners automatically became guards—criminals as well as political prisoners, and even women. Long live the Grizzlovite national guard!!

(*No one cheers. The prisoners and the "prisonerettes" run to their families and friends. Greetings and exclamations. General happiness.*)

LOPAK: Those were the criminals. Now they're going to let the political prisoners out.

(*Prince Padoval comes out wearing prison clothes and throws his arms around the Princess' neck.*)

GRIFUELLHES: Mother! See how nice I look in my new uniform.

IV. A scene from the Cracow production of *The Anonymous Work*, Act IV ("a square in front of the prison"). The political prisoners are let out. (Photograph by Wojciech Plewiński.)

I'm an officer in the Grizzlovite guard. At any rate I'm not one bit bored.

PRINCESS: My child, as long as you're not bored, I'm happy, completely happy.

GRIFUELLHES: And you know, mother, Uncle's in the clink. The officer of the day just told me. They got a phone call. Münsterberg's been crushed—he's retreating.

PRINCESS: Are you glad?

GRIFUELLHES: Of course I am, mother.

PRINCESS: In that case, I am too.

(*They kiss.*)

GRIFUELLHES: There's only one thing that bothers me: that's my unhappy love for Claudestina.

CLAUDESTINA: Don't say anything more about that, Prince. *I'm* waiting for Plasmonick.

GRIFUELLHES: Oh, that Plasmonick of yours is actually plasma, not a man. Mother, your Rosa made total psychophysiological mincemeat out of him.

(*Rosa comes out of prison in the same costume she wore in Act III.*)

ROSA: (*In a loud voice*) Isn't Baron de Buffadero here?!

FIRST MAN: Buffadero is at the castle. But he's not a baron any more; all titles have been abolished.

ROSA: Oh, is that so-o-o-o-o-o-o? That's too bad!

LOPAK: Ha, ha, ha, ha, ha! You won't be a baroness!

PRINCESS: You can take comfort, my dear: I'm just plain Mrs. Grifuellhes too.

(*Rosa greets the Princess.*)

BLÖDESTAUG: And how's my Plazy doing?

ROSA: He's having some kind of complications with his papers. But they say he'll be coming any minute now.

BLÖDESTAUG: Oh, those papers, those papers! In my ministry there won't be any kind of paper except the "perfectly pure article: water-closet paper," as the English call it. Poor Plazy! Lopak claims he never was a spy at all.

ROSA: (*Turning to Lopak*) Whaaat?! How dare you?!!!!

LOPAK: Careful, Miss Rosa! You're not Mrs. President yet, and maybe you never will be.

(*Rosa becomes flustered and quiets down. It grows lighter and lighter. A rosy glow begins to light the wall of the prison. Plasmonick comes out through the gates in prison clothes. The crowd made up of the relatives, friends, and mentors of the criminals breaks up slowly, as they take the prisoners home. Only those waiting for the political prisoners, who come out one by one, remain.*)

PLASMONICK: Good morning, everyone! How are you, father? I'm a bit dazed and I don't have any directions or any clear-cut line of action for the future. I'm waiting for my secret inner voice to tell me something.

CLAUDESTINA: I'll help you, Mr. Plazy. I know what you've got to do. I made a sketch of it yesterday.

PLASMONICK: You know—I'm not happy to be free.

(*They talk.*)

ROSA: (*Notices Sophie, whom Claudestina is holding by the hand.*)

Oh—my Sophie! How you've grown! How lovely you are! I'd completely forgotten about her.

(Caresses and endearments. Suddenly there's an uproar to the left. The clatter of many horsemen can be heard. Enter Tzingar, dressed in a riding outfit. He has a light-blue sash across his chest and a whip in his hand. The crowd grows larger again.)

TZINGAR: *(With forced gaiety)* Good morning, Rosa! How are you, Mrs. President? *(Kisses her hand. Rosa forgets about Sophie.)* Oh—we're here in full force. Mr. Grifuellhes, you'll excuse me for not having you released until now. Your uncle's already been done in. He was surprised half out of his wits. By the way, Mr. Plasmonick, is the portrait of Grizzelov done? *(He offers him his hand.)*

PLASMONICK: The portrait's done, but keep your distance. Would you mind paying me right now. I want to settle a debt I owe Miss Rosa. *(Tzingar gives him a bundle of banknotes, which Plasmonick hands over to Rosa.)* Here's that cursed ten thousand. Take it and may I never set eyes on you again.

TZINGAR: Friends, I must tell you in strictest confidence that the situation is far from clear. I left the palace on purpose, so that—how can I put it—so that things would settle down by themselves. Rioting has broken out among the lowest segments of the rabble. The fifth regiment began plundering the northern district. It's all being stirred up by some totally unknown people in black pointed caps.

LOPAK: *(Laughing)* Caps like mine maybe? Eh?

TZINGAR: *(Flustered)* That's right. How'd you get here? You're supposed to be at a meeting of the Committee for the Protection of Incapacitated Civilians now! What are you doing here?

LOPAK: I'm doing what I think is best, and I'm where I am most needed.

TZINGAR: What? How dare you! If that's how my subordinates are going to follow my orders there's no hope of keeping the rabble under control.

LOPAK: I knew you'd come here to get your Rosa, Mr.—*Tzingar!*

BLÖDESTAUG: Tzingar?

TZINGAR: *(Roars)* Whaaat?!!!

V. Another scene from the Cracow production of *The Anonymous Work*, Act IV. Lopak exposes Tzingar. (Photograph by Wojciech Plewiński.)

LOPAK: (*Taking two steps backward*) I'm that agent of yours you saw only once, and then I was wearing a mask. I'm the only one you didn't know personally, Mr. Tzingar! But I played that game so as to be able to put the blame on you when you weren't useful to us anymore—to *us!*—the people in the black pointed caps! The second regiment is ours!

TZINGAR: (*Roars*) Seize him!!

LOPAK: (*Roars to the soldiers standing guard at the gates, pointing at Tzingar*) Seize that scoundrel! That's Tzingar—chief spy for the Macerbators. (*The sentry grabs Tzingar, who seems more dead than alive, and holds him. Rosa cuddles Sophie in her arms. To everyone*) Fellow citizens! Men like this aren't our leaders; they're garbage waiting to be carted off! We—the real people—have made use of them for our own purposes. They made the first breach! We don't need a priest-run government camouflaged as mealy-mouthed democracy. We're going to create our own true self-government. We're going to get along without any parliament by organizing trade unions of loafers. We're going to create a true paradise on earth without any leaders and without any work! That's what we're going to do. We! The uniform, gray, sticky, stinking, monstrous mass: a new Separate Being, defying all metaphysics based on the concept of the individual and the hierarchy! There are no individuals!! Down with the personality! Long live the uniform MASS, one and indivisible!!!! Hurrah!!!!

THE CROWD: Hurrah!! Long live the uniform MASS!!!! Down with the individual! Down with the personality!!!!

(*Giers rushes in from the left accompanied by the officers. The first ranks of the army can be seen behind them.*)

GIERS: Where is Buffadero!! (*Because of the dense crowd, he cannot see that Tzingar is being held, and he shouts, pushing his way through the crowd*) Mr. Buffadero! The fifth regiment, along with the mob, is coming at us full tilt. The second has revolted too. Münsterberg's forces are supporting the rabble, not the Prince! (*Notices that Tzingar is being held by members of the guard.*) What the devil? What are they holding you for?

TZINGAR: (*In a trembling voice*) Sir . . . General . . . we're . . . lost. . . .

LOPAK: (*To Tzingar*) Shut up! Scum! (*To Giers*) Ho, ho, General, here's some good news for you. Do you know who this Buffadero of yours is? It's *Tzingar!* The chief spy!!

GIERS: That can't be! (*Grabs his head in his hands*) Oh—what an idiot I've been! It was so obvious all along, and I, like an utter ass, couldn't even figure it out!!

LOPAK: (*To the crowd*) String that mangy bum up to the lamppost.

THE CROWD: String him up to the lamppost! Hang him! Hang

him! *Hang both of them!* String the whole government up to the lamppost! Down with the priests! String Giers up to the lamppost! (*They rush at them both.*)

GIERS: (*Draws his sword and tries to run Tzingar through.*) Let him go! I'm going to kill that scoundrel!

(*They snatch his sword away from him and drag them both to the lamppost. At this point the following must take place: At the prison gates dummies, with sacks over their heads, must be ready, dressed exactly like Giers and Tzingar. The crowd swarms around the two live characters and conceals them from the audience. Meanwhile the dummies must be put in their places, and the live actors who play Tzingar and Giers must crawl off unnoticed, concealed by the crowd, through the prison gates into the wings. Sorry—it's indispensable.*)

THE CROWD: String the rascals up to the lamppost. Hurrah!!!!

GIERS: (*As he is dragged off*) Mr. Plasmonick! Forgive me! Oh! The compromise I made has exacted its full vengeance on me!!!

(*They completely swarm around them. Both the hanged figures are pulled up on the lamppost, over which ropes have been thrown. From the left the sun floods the square, the lamppost, and the wall of the prison with a glaring orange light.*)

LOPAK: (*Whose black cap falls off his head*) And now on to the palace! Hang the whole government!!! Hurrah!!!!

(*He goes out, surrounded by the crowd to the left. There remain only the Princess, the Baroness, Rosa and Sophie, Padoval, Claudestina, and Plasmonick—plus the two [false] corpses on the lamppost too.*)

BLÖDESTAUG: (*Rubbing his hands with satisfaction*) They forgot about me. That's marvelous! Well, Plazy—we're starting a new kind of underground existence.

ROSA: Plazy, I'm yours—*only* yours. I've woken up from a horrible nightmare. I don't love *him* any more.

PLASMONICK: It's too late, Miss Rosa, it's too late. I love Miss Claudestina de Montreuil. I've finally woken up from a dreadful nightmare too—the nightmare of loving you. I'm starting to paint in a completely different way.

BLÖDESTAUG: Then let's go home for morning coffee. I'm inviting all of you.

PLASMONICK: No, papa, I *cannot* live in a society run by Mr. Lopak and the mob from across the tracks. I've come to like

my room in that building very much. (*Points to the prison.*) Art
has come to an end, and no one is going to produce an artificial religion—not even the late Tzingar with the help of
Grizzelov, or even *Lopak himself.* I'm going back to prison.
And in order not to be tempted to get out again, I've got to
do something appropriately monstrous. I assume that even
in a new state based on the Lopakian rabble and the myth
about cattle-like worklessness, certain crimes will have to be
punished. (*He pulls out from inside his jacket his razor blade in a
wooden holder, from which he is inseparable, and shows it to the assembled group.*)

BLÖDESTAUG: Plazy! Don't kill yourself! Art!!
(*He tries to grab him. Plasmonick pushes him away.*)

PLASMONICK: Wouldn't think of it, father. (*To Rosa*) Miss Rosa—
your turn now. (*Rushes at her and slits her throat with lightning
speed. Rosa falls dead. Calmly*) My secret inner voice told me to.
She already had composed herself out anyway. She told me
so in her moments of sincerity, so it's no loss to art. In our
times there are only two places for metaphysical individuals:
prison or the insane asylum. (*They are all petrified, including
Sophie.*) Are you coming with me, Miss Claudestina?

CLAUDESTINA: Anywhere you want. We're still going to get out
of here: to another world, which I see dimly somewhere in
the future. What exists now—cannot last.

PLASMONICK: No, thanks. I won't get out, since I don't believe
in any of that. Social phenomena are *ir-re-vers-i-ble.* (*He syllab-
ifies the last word.*) Good-bye father. You can come visit me
tonight.

(*He goes in through the prison gates. Claudestina goes in after him,
closing the gates with a bang. In the distance the rattle of machine guns
can be heard again.*)

PADOVAL: (*Picking up Lopack's black pointed cap off the ground*)
Well—if that's the way it is, then *I'll* become "the unknown
man in the pointed cap." I'm leaving now to incite my regiment of grenadier guards to go all the way. (*Puts the cap on his
head.*) Compared to me, Philippe-Egalité will be just a
harmless little joke. Is that all right, mother?

PRINCESS: As long as you're not bored, dear boy. Do whatever
you want, whatever you think is best.

BLÖDESTAUG: That Plazy really *is* a madman. Did you ever hear of slitting a woman's throat that way like a chicken, and in the *morning* at that? In the morning! And that Claudestina— she's a real demonic fairy godmother. They're not normal types. (*Takes Sophie by the hand*) Come along, Sophie! I'm inviting all of you for coffee and nice fresh rolls.

Curtain
(End of Act IV, the epilogue, and the last act)

"A Few Words about the Role of the Actor in the Theatre of Pure Form" (written 1919; published 1921)

by STANISŁAW IGNACY WITKIEWICZ

In Warsaw recently there has been a revival of the art of the actor, initiated by Mieczysław Limanowski, a geologist well known throughout the whole of Europe.[1] We are obliged to debate the matter with him—we being (in the *pluralis doppelgängerus*) a painter virtually unknown even in Poland. This seems farcical, but that's the way it is—there's no help for it. The theatre really must be in bad shape if people from such diverse specialties have something to say on this subject.

The theories according to which this "renaissance" is taking place are closely related to the principles set forth in Kommissarzhevsky's book *The Art of the Actor and the Theatre of Stanis-*

Translated by Daniel Gerould from Stanisław Ignacy Witkiewicz, "Parę słów o roli aktora w sztuce teatralnej w czystej formie," in *Nowe Formy w Malarstwie, Szkice Estetyczne, Teatr* (Warsaw: P.W.N., 1974). An earlier version of this translation appeared in *Theatre Quarterly*, V (June–August, 1975).

[1] Mieczysław Limanowski (1876–1948) as a student of geology at the University of Lwów spent much time in Zakopane studying the Tatras Mountains, and while there served as Witkiewicz's tutor, helping to prepare him for his high school examinations. Long interested in the theatre, Limanowski wrote drama criticism and made plans for projected productions before World War I. When in 1915 he was deported to Russia, Limanowski had the opportunity to meet Stanislavsky in Moscow, and became acquainted with his method of training actors, even taking part in some Moscow Art Theatre rehearsals. On his return to Poland in 1918, Limanowski worked in the theatre as a director and manager, while at the same time continuing his scientific research and eventually becoming a professor of geology.

lavsky. Following these views, the actor is supposed to "experience" totally the inner life of his role; his words and gestures are supposed to result naturally from his feelings, just as would happen in real life to people under the influence of strong emotions. All this they call *pieriezhivaniya* (experiences), plus *voploshcheniya* (embodiment).

A second principle of the Stanislavsky school (in our view a correct one, as opposed to the first, which we must categorize as totally false) has as its aim the creation of an absolutely unified company in which no star tenor can hog the front of the stage and push the other actors into the role of accompanists, turning the play into a solo display piece for a particular actor or actress and destroying it as a work of art. It goes without saying that in the staging of the sort of Pure Form play which we have previously attempted to describe, this second principle is altogether indispensable. Despite the dominance or subordination of certain moments and individuals on the stage, it is impossible to think of any purely formal whole where unity in plurality in and of itself is not the most important goal. But, in our opinion, all kinds of "experiences" are totally irrelevant.

In the genre which we are proposing (and even for performances of the old masters of dramatic literature), the actor should be, in all he says and does, a part of the whole, without feeling any necessity to "create" the role in a realistic sense; that is to say, he need not enter into the real-life feelings of the hero and imitate onstage such a person's supposed gestures and tone of voice at various important moments in his life. Instead, the actor should truly *create the role,* which, in our interpretation, entails the following. First, the actor must understand the whole of the play, with particular reference to all the lines spoken by all the characters who appear in the work, as well as their gestures and also the different settings as they unfold during the course of the action; or, in other words, he must first understand the *formal conception* of the work (as distinct from its real-life mood) and its character, apart from all real-life probabilities. Next, he should build his role in such a way that—quite independently of his own frame of mind, his own inner experiences and state of nerves—he can execute with mathematical precision whatever is required by the purely formal conception of the particular work in question. This may mean that he is to say a given speech with special stress on certain words, at one moment emphasizing their logical content, at another their sound value, or to offer the spectator a new image which contrasts with the real, fluctuating picture of the given situation. His work will be genuinely creative only when he considers himself an element in the given whole.

Once he is onstage, the actor does nothing but give a performance, which of course may be increasingly perfected throughout the rehearsals and the actual production itself, but he will continue to do nothing but give a performance, comparable to other performances, such as the actual painting of a picture which has already been composed, or the writing down of a symphony and its performance by an orchestra. However, the relationship between conception and execution is different for each of the arts; their moments of invention and technical realization are differently coordinated. In painting and poetry, the most—relatively speaking—happens while the work is actually in progress; less takes place during the physical writing of music, although even here various changes and improvements of initially foggy conceptions are also possible. In the theatre there should be a minimum of this, unless of course the theatre is to be nothing more than a servile copy of reality. If that is the case, then "experiences" can be immensely useful, although if we imagine a successful play in which a certain character commits two murders and is condemned to death, we may well ask what kind of a superman or superwoman would be able to experience all that, say three hundred times, without becoming seriously disturbed or, quite simply, going insane.

In our opinion, for the actor who does not have to imitate a character, but who can create his role according to his own creative intuition, the psychology of the hero as well as the lines which he has to speak should be only subsidiary means. Once he appears onstage, the actor must be like a painter who has so thoroughly thought out all the details of his painting and has such a sure hand that the execution of the picture requires nothing from him but the mechanical application of several coats of paint. It goes without saying that such a procedure is almost impossible in painting; in the art of the actor, however, the creative process should ideally proceed in that fashion, and it is in fact quite within the realm of possibility. Naturally, unavoidable small variations are of no concern.

The actor should keep himself firmly under control the way a musical virtuoso does. The only difference is that the actor has much greater scope for his creativity, but always within the limits of the *given work's remaining true to itself*—which is the director's responsibility. Every play, like every poem, contains only a certain limited number of interpretations, beyond which it stops being the work created by the author. However, we have no objective measure for this limit. In our opinion, Shakespeare staged with Stanislavsky's realism stops being Shakespeare, Beethoven played sentimentally stops being Beethoven, but unfortunately we have no objective criterion for any of this. There will always be the possibility of more or less emphasis on real-life content, and every work of art, even the purest, faces inevitable defilement—in the performance and the hearing or viewing in music and theatre, and in the very visibility of the world of objects in painting.

Of course, it all depends on whether the author has stressed the formal content or the real-life content. Any play in Pure Form can be staged realistically, but a purely formal whole cannot be made out of every realistic work, even if the director were to stand on his head. But whereas in painting and sculpture there are only the works and those who view them, music and theatre are further handicapped in that they must depend on the performance, and in the case of theatre the complications arising from this reach quite colossal proportions.

Setting the *formal tone* depends, of course, on the director. Grasping the purely formal content of the work and creating a unified structural whole is an incredibly difficult task. But as a general guideline we could formulate the following purely negative principle: *Forget completely about life and pay no attention to any real-life consequences of what is happening onstage at any given moment as it relates to what is about to happen at the next moment.* It goes without saying—at the next moment onstage. Naturally we're not talking about real-life consequences beyond the stage, such as the possibility of an empty cash drawer, or the director, actors, and author being beaten up by the crowd, or other similar happenings which, in our opinion, the management of an experimental theatre should, at the present time, accept as the facts of life.

We should point out that in this kind of play the manner of speaking the lines, or the delivery, ought not to be uniformly a matter of the emotions. From time to time this sort of emotional emphasis might serve as a purely formal effect (for example, saying something sad in a joyful fashion or the reverse, which incidentally happens even in life when one gets upset over something totally insignificant or treats indifferently a real atrocity); however, compared to the roar of animal passions heard on the stage nowadays, compared to this hyperintensification of life, the delivery of the lines in the theatre of Pure Form must be very restrained, and all the same principles which we formulated when discussing the declamation of poetry must be applied to this question. Each play should have its own "tone," its upper and lower limits to be respected in accordance with the author's intentions which must be felt or understood by the director. We do not maintain that volleys of shots, roars, and groans are inadmissible on the stage, but only that everything must be interpreted and incorporated within the limits set by the tone of the whole, rather than be the expression of purely real-life associations. Whereas authors can afford to let themselves be carried away, the challenge of creative work on the stage depends on its rigorous limits.

If actors could only give up their ingrained bad habit of displaying emotions, the whole creative process of acting would consist solely in maintaining the agreed-upon tonality. On the one hand, this seems to be something so trifling that it is not worth talking about; on the other hand, it is infernally difficult—so much so as to be virtually impossible. However, we maintain that as soon as the tone is properly understood as a part of the formal conception, the details of the execution should fall into place of their own accord. Of course, actors would have to give up their long-standing practice of trying to send audiences into convulsive emotional twitchings, spasms, and fits—and that is one of the principal difficulties in the proper staging of a play in this new mode. The actor's need to direct the audience's attention to himself and to feel the satisfaction of being able to hit them in their innermost recesses and guts would have to become transformed into a genuine desire actually to create a whole in dimensions totally different from real-life ones, even though each actor's contribution would be only partial. To accomplish this, the actor would have to forgo his desire to impersonate, to pretend to be somebody real about whom someone else was tactless enough to write— which is what "experiencing" *à la* Limanowski ultimately amounts to. Despite all the lack of expertise in theatre of which we can be accused, we hold that the gist of what we have said is correct—from the formal point of view of course—and that the whole thing which we have outlined is completely feasible.

Let's assume that people at the first performance actually roar with laughter because they expect the play to make the kind of sense which they have always been accustomed to look for in the theatre and which *au fond* already bores them to death. Quite possibly sophisticated connoisseurs and professional theatregoers will make faces in disgust and use abusive language. But we are of the opinion that after a certain purely superficial getting used to the outer trappings of the thing, it should be possible to take far greater pleasure in performances of this kind than in French farces which already make people sick to their stomachs, or than in dramas with so much "truth" in them that they outdo life itself in truthfulness, sublimities hobbling on crutches, or various other tidbits under the rubric "renaissance."

Now we have absolutely no desire to depreciate the great masterpieces of past ages. But isn't it time to stop repeating what was created a long time ago in its most perfect form? What we propose is twofold: to cultivate the classics with a proper feeling for their essence—but only those works of outstanding value which have stood the test of time—and to launch out on the (at least seemingly) boundless sea of experiment. In painting nothing more remained to be created in the realm of subject matter, from the point of view of life undeformed, except for inane naturalism which amounted to beating one's head against a brick wall—in other words, against the unachievable perfection of nature. Likewise in poetry, sense— worked over for the millionth time—became an obstacle to new formal combinations. In theatre the situation is exactly the same now. Don't anyone tell me that this will produce private gibberish unintelligible to others, an individual language which only its creator will understand, or actions characteristic of people suffering from schizophrenia. All these accusations may be true if we look at art from the point of view of life. In our understanding of the term, form is something higher than subject matter and real-life sense, which are only means in the purely personal process of creation.

There is need to unbind hands and feet, ungag mouths, and shake all the old bad habits out of our heads. Let's assume that nothing comes of it and that it all sinks down again into the same boredom and grayness typical of the creative work going on around us now and reverts to that endless rehashing of the same old thing to the point of nausea. Let's assume that it's the figment of the imagination of a sick brain—the brain of an individual who does not understand that the theatre can never be anything but what it has always been up to now. Still, isn't it worth trying?

The force with which we resist the temptation to try anything new and unknown is truly diabolical. Or has the temptation really grown too weak? That would prove that the mechanization of life has really gone so far that the theatre as a social institution *par excellence* can no longer resist the petrification of everything into a uniform, gray, undifferentiated pulp that is only superficially heterogeneous.

II

Andrzej Trzebiński

To Pick up the Rose

A Drama in Three Acts (1942)

Translated by Daniel and Eleanor Gerould from Andrzej Trzebiński, *Aby podnieść różę* (Warsaw: Pax, 1970). An earlier version of the translation of Act I appeared in *Poland*, No. 9 (September, 1970).

CAST OF CHARACTERS

Vozup Teneroit, dictator *in potentia;* an almost mythical figure
Deromur Ilfare, dictator *in potentia*
Ralf Arioni, instructor, or maybe professor, of sociology
Riza Oblivia, girl of decidedly loose morals, a nudist
Garpadatte, world chess master
Ernest Kangar, heavyweight boxing champion
Lamo Bazarra, Deromur Ilfare's right-hand man
Elevator Boy
Followers of Bazarra and of Vozup

The action takes place in the international Hotel Morocco.

ACT I

(*A small game room, furnished in ultramodern style, in the Hotel Morocco. In the middle a regulation ping-pong table with the net set up. On the walls cubist sport compositions in dark and dense tones. In the window, which is closed for the moment, a zigzag-shaped black stand with a couple of cactuses. Garpadatte, chess player, world master, in a white tennis outfit. Ernest Kangar also in a tennis outfit, in white. Ralf Arioni, professor, or maybe instructor, of sociology, in a dressing gown, with a cigarette between his teeth. Riza Oblivia, a disconcertingly beautiful girl with a perverse ribbon in her hair, bare legs; reputedly a nudist.*)

GARPADATTE: (*To Arioni*) Professor, we're starting the game again. Your cigarette could burn our ball up, and it's the last one in the Hotel Morocco. (*To Oblivia*) So you think this is really the end of the world? (*Very cleverly*) The world whose master I am at chess? (*Going over to the table*) I must admit I've always felt that dependence of mine on the world as a lack of independence, but today . . .

KANGAR: Your serve, Master! Careful with the ball!

GARPADATTE: Ready! (*He serves, a light, white game begins.*) Seventeen–seventeen . . . don't worry about this ball, it's a strong one . . .

KANGAR: We already seem to have demolished seven of these strong balls today . . . (*To Oblivia*) Well, how about it, Oblivia? The end of the world?

OBLIVIA: (*To Kangar*) You must have gotten an F minus in religion! (*With native wit*) I mean, no self-respecting end of the world ever looked like this. (*To Arioni*) Do you know who they are, Ralf? (*She points to something out the window.*)

ARIONI: Oh, what can you hope to find out or understand by looking out the window?

GARPADATTE: (*Mimicking him*) Find out, understand? Don't ask me . . . looking out the window too . . . Well, still I have the impression . . . (*He doesn't finish.*) Because . . . (*To Kangar*) You know, Champ, I like those diagonal shots; they remind me of the way the bishop moves . . . (*To Arioni*) It's just a

VI. A scene from Andrzej Trzebiński's *To Pick up the Rose,* Act I ("a small game room in the Hotel Morocco"). Kangar and Garpadatte play ping-pong. Presented at the Ateneum, Warsaw, in 1970. Directed by Janusz Warmiński. (Photograph by Zofia Myszkowska.)

revolution, Professor . . . You don't even have to read the newspapers to know that!

KANGAR: (*Lightly during the game*) You guessed wrong, Oblivia. In religion I always got a D minus, but in history—wow! And now the result is I don't have even the vaguest opinions on all these political questions . . .

OBLIVIA: (*To Kangar*) You need opinions? People shoot people, and you need opinions for that? Ralf, you've got to explain it all to him!

ARIONI: Riza, dear child, you're really the one who doesn't understand any of it . . . Perhaps I could say a little something about it, since I actually do have opinions, but those questions—out there (*pointing out the window to the street*)—are somehow different . . . (*To Kangar*) I'm like you; I don't have any opinions about those questions. I just have opinions, period, all by themselves! . . .

GARPADATTE: Eighteen–seventeen, Champ! (*Absent-minded and offhand—to Arioni*) You're right, we've got to treat these things with utter disdain. (*To Kangar*) Your serve, Champ.

ARIONI: No. We're talking about different things. It's not a question of treating anything with disdain. The point is that our whole common history stopped back there somewhere, behind us, and we modern people with modern souls and ideas can't really live in such times. And yet we still have to go on in an incredible, grotesque fashion.

KANGAR: (*Completely off the subject*) Wait a minute, what's today's revolution like—very good, or very bad?

GARPADATTE: Honestly, can't you understand? Because of the revolution we won't be able to get a new ball if this one breaks on us!

ARIONI: Yes, but you're forgetting something, Master. The revolution is history's way of catching up with us. That shooting other people up is actually . . .

KANGAR: (*Business-like*) Then we've got to be careful if we can't buy a new one. (*Out.*) Damn it. Seventeen–nineteen! I'm hitting it too hard . . . (*Amazed*) In boxing, that would be quite absurd.

OBLIVIA: Ralf, they're behaving like children with that ping-pong of theirs! (*To Garpadatte*) And you know, Pablo, how afraid of children I am.

GARPADATTE: (*To Oblivia*) Better stay by the window and . . . keep your eyes peeled. Riza, tell me, what do you want? (*To Kangar*) That's right: nineteen–seventeen. (*To Arioni*) Who are you betting on, Professor?

ARIONI: (*With polished irony*) The truth always wins. I'm betting on that.

GARPADATTE: (*As they hit long, hard shots*) Oh, in that respect, you remind me of my late predecessor, world master Dr. Karl Doro. He too was in the habit of repeating the aphorism that the truth always wins. (*Whacking the ball into the net*) Well, he finally lost to me!

OBLIVIA: (*Piqued*) You didn't understand the professor's irony.

(*To Arioni, very little-girlish*) That was a dig at the phoniness of both the players, wasn't it? Because in ping-pong only the true ping-pong player always wins, isn't that so, Ralf? . . .

KANGAR: Eighteen–nineteen. My serve, Master.

ARIONI: (*To Oblivia*) Oh, no. That was only a little philosophical joke: I applied pragmatism to ping-pong and expressed it in the language of the Middle Ages.

OBLIVIA: You did? But that's marvelous! (*Claps her hands, like a big, beautiful doll.*) So there's all that joking and philosophy in those four words?

KANGAR: Professor, for love of a joke—your cigarette!!! Remember, we can't buy a new ball because of this damned revolution.

ARIONI: Champ, I see that thanks to ping-pong you've acquired some political opinions of your own. (*He quotes him.*) Because of this damned revolution . . . hm . . . this damned revolution . . . In other words, you're turning into a rabid counter-revolutionary. (*To Oblivia*) The truth always wins—that means that victory and only victory can be the truth. That's the secret meaning of my joke. (*He puts out his cigarette urbanely.*)

KANGAR: (*Uncertainly*) No. I still don't have any political opinions, Professor . . . What I said about the revolution . . .

GARPADATTE: Forget it, Champ. After all, it would be possible to catch the professor with words . . .

(*Kangar makes a backhand smash and wins the point.*)

KANGAR: Nineteen–nineteen! A tie!

ARIONI: (*To Garpadatte*) Oh, catch me with words? What words, Master?

GARPADATTE: Say, for example, that tie, or any kind of draw. Victory and only victory can be the truth! Isn't that so?

OBLIVIA: But, Pablo, you can't have a draw in ping-pong!

GARPADATTE: But what about chess or boxing? What happens to the truth, Professor, if it's a draw?

ARIONI: (*Intellectually carried away*) Master, with that single question, you're opening up marvelous horizons for me.

GARPADATTE: But what becomes of the truth, Professor? (*To Kangar*) What's the score—nineteen–nineteen?

KANGAR: That's right. Ready. My serve . . . (*He serves.*)

ARIONI: (*Carried away*) Well, then: two truths are born at the same time . . . (*To Oblivia, pointing to something out the window*) You see, down there! Oh, if only that window weren't there, if we only knew who they were!

GARPADATTE: (*To Arioni*) Are you saying that they're twins, professor? A draw means twins?

OBLIVIA: (*Intrigued; quietly*) If we knew? Then what, Ralf?

ARIONI: Do you know what might happen?

OBLIVIA: (*Racks her brains.*) I guess . . .

ARIONI: (*Excited, repeats*) Riza, do you know what might happen? Have you ever thought how frightening and marvelous it is that anything at all can happen? Have you, Riza? The end of the world? What if it's just the beginning? Couldn't it be the beginning of our life in the real world? (*Grandly*) No. Enough looking at everything through window panes. (*Rushes to the window.*)

OBLIVIA: (*Terrified*) What are you doing, Ralf?

ARIONI: (*With a final trace of grandiloquence*) Enough. I've had enough. I've got to open it now. (*Suddenly comes back to earth; ironically*) You heard me, I'm opening the window!

OBLIVIA: (*Without noticing the irony*) Ralf, I beg you, tell me— what can happen?

ARIONI: (*Excited once more*) Anything. Literally anything. This obsolete life can finally catch up with us and then Riza, we'll master it . . . Then I could be . . . even . . . a dictator!

OBLIVIA: (*Dazed and enraptured*) Ralf!

(*Ralf Arioni finally opens the window. A hideous glare, yelling, and commotion surge in through the window from outside. Garpadatte and Kangar, magnificent men in white tennis trousers, keep on playing, deaf to the sounds of the city, fascinated by the little white celluloid ball, blurred in flight to one long streak.*)

OBLIVIA: (*Somewhat mesmerized, quietly*) A moment ago you were talking about the truth, like . . . Socrates . . . and now again you're so unbelievably modern, so impossibly modern that . . .

ARIONI: (*Softly, in a completely different tone*) Am I?

OBLIVIA: (*Softly, delicately*) That's right . . . Yes . . . Our whole love affair is so marvelously and scandalously up-to-date.

ARIONI: (*In a still different tone*) It must have been a premonition

on your part, Riza. To other people I've always been an
anachronism. I'm as much behind the times as all that going
on outside. But today, Riza . . . something tells me in spite
of everything, that today . . .

OBLIVIA: That today?

ARIONI: That finally the world will take a great flying leap or
running jump and catch up with all of us . . . Then, in such
a modern world, I can be . . .

OBLIVIA: (*In a daze*) Ralf . . . Ralf . . .

(*Silence. The sound of the ball and the commotion of revolution from
the street.*)

KANGAR: (*To Garpadatte suddenly, in a louder tone of voice*) Hear
that, Master?

OBLIVIA: (*"Coming to"*) Oh, so at last you hear it too, even with
your ping-pong. The window's been open a good five minutes . . . Pablo . . . The professor says that this revolution . . .

GARPADATTE: (*Impatiently*) What the hell's the revolution to me,
dammit!! (*To Kangar*) Of course I can hear . . . The last ball
in the Hotel Morocco is cracked . . . We'll have to stop the
game! Let me see it, Champ.

(*They approach each other. Kangar gives Garpadatte the ball. Garpadatte examines it all over, looks for the crack, automatically reads the
lettering.*)

GARPADATTE: (*Reads*) Champion . . . (*Looks up.*) The Champion
Ball Company . . . but I just don't see the crack . . .

KANGAR: It's nineteen–nineteen. We still should be able to play
those last few points.

GARPADATTE: Let's play then . . . Your serve!

KANGAR: Rea . . . (*He serves.*)

ARIONI: (*Leaning out the window, turning around for a moment*)
What? They're playing again? I thought the ball was cracked.
(*Looking out into the street*) Oh, if we only knew who they were.
(*He rings.*)

OBLIVIA: (*To Garpadatte*) Pablo, just think . . . (*Rhetorically*)
After all, you too once had a mother, a sense of honor,
ideals . . .

GARPADATTE: Huh, and now I've got a few screws loose! Nineteen–nineteen, Champ! Take it easy with that ball!

(*Enter the elevator boy in answer to Arioni's call.*)

BOY: Did someone ring?

ARIONI: Yes, I did . . . Say, boy, maybe you can at least tell me who those characters are (*pointing to the window*)—you know, the ones down there?

BOY: (*Warming up*) They're going to attack the south bridge. The shock troops. Deromur's men . . . Deromur Ilfare has proclaimed that . . . every . . . Oh, it's just two steps from the station to the Morocco . . . If they come here . . .

ARIONI: What? I don't understand a single thing you're saying . . . What are you trying to tell me?

BOY: (*In an increasingly impudent and rabble-rousing tone as the din from the street grows louder*) Anyone who doesn't understand us doesn't understand the voice of the people, and the people are no artists who can be misunderstood . . . If you gentlemen don't understand us . . .

ARIONI: (*Astounded*) *We* understand *you?* Elevator boys? (*Shouting heard beneath the window; he leans his head out.*) But they're occupying the Morocco!!!

BOY: Where? (*Leans his head out the window.*) Oh yes, they are. That's it! (*Jumping up and down*) Now the hotel's in our hands. Long live Deromur Ilfare!

ARIONI: (*Grabbing the boy by the arm*) Listen, what's this all about? Tell me what this Deromur wants!

BOY: (*Pulling himself away*) W-e-e-e-ll! You'll see what he wants, all right! Just ask him! Let go of me! Now the hotel's in our . . .

ARIONI: (*Keeps holding onto him*) What does Deromur Ilfare want?

BOY: What does he want? Well, different . . . different things . . . I'll remember in a minute! Aha! (*Recites*) Deromur says: our history means pushing man into competition with the machine; it means compelling everyone to become a god, to double and triple his strength for more and more frightful work. For work under the threat of losing one's bearings in the thick of life. If between the physical reality created by the machine and the conceptual or psychological reality devised by us, a rift appears—an abyss—then all the nongods, foreign to the reality of our people, will perish in it. And that will be the new Tarpeian rock which will preserve the people from degeneration . . . (*He stammers and blushes.*) Oh, I forgot, there was something more, at the very end . . .

ARIONI: Oh for God's sake, are people still carrying on about that crazy machinocracy nowadays? Experiments like that! Do you know what you're talking about?

BOY: What do I care about experiments? . . . They're the brains; it's their business . . . Let them take care of it . . . We're winning the victory and that's enough . . . Let go of me . . . They're in the Morocco already!

(*Pulls himself loose and runs out.*)

ARIONI: Yes. Now I understand. Deromur Ilfare. And they're in the Morocco already, Riza!

OBLIVIA: (*To Garpadatte*) Pablo, I think you're doing it on purpose . . . I'm ashamed, I could blush for shame . . . Pablo!

GARPADATTE: (*To Oblivia*) Just a minute, . . . just a minute . . . (*To Kangar*) It's nineteen–nineteen. What's the professor claiming is in our hands? (*To Kangar*) So you're starting that way too, Champ—on the diagonal, like the bishop?

ARIONI: Not in our hands, Master, in theirs.

KANGAR: (*With simple-hearted malice*) Does it matter in whose hands? It's enough that, in addition to having control of us, those hands also have right on their side and the truth, since, as the professor says—they've won.

ARIONI: (*Craftily and gaily*) You'd like to beat me with my own jokes? You should avoid that, Champ. After all, I too could get the best of you and make you look foolish with your publicity photos.

KANGAR: (*To Garpadatte*) How about that one? (*He makes a smash.*)

GARPADATTE: Even that I can get. (*He gets it, but hits wildly in Oblivia's direction.*)

KANGAR: (*Almost at the same time*) Point nineteen. I really slammed it!

(*The ball hits Oblivia, who is standing near the window.*)

GARPADATTE: (*Beside himself*) Get it!!! It's the last one!!!

OBLIVIA: (*She bends over and picks it up. She stares at it, as in a trance, and reads*) . . . Champion . . . (*Still as though in a trance, she goes over to the window and throws the ball out into the street.*)

GARPADATTE: Riza, have you gone mad? That was the last ball, Riza!

KANGAR: (*Absolutely dumbfounded*) In boxing, a situation like this would be inconceivable!

OBLIVIA: (*Indignant*) Oh! (*She keeps quiet for a moment, smiling insincerely.*) I made a mistake.

GARPADATTE: (*Excited*) What do you mean, you made a mistake? Think of the spot you're putting me in: it was point nineteen. (*Going over to her*) Riza, you're lying! You threw it out on purpose . . .

OBLIVIA: (*Weakly and insincerely*) I tell you . . . I made a mistake . . .

GARPADATTE: I want to find out the truth! I'm strong enough to take it . . . Why are you lying, Riza?

OBLIVIA: (*She finally explodes.*) Oh, the truth? All right then, be strong enough . . . I'll tell you the truth. If you want, not only about the ball, but about a lot more too, about myself, about us—everything.

GARPADATTE: (*Trying to outtalk her*) You're clearly trying to talk your way out of this, Riza, so you won't have to tell the truth about the ball. (*In a rage*) But I want you to tell me the truth about the ball, and only about the ball—understand?

OBLIVIA: No, I'm not trying to talk my way out of it. But the revolution—that's something great. We should honor it in some way. (*Looking at Arioni*) I mean, it's like a second creation of the world, Grand Master—of the world that already exists.

GARPADATTE: (*Ironically*) Well, that's just it . . . I've been waiting for this new world . . . (*Nervously*) But that's not the point here! (*In a rage*) I want the ball!

KANGAR: No use making a big fuss, Master; the game's almost over and I've won. You've been defeated, Master.

GARPADATTE: (*With almost unrestrained fury*) Riza, do whatever you want now. I demand that ping-pong ball.

OBLIVIA: Pablo, try and understand . . . Stop and think for a second . . . (*Giving in*) Anyhow, how could I get it for you now?

KANGAR: Admit you've lost, Master . . . After all, I had the advantage in a situation like that!

GARPADATTE: I can agree to a draw . . . but if you're suggesting that I . . .

KANGAR: (*Interrupting him*) But I can't agree to it. First even the score; only then can there be a draw.

GARPADATTE: (*To Oblivia*) Riza! (*In a rage*) Riza! . . .

ARIONI: (*For the moment, with the cultured, humanistic attitude of an ironist*) Gentlemen, your predicament rather amuses me. (*To Garpadatte*) Grand Master, did you ever play chess without the chessmen?

GARPADATTE: (*Brightening*) Why, of course. Whenever I was in a big hurry. I even played that way recently with the son of my late predecessor, Grand Master Dr. Karl Doro . . . But what does that have to do with it?

ARIONI: A great deal, Master. Because in a pinch wouldn't it be possible to do the same thing with ping-pong?

KANGAR: (*At cross-purposes*) How's that—ping-pong without chessmen?

ARIONI: Why no, that's going a bit too far, Champ. But what about ping-pong without the ball?

GARPADATTE: What!? What do you mean?

OBLIVIA: (*Clapping her hands*) Oh, that's marvelous. Ralf! You've really got something of (*she thinks hard*) the Socrates in you . . . (*Her ribbon slips out of her hair and falls on the floor. She picks it up and holds it.*)

KANGAR: If there were a ball, I must admit I'd like it better.

ARIONI: But there isn't one.

GARPADATTE: (*To Arioni*) You could convince me of anything. I've got a feeling it'll be a great game. Great because it won't have any of the trappings. (*Going over to the table*) Anyhow, ping-pong is always played without the ball, solely by intuition. The ball is just a concession ping-pong players make to the public—just part of the setting.

OBLIVIA: (*Getting extremely enthusiastic*) My God, my God, what you're saying is so wonderful, Pablo. You really have something of . . . (*thinks hard*) the Socrates in you. This ribbon . . .

ARIONI: (*Urbanely jealous and critical*) Oh, undoubtedly, your

aphorisms, if they didn't deal with ping-pong, but with sociology or politics . . . (*He doesn't finish.*)

OBLIVIA: (*Getting the idea*) Or especially with philosophy. Ralf
(*she makes up her mind and goes over to Arioni*), Ralf, I really
can't understand any of this anymore . . . but as long as I
still know you are a genius . . . (*Hands him her ribbon as a
reward.*)

GARPADATTE: The idea is truly daring. We'll try it out right
away . . . So then it's nineteen–twenty, Champ?

KANGAR: (*Laughing*) Yes. At least I can belt it with all my
strength. Ready—I'm serving. (*He serves.*)

(*The game goes on with gestures only, and empty paddles. Incredibly
picturesque and at the same time almost musical; in absolute silence.*)

OBLIVIA: (*Enchanted, softly*) They're playing so mysteriously,
Ralf . . . You'd think we were at a seance.

ARIONI: Riza, are you beginning to believe that the new reality
is really catching up with us?

KANGAR: (*Shouts*) It went over!! Master, you've forgotten that
my recent shots would go through a stone wall, to say nothing of a little net like that.

GARPADATTE: All right then! (*Smashes with a marvelous jump.*)
Twenty all.

(*A new series of cries and sounds of shots from the street; with Oblivia
and Arioni wide-awake and watching intently, the masters keep on
playing.*)

OBLIVIA: (*Remembering*) Ralf, for goodness' sake! It's the same
thing all over again: Out there in the city a revolution's going
on, and here they're playing that game of ping-pong of
theirs . . . Ralf, what have you done?

ARIONI: Oh, you don't understand anything, Riza! Now that
they've occupied the Morocco—we're nothing but their prisoners . . .

OBLIVIA: Deromur Ilfare's?

ARIONI: Oh, if he were the only one! But no, it's much worse:
we're in the hands of his henchmen! And since the employees of the Morocco go along with them, they could denounce us to them as foreigners.

GARPADATTE: (*More loudly*) Out. It didn't hit the edge. My advantage!

(They keep playing. Silence. The world masters, dressed in white, hyp-notized by emptiness, paddles slamming a nonexistent ball, move around the table mysteriously, with great concentration. Arioni absent-mindedly sniffs the ribbon pinned to his dressing gown like a rose. Foot-steps on the stairs behind the door. Arioni listens intently.)

OBLIVIA: Denounce us?

ARIONI: *(Pretending to smile, in a transparently artificial manner)* This rose of mine has such a heavenly odor. *(He sniffs the ribbon carelessly, listening intently to the footsteps on the stairs.)*

OBLIVIA: *(Amazed)* A rose? *(Figuring it out)* Aha! *(Silence.)* And it doesn't even have any thorns!

(The footsteps reach the door. Enter Bazarra and Deromur's armed men.)

BAZARRA: *(To the people in the room)* Hands up! *(Watching the world masters who, without thinking, keep on playing for a while)* Hey, you, there!

(The masters come to their senses, drop their paddles, put their hands up.)

BAZARRA: *(To them all)* I demand that you hand over the head of the spy ring. You're all as good as dead anyhow. *(Conster-nation; choked, paralyzed silence. To Arioni)* Why in hell are you so quiet? . . . You the ringleader?

ARIONI: *(His voice sticks in his throat. Gestures with his hand, as if to say, "What's that?")*

BAZARRA: Talk, or I'll shoot everyone here for conspiratorial silence! *(A perceptible shudder of fear runs through the prisoners, who remain nailed to the ground. They turn pale and remain silent.)* I'm telling you for the last time, if you don't tell who this champion is . . .

KANGAR: *(Staggering two steps toward Bazarra, in a voice as if from beyond the grave)* The champion? But of course I'm . . .

BAZARRA: So it's you? *(Relieved)* At last . . . *(Finding something wrong)* But such diabolic secrecy . . . In disguise too . . . Of all the people here, you're the one who really looks least like the brains of the whole spy ring . . . *(Arioni makes a gesture with his hand, but doesn't even dare interrupt him.)* If this Ten-eroit of yours is disguised anywhere near as well, he must look like a baby, or a woman, at the very most . . . *(He laughs nastily and obscenely.)* Ha . . . ha . . .

KANGAR: (*Unintelligibly, in a voice not his own*) But really I'm, I'm only the champion—nothing else . . .

BAZARRA: (*Indulgently*) Oh, I'm not trying to talk you into believing you're Teneroit himself. (*Harshly*) You're the most important person here, that's enough.

(*They all take the insult calmly and without protest. They keep on standing by the table and at the window just as before.*)

KANGAR: (*Still in a voice not his own*) I'm a simple, ordinary boxer . . .

BAZARRA: (*Irritated*) Cut that modesty, dammit! You're the Champion. The message thrown out of here was about you. That's enough to get you killed.

(*They are all electrified, as if a current ran through them. The same gesture of physical shock.*)

ARIONI: A message?

GARPADATTE: A message . . . from up here?

KANGAR: (*Woodenly*) But I was playing ping-pong all the time.

BAZARRA: Yes. Of course: you were pretending to play to pull the wool over our eyes, to have an alibi to give us . . . But you were pretending. You didn't even have a ball . . . Because your ball . . .

OBLIVIA: Their ball . . . ?

(*Bazarra silently and contemptuously takes the ping-pong ball out of his pocket; holds it between two fingers and shows it to the prisoners. They all stare at the ball, then gradually turn their eyes toward Oblivia.*)

OBLIVIA: (*Pale, the blood drained from her face*) I've got to clear this up: I threw the ball out . . . You wouldn't believe me anyhow if I told you it was a joke, or that it was in your honor . . . but that's the way it was . . .

BAZARRA: (*Sullenly, icily*) I don't believe it.

OBLIVIA: (*Naively*) They were all furious at me because of it . . .

BAZARRA: (*With a dark, pitiless smile*) I understand—the sacrifice of a woman in love? Ha . . . ha . . . ha . . . So you two want to die together!

KANGAR: (*Nervously*) You said, a message . . . But it was a ping-pong ball . . .

BAZARRA: With your title on it—"Champion."

VII. Another scene from the Ateneum production of *To Pick up the Rose*, Act I. Oblivia talking to Bazarra after throwing the ping-pong ball out the window. (Photograph by Zofia Myszkowska.)

OBLIVIA: (*Covering her face with her hands*) Oh, my God! Of course . . . that "Champion" . . .

KANGAR: (*In a daze*) It's just the name of a factory that makes celluloid ping-pong balls . . . Haven't you ever heard of the Champion Company?

BAZARRA: (*Icily*) No, I haven't . . . (*Pointing to Garpadatte*) And what about your partner in this ping-pong hoax of yours?

OBLIVIA: That's Pablo Garpadatte, chess master of the world.

BAZARRA: Of the world? And who says the world exists at all?

GARPADATTE: (*Modestly, not so much explaining as justifying himself*) Well, that's how the saying goes. Of course, it means the round ball earth . . . only . . . the round . . .

BAZARRA: (*Laughing vulgarly and crudely*) Watch it, or a round ball'll finish you off. A little round ball right between the eyes, as the saying goes . . . The world's too small to have masters! The people are great. Got it?

GARPADATTE: (*At a total loss*) How's that? The world is smaller than the people? I don't understand.

BAZARRA: (*Passionately and ironically*) You want me to explain it to you? I won't explain much actually, just that you aren't allowed not to understand us, the people, because the people are no artists who can be misunderstood . . . What about that, master of the round ball earth?

OBLIVIA: (*to Garpadatte, terrified, tragic*) My God, my God . . . Pablo, why did I say you were the world master? I thought it would help you, and now it's ruining you.

GARPADATTE: (*Ironically, with a kind of "under-the-skin" cleverness*) If I die . . . it'll be for the world . . . Riza!

OBLIVIA: No! I can't stand it any longer! No! You are a true Socrates! That ribbon that I just gave Ralf . . .

BAZARRA: (*Looking at Arioni, or rather at the red ribbon pinned to his robe*) You forgot to conceal that ribbon of yours, Mister . . . Maybe you thought if it was in plain sight it wouldn't be noticed. Is that it?

ARIONI: (*Nervously, coming back to reality*) My ribbon? My red ribbon? Is that the badge of Teneroit's side?

BAZARRA: If you wear it even on your dressing gown, that means—yes . . . a red ribbon on the breast . . . Maybe finally, thanks to you, thanks to today's unmasking, we'll find out something definite about Teneroit and his organization. You'll be shot along with the rest of them. All at the same time. It's what I suspected before, down in the street: a spy ring . . . !

ARIONI: I can see there's no point even trying to convince you. (*Counting*) A ball with "Champion" printed on it, a world master, a red ribbon . . . That's enough, so many proofs of guilt . . . (*Glancing at the ribbon*) Especially this ribbon . . . Only I wonder if it had been a rose, instead of a ribbon? (*To Oblivia*) You see, Riza, even such unreal roses have their thorns . . . and we thought it was the other way around!

OBLIVIA: (*Still convulsively*) Ralf, Ralf . . . don't talk to me that way . . . You know I'm the one . . .

BAZARRA: (*After a moment's silence, astounded by it all*) You're lying, lady; you're the only person here who's actually innocent. All that about throwing the ball out is nothing but a lie on your part. (*On a final note of contempt*) The hysterical sacrifice of a woman in love who longs to die for her man.

OBLIVIA: (*Still convulsively*) Oh, no . . . no . . .

BAZARRA: (*Mistrustful*) Then—?

ARIONI: (*As a final attack*) We're the ones who are asking you: How? How is it possible that everything involving us immediately has some connection with Teneroit? Just who is this demonic enemy of yours who's taking vengeance on us? Who is it that's so mercilessly and relentlessly persecuting us?

BAZARRA: You're the ones who are supposed to tell us who this mysterious Vozup Teneroit is and what he wants.

ARIONI: I swear to you, none of us knows him!

BAZARRA: So, you don't know him? Well, we know about his monstrous plot. And, as his spy ring, you know what he wants, what his political philosophy is, how he's swaying the mob. (*To Kangar*) As the ringleader, you must know it . . . You know it, you believe in it. If you tell us the truth, I'll save you from the death penalty. All right? What are your views?

KANGAR: I don't have any views at all. I never stopped to think about it . . . We boxers have so little time . . .

BAZARRA: (*To Garpadatte*) And you?

GARPADATTE: Me? I'm no politician . . . *I* believe in different chess combinations and systems.

BAZARRA: (*Triumphantly*) Ah, now I have no doubts whatsoever. (*Shouts.*) The Teneroit spy ring! The inscrutability of everything concerning you constitutes your views, your political philosophy, your whole strength. Nobody knows whether you exist or not and that attracts people to you. But you know the source of your power and you hide it. Well, go ahead, hide it forever, even after your execution.

(*Silence; the prisoners don't even defend themselves any more. Bazarra paces the length and breadth of the room in the Morocco with the air of a conqueror.*)

ARIONI: (*Apathetically*) Is there anything left that can save us?

BAZARRA: (*Icily*) No, nothing!

ARIONI: (*Coming to life*) So we're irrevocably condemned to death without a trial for a man about whom nothing is known, whose political philosophy no one knows, whom none of us has ever even seen . . .

BAZARRA: (*Drily*) We know he's taking people away from us. We know he's sabotaging the revolution. That's enough.

ARIONI: And suppose Teneroit doesn't exist at all?

BAZARRA: (*Bluntly and forcefully*) Vozup Teneroit exists, because we feel his sabotage. And you threw a message to him on that ping-pong ball. He exists irrevocably and monstrously.

ARIONI: And suppose you're Vozup?

BAZARRA: (*Cynically*) Ha, ha, ha! The execution's still a long way off, and he's gone crazy already.

ARIONI: (*Carried away*) Oh no! It's you we threw the ball to out the window. The red ribbon is an eternal symbol of revolution, and so it's yours too. And you're the ones who don't have any political philosophy.

BAZARRA: Ha, ha, ha! Every revolutionary has to know our political philosophy by heart . . . It's been put within everybody's reach.

ARIONI: Well, so what is this political philosophy of yours? One of the hotel employees was bragging about it a while ago, but he couldn't remember how it ended . . . A belief that can be learned by heart can be forgotten so easily.

BAZARRA: (*Still cynical*) What? Maybe you think I don't remember our political philosophy either? Just a second! I don't even need time to refresh my memory . . . (*Rhetorically*) Deromur says: our history means pushing man to compete with the machine; it means compelling everyone to be a god, to double and triple his strength for more and more frightful work. For work under the threat of losing one's bearings in the thick of life. If between the physical reality created by the machine and the conceptual or psychological reality devised by us, a rift appears—an abyss—then all the nongods, foreign to the reality of our people, will perish in it. And that will be the new Tarpeian rock which will preserve the people from degeneration. We are creating the highest incentives and bases of work that have ever existed. Turning the whole of reality into a machine once and for all! How's that?

ARIONI: But just a minute. Industrial overproduction will lead to a depression; the depression will lead to unemployment; unemployment will turn gods and colossi back into people; the people will begin to seek forgetfulness after such a period of grandeur and happiness.

BAZARRA: What do you know about it? What can you possibly know about Deromur's political philosophy, buddy?

ARIONI: (*Reproachfully*) What about my sketch of the twilight of the gods?

BAZARRA: Shut up . . . shut up . . . you . . . you . . . defeatist! We're winning.

ARIONI: Oh, if you're winning, that's another story. But what are you winning for?

BAZARRA: What? (*Reaching for his revolver*) I'll shoot that scum right between the eyes! I'll blow your brains out if you say one more . . . word! I'll take care of all of you, dammit! I'll get Deromur in here himself. So he'll finally see what Teneroit's people are like. (*A knocking at the door.*) Who's there? Come in! (*Enter the elevator boy.*) Oh, what now?

BOY: Deromur Ilfare is already in the Morocco!

BAZARRA: I know. We planned it that way, my boy. We took this hotel of yours to make it into our headquarters.

BOY: Deromur Ilfare is asking for you. Shall I take you there?

BAZARRA: Did you already tell Deromur about uncovering the spy ring? He should be very pleased. Take me to him. (*To the revolutionaries*) See that they don't get away!

(*Silence. A kind of pantomime: the world masters dressed in tennis clothes sit down on the ping-pong table and start swinging their heads and legs. Arioni looks out the window. Oblivia paces around the table like a caged panther, going the length and breadth of the room in the Morocco. She stops in front of Kangar.*)

OBLIVIA: Great God, great God, it's all my fault.

KANGAR: (*Blankly*) Oh . . .

OBLIVIA: Sometimes I think that I'm that Vozup Teneroit. After all, haven't I ruined all of you? My God . . my God . . . And he did say that Vozup was in disguise, that he must look like a baby, or a woman . . . Ralf . . . ?

ARIONI: No. No. Riza. It doesn't matter whether Vozup really exists or not. What's important is that he's the first prophet in human history who, without resorting to martyrdom, knows how to arouse mankind to such active, contagious faith. As his means of converting—instead of haranguing anyone, he keeps quiet; instead of explaining anything, he makes everything obscure; in short, instead of converting people, he drives them away. And that's what people need if they're going to believe.

OBLIVIA: Ralf, what are you telling me this for? You know we all have to die before the day is over. From the very beginning I had a feeling that something was going to happen, remember? I kept telling Pablo it was the end of the world, but you all laughed then.

ARIONI: Oh, you don't understand anything. Riza! On the contrary, it's really the beginning of the world. This almost mythical enemy of theirs—Vozup Teneroit—he's something that never existed before, he's the greatest man in the world.

End of Act I

ACT II

(*Nothing has changed. Even the acts are not divided by lowering the curtain. Just a prolonged moment of silence and motionlessness on the part of those condemned to death. Shots are fired outside the window. After a moment the sociologist Arioni pulls out a cigarette and smokes it nervously without paying any attention to what he's doing. The world masters, like two colossi supporting balconies, sit on the table, stony, backs bowed symmetrically. Oblivia naively woebegone.*)

ARIONI: (*Turning toward the others, desperately*) That's right. Vozup Teneroit . . . But what if they only tricked us? What if he's not at all like the man we believe in? We've got to know—and be absolutely sure! Our whole situation is ceasing to be a mistake or a mix-up anymore. We're really going to die for Vozup, because we really believe in him. The facts are clear: a spy ring of his people turns up in a room in the Morocco. Listen: these revolutionaries now suspect us in earnest!

KANGAR: (*Pointing conspiratorially at the door, beyond which the revolutionary guard is posted*) Professor!

ARIONI: No. It's too late now for any clever schemes. They exposed us even before we could assume false identities. We hadn't even heard of Vozup Teneroit then, and now that we do know . . .

OBLIVIA: Ralf, for goodness' sake! We don't know anything at all! Who is he?

ARIONI: Oh, who is he—Oblivia! My dear woman, I've been trying to tell you. He's the greatest man in the world . . . Why, he's the one who understands modern life, whose conception of the world is catching up with modern individuals . . . He alone knows how humanity has got to be converted today— and perhaps even yesterday too, and forever . . .

GARPADATTE: What do you think? Will he be able to convert us before our execution?

ARIONI: That's just it. He doesn't even have to do the converting, we do it ourselves. By using all the inscrutability he's stirred up, plus the power of something or other, humanity is to create a faith on its own that will be unconsciously and profoundly modern and truly suited to its needs. Religion will develop out of the living faith of each and every individual . . . He's just the catalyst who speeds up the process. Thanks to him, peoples' beliefs nowadays can become religion for them.

OBLIVIA: But we're the ones who have to die for it! I don't want to die for anything. Not for anything at all!

GARPADATTE: You're making fun of us, Professor . . .

ARIONI: (*Astonished*) You don't believe it?

KANGAR: Believe what? Just because I don't know anything about politics and don't have any opinions—I'm supposed to be the ringleader of some kind of deep, dark spy ring? If the ball factory got in their way, let them gun down the factory, not me. The ping-pong ball factory and I are not the same thing, so why should we be punished together? . . . There's absolutely no connection between us . . .

ARIONI: Oh, oh, but there is! An illogical connection, an irrational connection, but one that damn well exists no matter what anyone thinks about it . . . After all, our death will come about precisely because you and that ping-pong ball factory . . .

KANGAR: Such a philosophy is pulling you toward death. I don't understand what you want from me.

OBLIVIA: Ralf . . . we've got to defend ourselves against death. Mr. Kangar says such a philosophy is pulling you toward death.

ARIONI: No, no. It's death that's pulling philosophy along with it. Death came first and foremost; because he (*points to Kangar*) and the ball factory . . .

KANGAR: Stop it . . . Stop it . . .

ARIONI: There's no stopping it anymore. Now they've absolutely got to shoot us. We really are a spy ring . . .

KANGAR: I don't understand a thing! But if I am to be shot for it, I have to understand, I absolutely have to understand why the ping-pong ball factory and I are supposed to be one and the same thing. (*In despair*) Everything I see is grotesque, grotesque, do you understand! To die for one silly grotesquerie with a ping-pong ball!

ARIONI: Oh, none of you understands me! (*To Kangar*) But I understand you! For one stupid grotesquerie? Yes, of course . . . and what if it were for two . . . or three . . . or a whole world of stupid, but inevitable and necessary grotesqueries . . . what then? What if the whole world was one big grotesquerie—and maybe even a stupid one at that . . . what then?

KANGAR: (*Stunned*) If that was so? Then . . . then . . .

ARIONI: (*Without waiting*) You can intensify and multiply all that! Look! (*Holds up his cigarette butt, displays it, and throws it out the window.*) Now that's intensification too.

KANGAR: (*To Arioni, no telling how*) Professor! (*To Oblivia*) Why don't you . . . ?

ARIONI: (*Unpinning Oblivia's red ribbon from his dressing gown*) And this too. (*Throws it out the window*) That's how you can intensify and grotesquify . . . all of life . . . and . . .

OBLIVIA: Ralf . . . !

KANGAR: Watch out, or I'll start intensifying too . . . I'll pick *you* up and throw you out bodily along with all that rubbish.

ARIONI: All right. (*Archly*) But they can't prove anything against

me . . . I'll say it was only the red cord from my dressing
gown . . . (*Pulls it out of his pocket and displays it.*) Look! It
disappeared somewhere around my collar . . .

KANGAR: Oh, so that's how it is? So this whole grotesquerie was
just your way of saving yourself!

GARPADATTE: What's that? Professor! You're just saving yourself?

ARIONI: Listen, all of you!

OBLIVIA: Ralf, what am I to think of you?

ARIONI: How naive you all are. It's just a joke. They'll bring it
back to me the way they brought the ball back to you . . .
No, no. And anyhow, I *am* Vozup's secret agent now. I
started believing in him a moment ago and I've become his
agent. Exactly the way all of you did.

(*Silence. Shots are fired. Lights in the window. They prick up their
ears. Steps draw nearer on the stairs.*)

KANGAR: Here he comes now. Professor, promise you'll be on
our side!

GARPADATTE: Professor, promise!

ARIONI: But what am I supposed to be? Teneroit's spy ring?
Huh?

KANGAR: Hurry up. There's no time. They're coming now . . .

ARIONI: All right. I promise. We're the spy ring, all of us . . .
including me.

(*Enter Deromur Ilfare in person, dictator in* potentia; *for the present,
a gentleman in a black suit—it has to be black, of course—with a
baroquely handsome and leonine face, accompanied by his right-hand
man, Bazarra*).

DEROMUR: (*To Bazarra*) So here they are. The first unmasking
of Vozup's subversive activities! We must talk with them for a
bit. Then, I'll pass sentence as usual—shoot the men, rape
the women . . .

OBLIVIA: (*Quite sincerely*) But, Dictator, that's inhuman . . . it's
barbarous . . . No civilized victors rape women nowadays.
And anyway it's dreadful to do it without a trial . . .

DEROMUR: (*Questioningly, but at the same time not committing himself*) You don't say?

OBLIVIA: What do you mean? You still have to ask about things
like that? . . . You don't understand what's so atrocious and

grotesque in this whole situation that you've created around us . . .

DEROMUR: (*As before*) You don't say?

OBLIVIA: (*Warming up*) You know almost all that from history, Dictator. Not from the direct course of events . . . And, after all, history is made by the victors . . . (*Deromur smiles leoninely.*) So all this grotesque absurdity is your work. Then what are you condemning us for, Dictator?

DEROMUR: (*In the same way*) You don't say?

OBLIVIA: You won't even answer me?

DEROMUR: (*Automatically*) You don't say? (*Waking up*) I'll answer you; just say what you've got to say and get it over with. Yes. I'm in the habit of giving synthetic answers. (*Shots, shouting. To Bazarra*) Is anything known yet about Teneroit?

BAZARRA: Nothing, Chief.

OBLIVIA: The whole sentence against us is practically by default. Dictator, I'm sure you don't know anything about the ball factory . . . and about the game without a ball . . . the game that's become the chief piece of circumstantial evidence . . . He (*pointing to Garpadatte*) is chess master of the world, and chess is often played without chessmen. And you don't know anything at all about any of this, Chief, you just don't know . . . You don't know anything, and you condemn . . . and that's how . . . Why don't you say something, Dictator? All right, I've finished.

DEROMUR: (*To Bazarra*) Bazarra, is it true that I don't know about anything here? What's been going on?

BAZARRA: (*Automatically*) A hotbed of cosmopolitanism, Chief . . . a spy ring unmasked, belonging to that . . . It's a fact!

DEROMUR: (*Automatically*) Yes. (*To Oblivia*) So you see. A hotbed of cosmopolitanism . . . Yes. I'll answer you right now. Bazarra, are the prisons already in our hands?

BAZARRA: Combat Squad C is mopping up the district where the prison is . . . I think so, Dictator. I'll have to call and find out. (*Goes out.*)

DEROMUR: (*To all of them*) I'm giving you a synthetic answer. History is no operetta, ladies and gentlemen. Our history means pushing man to compete with the machine; it means compelling everyone to become a god, to double and triple his strength for more and more frightful work. For work—I repeat—under the threat of losing one's bearings in the thick of life. If between the physical reality created by the machine and the conceptual or psychological reality devised by us, a rift appears—an abyss—then all the nongods, foreign to the reality of our people, will perish in it . . . And that will be the new Tarpeian rock which will preserve the people from degeneration . . . We are creating the highest incentives or bases of work that have ever existed . . . Turning the whole of reality into a machine once and for all! What? Are you trying to interrupt me?

ARIONI: Not at all; only I don't understand . . . I just don't understand . . . What's it really going to be like?

DEROMUR: Oh, you don't understand? But you know that not understanding us is not allowed. That our voice is the voice of the people, and the people are not a woman who can be misunderstood. That the people take their vengeance and punish? What about that?

ARIONI: And what does the voice of the world say to that?

DEROMUR: The world . . . ? The world hoax, not the world! Up till now there have only been world swindles and world frauds . . . (*To Garpadatte*) And as for you, Chess Master, I believe the only thing you've got coming is a little journey to the other world. What do you say about that?

GARPADATTE: But what we're talking about is the little round ball earth.

DEROMUR: Shut up! What we're talking about is a little round ball right between the eyes! (*Screams.*) History is no operetta. Our voice is the voice of the people, and a woman isn't . . .

ARIONI: (*His nerves giving way*) But that's not it, Chief! You've got it all wrong . . . It's that the people are no woman . . . And anyhow, it's not about any woman, but about the misunderstood artist!

DEROMUR: I am never wrong! How dare you . . . ! Do you understand?

ARIONI: (*Interrupting*) How can I help but understand? Your voice is the voice of the people, and the people . . .

DEROMUR: (*Terrifyingly*) You're making fun of me! (*Pulls out a revolver.*)

ARIONI: I'm not doing anything, Dictator . . . not anything at all . . . I'm just repeating . . .

DEROMUR: Repeating like that without believing is . . . irony.

ARIONI: (*Imploringly*) But they all repeat those slogans, all that political philosophy without believing any of it, Dictator . . . Bazarra even repeats every single word you say, because he's so impressed with you, but here's the truth, Dictator: no one believes you, not even Bazarra . . . !

DEROMUR: (*More seriously than he should*) What? (*Ironically*) So you want to stop being my enemy and become my spy?

OBLIVIA: Ralf, what sort of nonsense are you talking! (*To Deromur*) They simply don't understand you, Dictator.

DERMOUR: (*Grandiloquently*) They don't understand? But my voice is the voice of the entire people, and the people are . . . no woman . . .

OBLIVIA: (*Bursting out laughing*) Oh, not that again, not again. It's so fiendishly, so hysterically . . .

DEROMUR: Funny, eh? (*Ironically*) But we're creating these grotesque situations for you.

OBLIVIA: (*Terrified*) No . . . I wasn't thinking about anything like that . . . Now I don't know what . . .

DEROMUR: You're lying! It's . . . really . . .

(*Breaks off, Bazarra's footsteps are heard.*)

ARIONI: How's that! Dictator, you said yourself . . .

DEROMUR: . . . tremendously funny even . . . Yes, I can see that myself . . .

ARIONI: (*More impertinently*) You said that repeating without believing is irony . . . Well, then . . . this whole revolution they've produced is nothing but irony directed against you, Dictator.

DEROMUR: (*Automatically*) Yes. (*Waking up*) Shut up! Shut up! Bazarra!

BAZARRA: (*At the door*) Yes, sir?

DEROMUR: Is the prison taken yet?

BAZARRA: Assault Squad C is fighting for it now . . . They've almost got it . . . They need help to turn the tide!

DEROMUR: (*As though awakened*) The presidium of cabinet ministers?

BAZARRA: Half an hour ago . . .

DEROMUR: The central train station . . . ?

BAZARRA: Already taken. The south station begs for help.

DEROMUR: Vozup Teneroit?

BAZARRA: Nothing. No one knows a thing. He could put one over on us at any moment. They say he's got thousands of followers . . .

DEROMUR: Yes. So we've got to send help. The battalion of volunteers from the arms factories. And what about the company guarding the hotel, Bazarra?

BAZARRA: Untouched. They're looking after your safety, Dictator, and protecting the Hotel Morocco—in disguise.

DEROMUR: (*Suddenly uneasy*) Are you sure no one knows I'm here, Bazarra?

BAZARRA: No one. Except for them. (*Pointing to the prisoners*)

DEROMUR: And the message they threw out . . . ?

BAZARRA: Impossible. It fell right into our hands.

OBLIVIA: Dictator, you really don't know anything about what's been going on here. It was just an ordinary ping-pong ball.

DEROMUR: Bazarra, they keep saying I don't know anything about what's been going on here. Was it really just an ordinary ping-pong ball?

EVERYONE: (*Shouting Bazarra down*) We swear it was an ordinary ping-pong ball . . . No one even dreamed of throwing out a message.

BAZARRA: I can assure you there was a message . . . They confessed it themselves immediately afterward. What's more, they were completely exposed.

OBLIVIA: But, Dictator, is being found playing ping-pong without a ball being exposed? If I threw the ball out the window and they had to finish the set, what else could they do?

DEROMUR: (*Automatically*) Yes. Naturally. (*Coming back to life*) What do you mean, ping-pong without a ball?

ARIONI: Oh, it's nothing . . .

DEROMUR: What do you mean, it's nothing? It's completely impossible. It's a lie.

ARIONI: Dictator, I'll admit that even I find it improbable now. But that's the fault of all the fossilizations of life, of each and every one of its by-products. They're always incomprehensible and full of nonsense if seen through the eyes of life. Isn't it nonsensical and paradoxical that all creators, leaders, and dictators, all those who have lived the most intensely, the most restlessly, the most dynamically, are commemorated by fossilized, deadly stiff statues and monuments? It's exactly the same way for us . . . Only life itself can excuse in our eyes the strangeness and absurdity of all its works . . .

DEROMUR: Yes. (*More intelligently*) I see you're beginning to adopt our philosophy.

ARIONI: What do you mean? A moment ago you yourself said that it was just uproariously funny, Dictator, and now you demand . . .

DEROMUR: (*Interrupting*) So what if it is uproariously funny? If I said that, it means that it doesn't matter to me, that it's totally insignificant . . . What if it is uproariously funny? So what?

ARIONI: A funny political philosophy?

DEROMUR: Well, yes. So what? I said it could be funny, so it is. (*To Bazarra*) Send couriers to the battalion of volunteers from the arms factories . . .

ARIONI: Dictator, I'm very impressed with you. That's where your greatness lies. And that's why I believe that you'll want to try to understand us too.

DEROMUR: (*Ironically*) You overrate my powers. Even if I wanted to, I couldn't believe you . . . As a boy I was an avid ping-pong player myself and I know that playing without a ball can only turn the game into a hoax.

ARIONI: Oh, but I was saying that the by-products of life are always incredible and absurd. Dictator, in order to believe, you've got to experience it yourself . . . (*Carried away*) Just change places with one of us and play with your own hands, see with your own eyes, take part in the course of events in person. Then it will be impossible for you not to believe.

(*Bazarra remains rooted to the spot. He keeps silent.*)

DEROMUR: (*Astounded*) What? Me play ping-pong with my own prisoners? Have you gone crazy?

ARIONI: Why no, Dictator, that's the only path to the truth! And for us it's the only defense. You don't believe our oaths, Dictator. Our explanations sound incredible . . . How else can we save ourselves, Dictator?

DEROMUR: Bazarra, if necessary, deploy half the company of

the hotel guard to the south station. Professor, you can show
me how it's done if you think it will do you any good . . .
(*Bazarra goes out.*)

ARIONI: Come now! It's the only thing that can do any good!
But, Dictator, you've got to take part in the game, you've got
to get completely swept up in it; only then can you see the
truth.

DEROMUR: (*Amused*) Well now, that's an interesting idea. Do you
have the ball?

OBLIVIA: (*Quickly*) Mr. Bazarra has it . . . You can still call him
back . . .

DEROMUR: (*Opens the door, calling.*) Bazarra, come back for a
minute!

BAZARRA: (*In the doorway*) Yes, sir?

DEROMUR: Bazarra, give us that celluloid ping-pong ball you
used as the chief proof of their guilt.

(*Bazarra silently hands over the ball and goes out again. Deromur
starts to get into a better mood.*)

DEROMUR: (*Lightly*) We'll find out everything soon enough . . .
You're playing for life or death.

GARPADATTE: Let's begin then. For serve! (*Throws the ball on the
table. The game begins.*)

DEROMUR: (*Repeating*) For death, rather.

KANGAR: (*After a moment's play*) Out. Serve, Dictator! You've got
a terrific forehand . . . Well, do you believe now?

DEROMUR: Not yet. It's too soon to start believing.

GARPADATTE: Let's keep on playing then. Your serve (*to
Kangar*), Champ, no questions, no interruptions: the effect
has to be authentic.

(*The game goes on and on, fluidifies, becomes more real. The absurdity
of the whole situation ceases to be felt. Kangar stands by the table and
referees. Oblivia and Arioni at the window.*)

KANGAR: (*After one of the smashes*) Your serve, Dictator. (*Recalling
the words from the first act*) Careful with the ball.

DEROMUR: (*Not knowing the course of the earlier scene in Act I, or
what to say, he looks at Kangar expectantly.*) Well, what do I say
to that?

KANGAR: (*Prompts*) You say, "Don't worry about this ball, it's a
strong one."

DEROMUR: (*Confidently and naturally*) Don't you worry about this ball, Champ, it's a strong one.

KANGAR: (*Continuing the previous dialogue*) We already seem to have demolished seven of these strong balls today.

BAZARRA: (*Coming into the room*) Dictator, we're gaining control of the bridges over the river . . .

KANGAR: (*Making it emphatically clear that he should get out*) Don't bother the dictator now. Can't you see he's busy?

BAZARRA: (*Looking incredulously at Deromur himself*) Dictator! All our men are itching to take those bridges . . .

DEROMUR: That's fine, Bazarra. I'll be finished in just a minute. But for the time being, don't bother me. I've got to finish with them somehow or other, find out something about them. (*All of this while they're playing*) It would be a hell of a kind of sabotage if we treated them as Vozup's spy ring and it turned out it wasn't true. And that seems to be the case, Bazarra.

(*Bazarra wants to object.*)

ARIONI: Don't bother the dictator. You can settle all that later.

(*Bazarra goes out stunned. The game proceeds without a break. Silence in the room, but outside, in the city, the sounds of shells exploding close by and the still nearer screaming of huge crowds grow in intensity.*)

DEROMUR: (*Impulsively, forgetting about the hoax*) What's going on out there? Professor, what do you see out there?

ARIONI: (*Unconsciously repeating the words from the first act*) Oh, what can you find out or understand by looking out the window? I'm very impressed with your game, but I simply can't stand not to know anything about what's going on . . . I've got to—

GARPADATTE: (*Getting into the swing of the first act*) What do you mean, not know? (*To Deromur*) You know, Dictator, I like those diagonal shots; they remind me of the way the bishop moves. (*To Arioni*) It's just a revolution, Professor. You don't have to read the newspapers to know that.

DEROMUR: Don't talk so much, or you'll lose. I already have a five-point advantage.

GARPADATTE: We'll see about that. (*To Arioni*) Don't be afraid . . . Champ! Who are you betting on, Professor?

(*Silence*)

ARIONI: (*Looking out the window; ironically and enigmatically*) The truth always wins. I'm betting on that.

End of Act II

ACT III

(*Exactly the same, only the window is growing upward and is getting considerably wider at the very top; it forms a trapezoid. Deromur and Garpadatte's set is nearing an end. Kangar counts as he keeps score. It's now close to twenty.*)

OBLIVIA: (*Metaphysically terrified*) Ralf . . . It's all mounting up in such a fantastic way . . . I'm afraid, Ralf . . . Tell me, what's going to happen?

ARIONI: (*Excited*) Anything. Literally anything. Our death—or our life.

OBLIVIA: But it's impossible that this is a matter of things like life and death. They're having fun, Ralf . . . They're playing ping-pong . . .

ARIONI: Riza, you don't understand a thing . . .

OBLIVIA: (*Interrupting him*) I do understand! I understand very well! Ralf, they're playing ping-pong again—there's nothing else . . . This ping-pong nonsense is getting atrociously nonsensical; it's getting more and more so . . . Ralf, I don't think you see what's going on here! The dictator himself, the leader of the people, the leader of the revolution is playing ping-pong . . . Ralf, I think I'll go crazy. If this is how the world must catch up with us to become modern, then . . .

KANGAR: (*Louder*) Ready . . . nineteen–fifteen . . . Dictator's serve. (*Corrects himself, turning the situation into a hoax.*) Excuse me, Champ's serve.

ARIONI: (*To Oblivia*) Then what? The most important thing is that we've got to live, Riza.

OBLIVIA: (*Going berserk*) Then—then I don't want to live in such a world!

DEROMUR: (*Butting in*) No one wants to live in such a world. It's absurd anyhow. We live only in the people.

GARPADATTE: (*Irritated, to Deromur*) Champ, if you're going to

keep making mistakes all the time, nothing is going to come
of any of this . . .

DEROMUR: You're right; that was a mistake. Sorry. (*He misses at
the same time.*)

GARPADATTE: Point fifteen! You're losing, Dictator. (*Correcting
himself*) Champ . . .

DEROMUR: (*Excited*) We'll see about that. Where's the ball?

KANGAR: (*Looking for it*) It's disappeared somewhere. It's not
anywhere. That ball has to be lying around here somewhere . . .

OBLIVIA: (*Helping him look for it and finding it*) It is. Here it is! I
found it. (*Suddenly growing serious*) But I didn't find it for you.
Not to feed the fires of nonsense . . . (*Powerfully*) I won't
ever give it to you.

DEROMUR: (*Furious, excited at losing*) Give that ball back this minute! (*Upset*) What do you intend to do with it? (*Runs up to
Oblivia.*)

OBLIVIA: (*Throws the ball out the window.*) Throw it into the fires
of revolution, not nonsense. Oh . . . it'll burn up there!

DEROMUR: How dare you!

ARIONI: Riza, what have you done!?

OBLIVIA: (*Flaring up*) I know what I've done now. I've made a
burnt offering to the revolution . . .

DEROMUR: Without my permission? Defying me? I'll have you
. . . raped . . .

OBLIVIA: (*Defiantly*) Because you don't have . . . the time yourself? You've got to play ping-pong.

DEROMUR: (*Automatically*) That's right. I don't have the time.
(*Coming to life*) But what can we do about our game now?

ARIONI: Oh, Riza . . . everything's ruined because of you. It's a
matter of our lives, Riza. (*To Deromur*) But you still hadn't totally lost yet, had you?

DEROMUR: You forget yourself, Professor. I never lose. It was
just a maneuver. I demand the ball. . . !

GARPADATTE: *I* demand the ball! The game's got to be finished
. . . I was winning anyhow . . .

DEROMUR: Shut up! It was a tactical maneuver. Now is when I
would have shown you how to play ping-pong! The ball! . . .

ARIONI: Well, what are we going to do? All the stores are closed—the one that was thrown out broke . . . Riza, the ball?

GARPADATTE: You would have lost the final point and so . . . I won.

DEROMUR: Shut up! I had a surprise for you. A shot no one's ever seen.

GARPADATTE: Just who do you take me for? I know all the shots and I can return them all!

DEROMUR: (*Seizing his paddle*) You don't know this one . . . (*Demonstrating the shot*) See!

GARPADATTE: Coming, hold on . . . (*Gets behind the table.*) Do that again.

DEROMUR: All right, here! (*Swings his paddle.*)

GARPADATTE: (*Pretends to return it.*) Got it.

DEROMUR: Right on the corner, twice in a row.

GARPADATTE: Got it, you can't beat me with that one!

DEROMUR: We'll see about that. Look! You missed it—point sixteen.

GARPADATTE: Keep playing! (*To Kangar*) You keep score . . . it's point sixteen . . .

KANGAR: All right; it's twenty–sixteen . . . (*To Deromur*) Your serve.

ARIONI: (*Captivated, beginning to get the picture*) Riza, you've saved our lives. They've forgotten they're just pretending and they're playing without the ball in earnest . . .

OBLIVIA: (*In despair*) But what's the point of saving our lives, Ralf? I didn't want that at all . . . What's the point of living in a world in which people like that are the dictators? (*Points to Deromur.*)

ARIONI: People like that? You mean?

OBLIVIA: I mean characters out of an operetta. People like that!

ARIONI: But, Riza, he's just grasped that for history to stop being an operetta—he's got to become a character out of an operetta himself. He's a man who has understood that ridicule not only is not threatening, it's inevitable.

OBLIVIA: I'm not talking about this game now . . . I'm talking about everything . . . About repeating his whole political philosophy inanely until it becomes grotesque. About turning the people's ideas into meaningless propaganda.

ARIONI: But was I *really* talking about that game? I meant everything too. It's just that you never understand anything, Riza . . . My point too is about his organizing the people and making some sort of social refrain out of a political philosophy. But that's where his true greatness really lies. He understands that that's the whole point. Get everyone to repeat the same refrain over and over again. Without thinking, or even as a joke, but all the same the refrain helps in the making of history, just as the rhythm of a song spurs people on to work . . .

OBLIVIA: Ralf, you're a genius! You're the only one who understands what's happening in this messy world . . . They don't even know themselves, do they?

ARIONI: No, Riza, if there's one thing that that Deromur Ilfare doesn't know, it's that he's the greatest man in the world . . . He thinks that only the people make him great and that the world as such doesn't exist!

KANGAR: Point eighteen!

(*Steps from down below are heard on the stairs.*)

GARPADATTE: Well, what do you have to say?

DEROMUR: At least it seems believable to me now. But don't spoil my sense of its reality. (*To Garpadatte*) My serve!

(*Once again the quiet, mysterious game with empty paddles—producing the effect of a dance. As an undercurrent to all this, footsteps. Footsteps on the stairs, closer and closer. Garpadatte, dressed in a white tennis outfit and Deromur Ilfare, in a black suit, create a strange chess board on which a game is in progress without the chessmen. Enter a man dressed like Deromur, in a black suit, on the thin side, intelligent-looking, likewise a bit baroque. A couple of armed men follow him in.*)

TENEROIT: Yes, it seems we've come to the right place . . . (*Uncertainly*) Is the champion really here?

(*Garpadatte and Deromur keep playing a moment more.*)

KANGAR: (*Forgetting*) That's me, what can I do for you?

DEROMUR: (*To Kangar, stopping the game*) Damn it all, have you forgotten? (*To Teneroit, continuing the hoax*) Excuse me, but I'm the champion.

TENEROIT: (*Confused*) What's that? Then there are two champions?

KANGAR: (*Apologetic*) No, of course not. I just mixed things up . . . I'm not . . .

TENEROIT: (*Amazed*) You mixed things up? Who are you then?

KANGAR: (*Disconcerted*) Well, well . . . I'm not . . . You're interested in the champion; well, there he is. (*Points to Deromur.*)

TENEROIT: No, excuse me, gentlemen, there's some mistake. It's obviously some other champion that's involved here.

DEROMUR: (*Getting caught up in the hoax with greater and greater zeal*) Of course it isn't! I'm the champion about whom the message was thrown out on a ping-pong ball . . .

TENEROIT: (*Incredulously*) Well, then it all holds together. But I heard you were taken prisoner . . .

DEROMUR: (*Treating Teneroit as part of the hoax*) Watch out, or I'll lose my patience. Can't you see that I've been taken prisoner . . . ?

TENEROIT: But you were playing ping-pong . . . What are you trying to put over on me?

DEROMUR: I was playing, but now I've been arrested, damn it all . . .

TENEROIT: Well, where is he?

DEROMUR: Who? Where is who?

TENEROIT: Well, whoever arrested you, damn it all?

DEROMUR: (*To them all*) No, that's going too far; I was just beginning to believe everything, but he's spoiling my sense of the reality of it . . . (*To Teneroit, still hoping to involve him in the hoax*) Well, now . . . see here . . . have you forgotten what the whole point is?

TENEROIT: You're clearly making fun of me, Champ. And here I've been running around the whole city gathering people and arms and rushing to help you . . .

DEROMUR: (*Ironically*) You don't have to lie so shamelessly. We threw the ball out when it was point sixteen. How, in the course of a few minutes, could you manage to run around the whole city, gathering people and rushing to help me?

TENEROIT: (*Confused*) Well, that was just the problem . . . I had to run like crazy.

DEROMUR: (*To all of them, indignant*) No, you've messed it up. The spell is broken. He's absolutely ruined my sense of the reality of it all . . .

TENEROIT: What's that? You don't believe in my reality? Up to now, it's true, I've been hiding my true identity, but to save you I have finally decided to reveal myself. This you can believe: I really am Vozup Teneroit!

DEROMUR: (*Dazed, utterly stunned*) Vozup Teneroit? You're lying!

TENEROIT: No, Champ, maybe I shouldn't have told you, but it seems some sort of misunderstanding has developed that must be cleared up . . . And now we're leaving the hotel as fast as we can . . .

DEROMUR: (*Dropping his hoaxing tone*) You're lying. In the first place, it's really impossible for you to have intercepted our ball. And besides, the revolutionary guard is posted outside.

TENEROIT: I didn't intercept it now, but when the revolutionary armies were still taking the hotel . . .

DEROMUR: (*Getting the picture with a terrible jolt*) What's that? So you really did throw out a message then? You were lying when you swore you didn't?

OBLIVIA: Of course not! No one threw out any message . . . I swear it.

DEROMUR: What was the message all about, Vozup? What sort of message was it?

TENEROIT: (*Surprised at Deromur's reaction, but continues to be polite and civilized.*) I must admit, I don't exactly know. I only heard it shouted by Bazarra to the revolutionaries.

DEROMUR: (*Pulling himself together, adopting a dictator's tone*) All right, that will do. As it is, your machinations have proved to be your undoing. You're through, Vozup; I'm having you arrested this minute.

TENEROIT: (*Surprised, not understanding a thing*) What? So you're one of Deromur's spies? You were put here as bait for me?

DEROMUR: No, Vozup.

TENEROIT: Well, what then?

DEROMUR: (*Bringing everything to a bombastic culmination*) To catch Vozup Teneroit one needs bigger bait than some box-

ing champion. I am the leader of the revolution—Deromur
Ilfare.

TENEROIT: Oh, Oh, Oh, Oh!

DEROMUR: (*Going over to the door*) Bazarra ! Bazarra! Whoever is
out there—come in here!

BOY: (*Rushing into the room almost instantly*) At your orders.

DEROMUR: Where's Bazarra? Call in half the company of the
hotel guard. Arrest these people!

BOY: General Bazarra is leading the attack on the railroad
bridge at present. Victory, Dictator! Every last man from the
hotel guard has gone to help and—to fight for victory.

DEROMUR: What? You've left me here alone? They went to
fight without my orders, eh?

BOY: Turning the tide in the battle for the railroad bridge
depended on them. But it's almost over now. There's no
doubt about the victory, Dictator . . .

TENEROIT: (*Gaining control of the situation; very ironically*) There's
no doubt about the victory, Dictator. But it's a victory for the
revolution, and you've lost . . . (*To his men*) Arrest him!

(*Vozup's armed men stand flat-footed, immobile. They look reproachfully at Vozup, but say nothing.*)

TENEROIT: (*A second time*) Arrest Deromur Ilfare immediately!
Did you hear me!

(*Silence, silence growing ghastly, strained, actively getting under their
skin until it hurts and most of all—unbearably rapid.*)

OBLIVIA: (*Hysterically*) Ralf, kill me, I've had enough . . . Stop
this . . . I can't take it any more.

KANGAR: (*Impulsively*) Neither can I. Why doesn't anyone arrest
anyone?

TENEROIT: (*Frothing at the mouth*) Why don't you arrest him? (*To
the first of his men*) Well? Say something, damn it all!

FIRST FOLLOWER: Forgive me, Chief, but I don't believe that
such uncompromising solutions are inevitable any longer. It's
opposed to my belief in the modern world.

TENEROIT: (*To the second of his men*) What about you?

SECOND FOLLOWER: I came here, Chief, to protect those who
had been arrested, but attack an unarmed man? No, Chief, I
don't believe a lack of gallantry can produce lasting
victories . . .

TENEROIT: (*To the third of his men, silently, with only a questioning gesture.*)

THIRD FOLLOWER: I believe the easiest way to wrest the weapon out of your enemy's hand is through forgiveness. Therefore, you should begin by pardoning everyone, Dictator . . .

TENEROIT: (*To the fourth*) And you too?

FOURTH FOLLOWER: I don't believe any of this is real. We've become the butts of a joke once more. We mustn't expose ourselves to ridicule, Chief.

DEROMUR: (*Defiantly*) Well? Now, what are you going to do?

TENEROIT: (*To his mutinous men*) What is this? You refuse to obey me? Is that right? (*Silence.*) Treason?

THE FOLLOWERS: No, Dictator, disillusion. When you organized us, we believed you had different goals, completely different principles . . .

DEROMUR: (*Ironically*) Well, I'm waiting . . .

TENEROIT: (*Desperately and ironically*) So am I . . . Oh, Oh, Oh . . . I'm waiting for your victorious army to return.

DEROMUR: Oh, Oh, Oh . . . Stop it! Go ahead, arrest me.

TENEROIT: You wanted to arrest me first . . . A trap for me . . . Oh, Oh, Oh . . .

OBLIVIA: (*Hysterically*) My God, why doesn't anyone arrest anyone? Let's get it over with.

(*Silence. The dictators* in potentia, *both in black, face each other, pale and dreadful to the third power of passion and impotence, spluttering out bile.*)

DEROMUR: (*Ironically, and helpless as a martyr*) You have impressed me, Vozup, with your men who still believe so strongly in something today . . .

TENEROIT: (*Picking up Deromur's tone*) You have impressed me, Deromur, with your men who still want to fight for something or other.

DEROMUR: (*Unable to contain himself, reaches for his revolver, takes aim.*) Watch out! (*Squeezes the trigger.*) Now at last a little murder will take place!

TENEROIT: (*Turning pale; defenseless*) Well, why don't you shoot? It's the only . . .

DEROMUR: (*Turning pale*) I . . . can't. (*Silence. Deromur staggers about in a daze, handsome, ambiguous, grotesque.*) Now I under-

VIII. A scene from the Ateneum production of *To Pick up the Rose*, Act III. Deromur Ilfare aiming at Teneroit with a revolver that contains no bullets. (Photograph by Zofia Myszkowska.)

stand . . . This bastard gun doesn't have any bullets in it . . . They were afraid I'd commit suicide if I was defeated, so they gave me a bastard without bullets. (*Flings the Browning on the floor.*)

TENEROIT: (*A dreadful puff of strong feeling, passion to the third power*) Deromur, of all ham actors, you are the greatest . . . I could throttle you . . . I won't let you out of here . . .

DEROMUR: Vozup, dictator of life's eunuchs . . . do they still go on believing in all that?

TENEROIT: Militarist, without a bullet in your Browning, totalitarian figure of speech! Stop it . . . stop it . . . Tell me, how shall I finish you off?

DEROMUR: Oh, oh . . . Don't worry, I won't let you get out of here.

TENEROIT: What? Are your men still busy taking that one bridge?

DEROMUR: Oh, Oh, Oh . . . Skunk, mistletoe growing on democracy . . .

TENEROIT: Oh, Oh, Oh . . . What is he saying?

DEROMUR: That I'll beat you with my bare fists if necessary.

TENEROIT: Just try, scum . . .

(They stand face to face, transformed into brutes, dedictatorized, but boxerizing more and more each moment. Fists.)

KANGAR: *(Desperately)* No . . . look here . . . that isn't the way at all . . . How are you going to box when even ping-pong is . . . *(Breaks off terrified.)*

TENEROIT: *(In a croaking voice)* Ping-pong? Without a ball?

DEROMUR: *(Still more hoarsely)* Without a ball? That toadstool of democracy will never understand ping-pong without a ball . . . Oh!

TENEROIT: I'll murder him . . . Where are the paddles?

(Weird, contorted, convulsive, hateful, misshapen, with stiff, shrunken muscles, wrinkles on their faces, the dictators take their places on each side of the table and without a word begin their black, infernal, inhuman game. At times they seem like the two black zigzag supports for the cactus. All present are bewitched, turned dumb. Woodenly and automatically, Kangar keeps score. Numbers, changes of serve—not one word more. After some moments of this condensed, mad absurdity, there comes floating through the open window a simple-hearted and lively song, played by the band of revolutionaries who have taken the railroad bridge.)

OBLIVIA: *(Waking up)* Ralf . . . Ralf . . . I'll bet you're going to say that now the world has caught up with us for good and all . . . That that's what everyone has been waiting for . . . That at last it's possible to begin living, Ralf . . . But I can't take it all anymore . . . Forgive me, but I really can't. The revolution is out there, and the dictators are in here . . . Ralf, it's beyond a woman's strength . . . even if that woman was a nudist once . . . Ralf . . . think well of me . . . try to understand . . . Kiss me once more with that compromising,

utterly contemporary kiss of the world. For you I'll intensify
to the maximum all that is grotesque and modern in the
world . . . A ball, a cigarette, my ribbon thrown out the window. They're nothing, Ralf; but a *woman* throwing herself
out the window . . .

ARIONI: Riza, have you gone crazy? (*Arioni rushes over, but Oblivia is too quick for him and jumps.*) That's my last . . . (*Stands
in front of the empty window.*)

KANGAR: (*Automatically and woodenly*) Seven–eight. Change
serve.

ARIONI: Riza? Last . . . love . . .

(*The song can be heard breaking off. A cry. A cry of horror. A com-
mand.*)

KANGAR: Eight–eight. All even.

(*Quiet; footsteps on the stairs, footsteps going up to higher floors. The
zigzag, black game of the dictators continues without a break.*)

GARPADATTE: (*Bitterly ironic*) Did you hear, Professor? It's even.

ARIONI: (*Blankly, apathetically*) I don't know . . . I don't know
anything . . . Riza's dead . . .

(*Footsteps outside the door; enter Bazarra.*)

BAZARRA: The bridge is taken, Dictator. The battle lasted a
good hour. I led the attack myself.

(*The players don't pay the slightest attention. Arioni rouses himself, undergoes an inner change; pale, unsmiling, but strong. His decision is
made.*)

ARIONI: (*In the tone of a dictator, a leader of the revolution*) That's
very good, Bazarra. I'm proud of you for showing such ini-
tiative on your own . . . We'll take a taxi immediately and
inspect the railroad bridge and the south station.

BAZARRA: (*Thrown off; to Deromur*) Dictator, we've also intercepted secret papers belonging to the former government
. . . Do you want to look them over?

ARIONI: (*Answering once more as the dictator*) Naturally, Bazarra
. . . we can't neglect those things . . . (*As though he just re-
membered something*) Only first, even before that car trip—I've
got to do one more thing . . .

BAZARRA: (*Astounded*) But I don't understand by what miracle
you became dictator.

ARIONI: Yes, Bazarra . . . a miracle perhaps . . . As I was say-

IX. Another scene from the Ateneum production of *To Pick up the Rose*, Act III. Oblivia jumps out the window. (Photograph by Zofia Myszkowska.)

ing, I've got to do one more thing: find the red ribbon on the
street the late Riza gave me for thinking up ping-pong without a ball.

BAZARRA: What do you want? (*Correcting himself*) What are your
orders, Dictator?

ARIONI: (*Bitterly*) Well, now . . . I figured you'd bring it to me
yourself the same way you brought them that ball then. I was
sure of it. Well, but, you see. Even such false roses have their
thorns . . . To be able to look for them freely on the street
you have to become dictator . . . (*To Bazarra*) Let's go, Bazarra.

(*They go out.*)

GARPADATTE: Professor, where are you going . . . ? Tell me
what all this really means!

ARIONI: (*Turning around*) It means that the world has finally
caught up with me, Master . . . I'm going down to pick up
the false rose, which must be lying somewhere near the body
of poor, naive Riza. But to be able to do that I've got to
become a man whom everyone laughs at as the creator of
social refrains and who they don't want to listen to, since they
still believe in something or other themselves. I've got to
become dictator, Master. (*Goes out.*)

(*The game of the dictators* in potentia *goes its ghastly way ad infinitum.*)

THE END

Selections from "From the Drama Laboratory" (1942)

ANDRZEJ TRZEBIŃSKI

MAN AND THE PING-PONG BALL: There have been dramas about people left face to face with themselves and dramas about people confronting fate. On the other hand, no need was felt to create a drama in which the contestants would be man and thing. While this fact may be regarded as odd and whimsical, we can just as easily discover in it a deeper philosophical undercurrent and the crucial Gordian knot of drama.

For all that, it would be difficult to expect a walnut chest of drawers to suffer a setback in a love affair or to torment some human being with fits of jealousy. That is true, and no one would ask a chest of drawers to do anything like that. Yet there is a source of drama in the interrelationship of man and thing.

Let us examine the entire question from the perspective of the history of drama.

Ancient drama, devoted to collisions between man and his destiny, simply did not feel the need to involve things in the conflict. Men of ethos and pathos were in fact huge projections of their own consciences on the screen of life. And as projections of conscience, it was not fitting for them, for example, to eat a lavish meal, clean a room, or dig a grave. The ancient hero was isolated from the world of things by the very fact that he never used any. It was contrary to the heightened style and psychological concentration required by the tragic struggle.

Shakespeare, Molière, and nineteenth-century bourgeois

Translated by Daniel Gerould from Andrzej Trzebiński, "Z laboratorium dramatu," in *Aby podnieść różę* (Warsaw: Pax, 1970).

drama introduced the thing as background. As something that is actually used. Background in a dramatic sense, serving to emphasize action and gesture, in that they are associated with objects of daily use which, like cashboxes, have stored up a little capital of the bustle of life, its movements, and everyday activities.

Symbolism, it would seem, finally gave things an important dramatic function and the leading role in drama. Things were scrutinized carefully; their language was listened to attentively. The common, ordinary use of things seemed almost a profanation.

But all this gazing at things was like gazing at a windowpane through which we see a landscape. The thing remained a medium for forces, meanings, and implications that were higher and more mysterious.

These forces and meanings were, it is true, manifested in things and spoke the language of things, but that does not in the least signify that the thing became dramatic and functioned as a contestant in the struggle.

And here arises a possibility as well as a necessity for contemporary drama: TO GIVE THINGS A DRAMATIC FUNCTION!

We could cite the prewar American play *Our Town* as an interesting venture in this field. It might be maintained paradoxically that in that play the thing truly did become a contestant in the drama.

Because in fact there were no things. Their absence was what was felt. They should have been there, but they weren't.

The ancients constructed their dramas in such a way that there were no things in them, nor should there have been. In ancient drama there was no place provided for things.

In *Our Town* there was a place for things, but it was empty. And precisely this emptiness, this palpable absence of things, had dramatic significance. Reality had an aura of the visionary, it unfolded like a dream.

It was a drama—perhaps not fully realized—but capable of occurring between two elements: the spiritual and the real. Between the reality of the spirit and the reality of the thing.

Things said a great deal in that play by the stress on their absence, just as in the diplomatic world, most is said by what is unsaid, by the empty chair.

That is a concrete example.

Further perspectives: Things can play their roles in the drama not only by being absent. Not only by being silent can things speak out. Although, parenthetically, this is an extremely clever way of doing it.

Things ought to speak and act directly. Like people, things operate on objective values. One thing has beauty, another ugliness not because we see them that way: the first is beautiful, the second ugly independently of us. Objectively.

[Two paragraphs are omitted.]

Things are mysterious accumulators of values, both good and bad. As people become attached to things, as they establish contact with them, they begin to shine.

Things impose their values upon us and challenge ours. Conflicts are everywhere in the air and are ours for the taking.

The question of the interrelationship of man and thing has still other aspects. Man could be regarded as the process of creating values, and the thing as the state of values already created. The dichotomy between man and thing is more or less the same as the dichotomy between reality as it is being created and reality as it already exists, between what is becoming and what is.

As a result, man is also a thing to a certain extent. The drama of man and thing can take place not only in the external world; the human conscience suffices for such a drama.

Man as a current of becoming, as a process of growth, as a potential, and man as an established thing, already finished and complete, can carry on a struggle in his own conscience.

With such a conception we can even regard as a thing the sphere of our inner traits, the sphere of our psyche—in a word, everything that already exists, that is formed and fixed. Whatever is not still in the process of being made.

With these new aspects to enrich it, the problem should become simpler and more concrete. It should facilitate the creation of a drama of man and thing. Or of man and the world of things, if a single, individual thing, such as an umbrella or a ping-pong ball, proves too light, lacking sufficient weight to be a counterforce and counterweight to man.

III

Konstanty Ildefons Gałczyński

Twenty-two Short Plays from The Little Theatre of *The Green Goose*

Translated by Daniel and Eleanor Gerould from Konstanty Ildefons Gałczyński, *Zielona Gęś*, in *Dzieła*, III (Warsaw: Czytelnik, 1958). Except for "Family Happiness" and "The End of the World," earlier versions of these translations appeared in the Special English Language Issue of *Dialog*, copyright 1969 by Daniel C. Gerould and Eleanor S. Gerould, copyright 1970 by Wydawnictwa Artystyczne i Filmowe, Warsaw.

THE LITTLE THEATRE OF *THE GREEN GOOSE*

Has the Honor of Presenting

"A Salvation Army Concert"

In which appear:
  BISHOP BURKE, drum
  MISS PETIT POOH
  JOHNNY BROWN, former alcoholic, trumpet
  A CROWD OF THE MORALLY MISGUIDED
  and RAIN

Scene: Boston, U.S.A., 7th Street.

BISHOP BURKE, MISS PETIT POOH, and JOHNNY BROWN: (*Beating on the drum, fiddling on the violin, and trumpeting*) Holy-holy-hallelujah!

CROWD OF THE MORALLY MISGUIDED: (*Undergoes a very slight moral rebirth.*)

RAIN: (*Starts to sprinkle.*)

BISHOP BURKE: (*Beating on the drum*) Oh, hell. Brethren. The end of the world is coming. The Gobi fish will come out of the depths of the waters and devour the Rockefeller Institute and the Peace Conference. So too will this fish completely devour the inventors of the atomic bomb and the inventors of the meat grinder. Then the vegetarians will be on the right, the meat eaters on the left, and I will be in the middle. Buy my pamphlet, *How I Became a Vegetarian.*

MISS PETIT POOH: (*On the violin*) Holy-holy-hallelujah.

BISHOP BURKE: Along with a color portrait of the Gobi fish, only four dollars. Four dollars. Four dollars. Four dollars. Four dollars.

JOHNNY BROWN: (*Trumpet*) Holy-holy-hallelujah. Holy-holy-hallelujah.

BISHOP BURKE: Thank you. Four dollars. Holy—thank you—hallelujah!

CROWD OF THE MORALLY MISGUIDED: (*Undergoes a total rebirth.*)

RAIN: (*Coming down in buckets.*)

JOHNNY BROWN: (*Every so often pours water out of his trumpet and gazes longingly at the sign in front of the bar, "The Jolly Owl."*)

211

Miss Petit Pooh: (*By mistake pours water out of a size 12 shoe into the violin.*) Blasted downpour. It's an absolute cloudburst. Boston's turning into an aquarium. I splash, you splash, he, she, it splashes. We splash, you splash, they splash.

Bishop Burke: (*Through the rain and darkness, stopping beating on the drum*) The hell with it all! Well, friends, one more "holy-holy" and we'll call it quits.

CURTAIN

1946

THE LITTLE THEATRE OF *THE GREEN GOOSE*

Has the Honor of Presenting

"The Drama of a Deceived Husband"
or
"Crushed by the Credenza"

Characters:
A MAN and A CREDENZA

(The stage represents a small room in which stands the above-mentioned antique three-tiered credenza with a drolly shaped ornamental railing and a cornice with trumpeting cherubs.)

MAN: "Cogito, ergo sum"—which means, "I think, therefore I am"—said our friend Descartes. But what if I am, if my wife never is. She sits and gossips all day long in a café.

And meanwhile:

> The mushrooms are not marinating,
> The socks aren't getting darned,
> The dust's not being wiped away,
> The beds aren't getting made,
> The fish aren't being scaled,
> The potatoes are not peeled,
> The eggs aren't being boiled,
> The faucets aren't turned off,
> So I stare at the bare wall,
> And swallow bitter tears.

(Swallows again and again.)

My only companion, my only friend is this old credenza, witness of all my sufferings and longings. Oh, if you could only speak, old credenza, credenza with your ornamental railing of indeterminate shape and your cornice on which two cherubs blow golden trombones!!

But I have the impression that credenza's starting to tip again. Pikus probably bit off the leg again. That damned Pikus! *(With a gesture of despair he straightens the credenza; the credenza falls over and crushes him.)*

MAN: *(From under the credenza)* Oh, this is great! Maybe now my sufferings will finally end. What's that? Aha, that's the jar of

213

horseradish that's come open, and the horseradish is dripping in my eyes. I forgive you, Marie. (*A pause.*)

Marie, where are you right now? At Alice's, maybe? Or perhaps at your favorite café? Or maybe you've enrolled in a course in gliding and are soaring now like a swallow through the clouds high above the commonplace chimney of our house and, as it were, all this *vanitas vanitatum?* Like a bright spirit you're beyond this earthy vale of tears. While I am underneath the credenza. Marie, I forgive you. And you, credenza, crush me all the way.

CREDENZA: (*In a human voice*) All right, here we go! (*Crushes him all the way.*)

CURTAIN

1949

THE LITTLE THEATRE OF *THE GREEN GOOSE*

Has the Honor of Presenting

"The Atrocious Uncle"

In which appear:

THE ATROCIOUS UNCLE
THE UNHAPPY AUNT
GENERAL VENDETTA

THE ATROCIOUS UNCLE: (*Drips with blood.*)

THE UNHAPPY AUNT: Well, what's your latest prank, Aloysius?

THE ATROCIOUS UNCLE: I murdered the Baroness.

THE UNHAPPY AUNT: (*In a hollow voice*) That's your sixth crime so far this week. Aloysius, what's happened to you?

THE ATROCIOUS UNCLE: Boredom. I'm bored.

THE UNHAPPY AUNT: So you're bored, are you? Oh, too bad I'm paralyzed, or I'd braid myself a narcissus wreath and dance you a dance of the South Sea Islands. Remember how in Junction City . . .

THE ATROCIOUS UNCLE: Where's our pussycat?

THE UNHAPPY AUNT: It went out on the roof.

THE ATROCIOUS UNCLE: Too bad, I wanted to strangle it. Strangle. Strangle. Boredom.

THE UNHAPPY AUNT: Oh, strangle me, miserable wretch. After all, there's little joy in life for me as it is, since you gouged out my left eye and I'll only see half the spring this year.

THE ATROCIOUS UNCLE: Spring? Spring will come when the general returns.

THE UNHAPPY AUNT: But will he return?

THE ATROCIOUS UNCLE: He'll return, sword in hand. On a white horse. And all the bells will ring. And there won't be any more boredom, only building for the future and the great inspired cry of regeneration. The price of eggs will go down. I'll become district governor of Smolensk. God save the general.

THE GENERAL: (*Doesn't return.*)

THE ATROCIOUS UNCLE: (*Strangles the cat.*)

CURTAIN

1946

215

THE LITTLE THEATRE OF *THE GREEN GOOSE*

Has the Honor of Presenting

A Bloody Drama in Three Acts
With Vinegar
Taken from Life in the Upper Reaches of Academic
High Society
entitled
"Pickled Alive"

In which appear:
GASPARON, the ghastly baron
GASPARINA, the unfaithful baroness
and JEAN ODOROUS, the faithful servant

ACT I

Setting: A secret gallery leading to the door of the Baroness'
bedroom.

BARON: (*Peeping through the keyhole*) By Jove, Jean, I've had my
fill. The Baroness is deceiving me with a full professor. I
won't live through the aforementioned, inasmuch as I'm having a moral breakdown. (*Has a moral breakdown, as well as tottering on his feet.*)

JEAN ODOROUS: Courage, my lord. Your fears will soon be laid
to rest.

BARON: (*Peeping through the keyhole once more.*) Whew. They already have been.

ACT II

Setting: the Baron's library. In the middle of the library a jar of
alarming proportions.

BARON: (*Suffering; aside*) If the soul weren't immortal, I'd say
my soul had been mortally wounded. Women, women! (*A
knock.*) Ontray!

BARONESS: (*Entering*) Don't you want a drink, Joevanny?

BARON: Yes, thanks. (*His teeth chattering*)

BARONESS: Oh, almighty God! What does that sinister jar mean?

BARON: Ha, ha! You'll find out about all that soon enough. Jean!

JEAN: (*Entering*) Did madam ring?

BARON: Nonsense. Madam didn't ring and will never ring again. Die, faithless woman. (*Aided by Jean, he grabs hold of the Baroness, and they both stuff the latter into the waiting jar, pouring vinegar over the contents.*)

Note: To spare the nerves of the esteemed Public, the remaining phases of the pickling process take place offstage.

ACT III

(*Conceived in an operatic style*)
ARIA OF THE BARONESS IN THE JAR
(*in verse*)

My career glittered like a star,
Today that star's gone out. For being fickle
The Baron's put me in a jar
And now I'm leading the life of a pickle.

CURTAIN
falls by mistake, so it goes back up again

ARIA OF THE BARONESS IN THE JAR
(*continuation*)

My prayers can never alter my fate,
I can't get out from where I've sunk.
Who'd fall in love with me in such a state?
Except maybe some drunk.

1947

THE LITTLE THEATRE OF *THE GREEN GOOSE*

Has the Honor of Presenting

"The Peculiar Waiter"

In which appear:
THE PECULIAR WAITER
FIRST CUSTOMER
SECOND CUSTOMER
THIRD CUSTOMER

PECULIAR WAITER: What did you have?

FIRST CUSTOMER: Lamb chops.

PECULIAR WAITER: Lamb chops two dollars.
No cocktails?

FIRST CUSTOMER: No cocktails.

PECULIAR WAITER: No cocktails five dollars.
Any beer?

FIRST CUSTOMER: No beer.

PECULIAR WAITER: No beer six dollars, chops two dollars; that's eight dollars; thank you, sir. (*To the Second Customer*) You had tongue with horseradish sauce?

SECOND CUSTOMER: No, three eggs scrambled.

PECULIAR WAITER: No tongue with horseradish sauce two-fifty, three eggs scrambled ninety-nine cents, no champagne sixty dollars; altogether that comes to sixty-three dollars and forty-nine cents; thank you, sir; good-night, sir.

THIRD CUSTOMER: (*Gets up and pokes a hole in the Peculiar Waiter's head with his oak cane.*)

PECULIAR WAITER: A hole in the head eight-fifty, pork chops two dollars; altogether that comes to ten-fifty; no beer a dollar, so that's eleven-fifty; thank you, sir; good-night, sir. Come back again, sir.

CURTAIN

1946

THE LITTLE THEATRE OF *THE GREEN GOOSE*

Has the Honor of Presenting

"The Burial of a War Criminal"

In which appear:
THE FUNERAL DIRECTOR
THE GRAVEDIGGERS
and THE PUBLIC

THE FUNERAL DIRECTOR: Ladies and gentlemen. In a moment War Criminal No. 8 will be buried. Quiet, please.

THE PUBLIC: Bravo!

THE GRAVEDIGGERS: (*Lower the corpse.*)

THE PUBLIC: Encore!

THE GRAVEDIGGERS: (*Raise the corpse up and let it down again.*)

THE PUBLIC: Encore!!

THE GRAVEDIGGERS: (*As above*)

THE PUBLIC: (*Completely carried away*) Encore!!!

THE GRAVEDIGGERS: (*Keep giving encores without stopping*)

THE PUBLIC: (*Delighted to have disposed of the war problem, demands further encores.*)

CURTAIN

1946

THE LITTLE THEATRE OF *THE GREEN GOOSE*

Has the Honor of Presenting

Act III of an Opera
called
"Judith and Holofernes"

In which appear:
  JUDITH
  HOLOFERNES
  CHORUS
    and TRUMPETERS

JUDITH:

> The day's heat is spent.
> The shadows deep.
> There in his tent
> Holofernes sleeps.

(*She goes into the tent where Holofernes is napping.*)

> And yet how sad it seems!
> My heart has almost stopped.
> Now, head, I'll cut you off.
> Chop.

CHORUS:

> She's cutting off, she's cutting off,
> She's cutting off his head.
> She's cutting off, she's cutting off,
> She's cutting off.

TRUMPETERS: (*Trumpeting*) Ta-ta-ta-ta.

JUDITH:

> The bloody work is ended,
> And joy is mixed with dread,
> Now, head, I've cut you off,
> Oh, Holofernes' head.

CHORUS:

> She has cut off, she has cut off,
> She has cut off his head.
> She has cut off, she has cut off,
> She has cut off.

TRUMPETERS: (*Trumpeting*) Ta-ta-ta-ta.

HOLOFERNES: (*With a missing head*) Wonder how I'll get along now. Unless I get used to it.

CHORUS: (*Casts doubt on Holofernes' assertion.*)

> Forsooth, forsooth,
> You dirty dog, forsooth,
> Get used, get used,
> You think that you'll get used?

CURTAIN

1947

THE LITTLE THEATRE OF *THE GREEN GOOSE*

Has the Honor of Presenting

With Horror
A Play in Prose and Verse
called
"When Orpheus Played"

Characters:
MAESTRO ORPHEUS
and MANY WILD ANIMALS

Motto:
"Orpheus, son of Apollo and the muse Clio, played so beautifully and ardently on his instrument that the wildest animals heard him with emotion and immediately grew tame, so to speak, automatically."

—Professor Bączyński,
Mytho- and Angelological Dictionary,
Fourth edition, Lumberville, 1878.

ORPHEUS: (*In a grotto*) Something tells me I feel like playing something. But what to play? Aha, now I know what to play. Well, folks, I'll play "The Turkish March" by Wolfgang Amadeus Mozart. (*Turning to his strings, which are strung on a pocket harp*)

> Say, strings, what could be finer,
> Than Mozart's "Turkish March" in A minor?

(*The strains of the well-known composition by the talented composer issue forth from the grotto in a flawlessly executed performance.*)
LION:

> When I hear Orpheus play his lyre
> It stirs me to the inmost fiber.

(*Weeps and is morally transformed to such an extent that instead of devouring innocent creatures, he masters with lightning speed the fine art of tailoring and sews Orpheus a winter overcoat.*)
EIGHT TIGERS:

> The way he plays affects us too,
> Friend lion, the same as it does you.

(*Become hairdressers.*)
Scandalmongering Old Hag:
  Maestro Orpheus, your art
  Finds its way straight to the heart.
(*Licks Orpheus' feet and undergoes a spiritual rebirth.*)

(*In a while the whole neighboring town enjoys the services of the animals, tamed and trained by the playing of Orpheus, son of Apollo and the muse Clio. A certain lion, brother of the tailor-lion, becomes a motorman-lion on the local streetcars; the tigers, on account of their colored coats, decorate the lawns for lack of flowers in winter; wild, towering giraffes are turned into street lights, etc.*)

CURTAIN
comes down, lowered by an anteater

1949

THE LITTLE THEATRE OF *THE GREEN GOOSE*

Has the Honor of Presenting

"The Flood That Failed in Winter"

In which appear:

NOAH
NOAH'S WIVES
NOAH'S CHILDREN
and NOAH'S ANIMALS

NOAH: Honored guests, friends, and relatives!

ANIMALS: Please make it brief.

NOAH: I'm just about finished. Now, as I've explained to you, our Biblical situation doesn't leave us any way out. As you can see, all the waters have frozen over, which makes the ark an absurdity. Do you all agree that we should turn the ark into a sleigh?

WIVES AND CHILDREN OF NOAH: (*Stamping their feet with cold*) Brrr-brrr! We agree.

NOAH: (*Turns the ark into a sleigh, attaches bells, and the whole group rides off up to Mount Ararat on a sleigh ride.*)

CURTAIN

1947

THE LITTLE THEATRE OF *THE GREEN GOOSE*

Has the Honor of Presenting

A Real-Life Drama
called
"In the Clutches of Caffeine"
or
"The Frightful Effects of an Illegal Operation"

In which appear:
ROBERT
ROBERTA, Robert's wife
THE JAMAICA CHARLATAN

(*Scenes I and III represent a villa on the edge of a precipice. Scene II
in the Jamaica Charlatan's office.*)

SCENE I

ROBERT: *J'adore le café. J'adore le café.* I love coffee. Drink.
ROBERTA: Robert, stop guzzling down that hideous coffee. You
know how terribly bad it is for your heart.
ROBERT: (*With a diabolical gleam in his eyes*) For what?

SCENE II

ROBERT: Are you the Jamaica Charlatan?
JAMAICA CHARLATAN: Yes, I am. I can change sex and height. I
can make hair grow. I can make people younger. I perform
miracles. On request I soar through the air as Miss Ophelia
in a transformed shape. Specialty, teeth and hearts.
ROBERT: Yank away.
JAMAICA CHARLATAN: What? A tooth?
ROBERT: No. A heart.
JAMAICA CHARLATAN:
You don't like love, but coffee? Drink!
Because at last you've found the man
Who'll cure your heartaches in a wink:
The famous Jamaica Charlatan.

225

X. "In the Clutches of Caffeine," from Konstanty Ildefons Gałczyński's The Little Theatre of *The Green Goose*. Presented at the Walden Theatre, New York, in 1975. Directed by William Korff. (Photograph by Warren C. Levy.)

Just drop ten dollars in the bank.
Thanks. The knives are on the cart.
With a snippety-snip, clinkety-clank;
Whoosh-whish! Good-bye, sweet heart!

(Takes out Robert's heart. Robert immediately goes out for a cup of coffee.)

SCENE III

ROBERTA: At last you've come back, darling. There's some marvelous bean soup in the mess hall.

ROBERT: Never. *J'adore le café.* From now on it's going to be nothing but coffee.

ROBERTA: Oh, that coffee again. You'll ruin your heart completely, Robert.

ROBERT: Oh, not anymore now.

ROBERTA: *(Notices the black hole in the place where Robert normally kept his fountain pen.)* Good heavens, you look strange! Come here, close to me. Kiss me. By Jove, I don't hear your heart beating at all.

ROBERT: And you won't hear it anymore. For only ten dollars I had my heart taken out, and now I can drink coffee night and day without having to worry about apoplexy. *J'adore le café.* Drink.

ROBERTA: *(Gives him a bucket of coffee.)*

ROBERT: *(Disappointed)** Coffee doesn't taste good anymore. I don't feel like kissing. It seems you have to put your heart into everything. But now I don't have a heart anymore. And that's why I can't love either coffee or you, Roberta. Then what is life? *(Throws himself over the precipice.)*

CURTAIN

1946

---

* Robert must be played by a consummate actor who can portray Robert's disappointment with all the resources of the art of pantomime (author's note).

THE LITTLE THEATRE OF *THE GREEN GOOSE*

Has the Honor of Presenting

"Miracle in the Desert"

In the principal role:
  ALOYSIUS PTARMIGAN
In an episodic role:
  A MALE BABY

Setting: Desert, palm trees, camels.

ALOYSIUS PTARMIGAN: Here I am in the desert. No water, no cool shade, not a single co-op. Desert, thy name is hopelessness. But what's that that's making such remarkable sounds under a cactus leaf? Aha, it's a male baby abandoned by a degenerate tourist. By Jove, I'd rather die myself than leave this babe uncared for! Courage, Ptarmigan! (*Takes the babe by the hand.*)

But how will I feed you, poor little thing? Not a brewery on the horizon, and personally speaking, I'm a man. The only thing left is faith in miracles. (*He has faith and immediately grows lady's breasts.*)

A miracle! A miracle! Oh, take some refreshment, my babe, and then go to sleep like an angel.

BABY: (*He's a realist and doesn't believe in miracles; starts to cry.*) Aaaaaaaaa . . . !!!

PTARMIGAN: (*Notices that the breasts are there but don't have any nourishment in them; gets upset.*) O-o-o-o-o-o-o-o-oh . . . !

BABY: (*Pulls out a package of powdered milk; takes some refreshment.*)

DESERT, PALM TREES, AND CAMELS: (*Split their sides laughing.*)

PTARMIGAN: I'm leaving, clutching my crumbling faith in miracles in my right hand and my shattered world view in my left. (*Leaves.*)

CURTAIN
gets caught on a palm tree as it falls

1947

XI. "Miracle in the Desert," from William Korff's production of plays from *The Little Theatre* of *The Green Goose*. (Photograph by Warren C. Levy.)

THE LITTLE THEATRE OF *THE GREEN GOOSE*

Has the Honor of Presenting

A Ballet
called
"The Poet Is in Bad Form"

(The stage represents the Poet's apartment. On the walls pictures of various things. The Poet's Relatives, both Close and Distant, sit on chairs against the walls. The Poet himself sits at a table, almost entirely buried in a mountain of manuscripts.)

POET: *(Executes the so-called* pas de quoi, *which is to signify that his writing isn't going too well; he tears up a manuscript; as a sign of protest he pours a bottle of green ink over his head; executes three* pas de quoi, *one leap* à rebours, *and three* châteaux d'Espagne.*)*

MOTHER-IN-LAW: *(Executes a gloomy tarantella, which is to signify a certain state of economic anxiety, or—if my son-in-law stops writing, what'll we live on? In addition the mother-in-law executes four pirouettes* à la saucisse *in a more optimistic spirit, or—perhaps my son-in-law will still go on writing.)*

DISTANT RELATIVES: *(Who have been helped out by the Poet with loans, both large and small [in the period of the great outpouring of his creative energy], express, in the form of the so-called* danse macabre, *their grief at the ebbing of his creative energy.)*

POET: *(Totally abandoned by Inspiration, tears out his hair, eyebrows, eyelashes, and other things.)*

CLOSE RELATIVES: *(Wag their heads in three-four time.)*

POET: *(Makes a superhuman effort of will; masters himself; his eyes flash like spring lightning, and behold, inspired works begin to cover the parchment.)*

CLOSE AND DISTANT RELATIVES: *(Joyful dance, a form of can-can and* pas de chose.*)*

CURTAIN

1950

THE LITTLE THEATRE OF *THE GREEN GOOSE*

Has the Honor of Presenting

A Play
About the Life of the Intellectual Elite
entitled
"Hamlet and the Waitress"

Characters:
   HAMLET, Prince of Denmark
   WAITRESS, that kind of woman
   MAURICE EVANS, no comment
   DEVILISH PETE, a pig

Place: A pub, "At the Sign of the Plucked Eyebrows."
Time: Indefinite.

HAMLET: (*Bass*) What can I have?

WAITRESS: Everything. (*Unfastens her brooch and takes off her shoes.*)

HAMLET: (*Soprano; firmly*) No. We'll put that off till Tuesday. I mean what can I have in the way of something to drink?

WAITRESS: Coffee, tea.

HAMLET: (*Lyric tenor*) Then I'll take coffee. No. Tea. No. Coffee. No. Tea. No. But why not tea? No. Coffee. Coffee. Tea. Tea. Coffee. Coffee. Coffee. Coffee. (*A pause; dimming of the lights; mezzosoprano*)
Tea!

WAITRESS: But why not coffee?

MAURICE EVANS: But why not tea?

HAMLET: (*Dies from a lack of decision and a twist of the guts at a sharp turn in history.*)

DEVILISH PETE: It's just ghastly. The women are going crazy. (*Writes in firm white chalk on Hamlet's black coffin:* HAMLET IDIOT.)

CURTAIN

1948

THE LITTLE THEATRE OF *THE GREEN GOOSE*

Has the Honor of Presenting

A Polish Drama
Of the So-called "Ponderous" Variety
entitled
"He Couldn't Wait It Out"

In which appear:
HE and SHE

ACT I

SHE: Do you love me?
HE: I love you.
SHE: And will you always love me?
HE: Always.
SHE: Even if I leave you?
HE: What? (*Has an epileptic fit.*)
SHE: Calm down, baby. For just a minute. While I go to the store. To get your great favorite—hot dogs.
HE: Oh, that's different. Get ten pounds. The night is ours.
SHE: Bye-bye, darling. And will you miss me?
HE: Yes, I'll miss you, dearest. I'll die I'll miss you so much. So come racing right back. Don't torture your turtledove.

ACT II

HE: (*Alone*) Waiting's a perfect hell! My feelings are a hurricane! No. I can't stand it any longer. (*He can't stand it any longer, goes cross-eyed, mad, after which he falls over on the floor with a crash and dies from longing.*)

ACT III

SHE: (*Without moving*) Oh!
(*She lets the hot dogs fall out of her hands and strews the aforementioned him with hot dogs as though with flowers.*)

CURTAIN

1947

THE LITTLE THEATRE OF *THE GREEN GOOSE*

Has the Honor of Presenting

Its Author Wielding a Terrible Pen
"The Tragic End of Mythology"

Characters:
    LEDA, the lawful wife of Tyndareus
    JOVE, a noted sex fiend
    and A FRYING PAN

LEDA: Jove! Ah!

JOVE: (*Grim; with a frying pan hidden in the folds of his chlamys*)
    What now?

LEDA: Jove, oh, how handsome you were as a swan! How you
    kissed me! How you kissed me!

JOVE: Well, what of it? That's enough rhapsodizing. What I'd
    like to know is, Where are the eggs, and how many are
    there?

LEDA: Here they are, darling. Here. Three. Written out,
    t-h-r-e-e. Just the way it is in all the handbooks on classical
    mythology. And the sequence of events is the same. First you
    changed into a swan. Then that night in Acapulco. And in
    just a minute now our three mythological children, Castor,
    Pollux, and Helen, will be hatched from the three mythologi-
    cal eggs.

JOVE: (*Very grim, nervously handling the frying pan hidden in the
    folds of his chlamys*) That's enough!
    (*Pulls out the frying pan from under his arm, turns on the electric
    stove, and using the three mythological eggs, whips up some realistic
    scrambled eggs with chives.*)

LEDA: What have you done, miserable wretch?

JOVE: What the conscience of my Jovian stomach dictated.
    You're an idiot, Leda. But maybe you'll understand this: we
    can't expect anything worthwhile from Castor and Pollux,
    and as for Helen, everybody knows the consequences—the
    Trojan war. And we've certainly had enough wars.
    (*Digs into the scrambled eggs.*)

THE CURTAIN
falls

1949

THE LITTLE THEATRE OF *THE GREEN GOOSE*

Has the Honor of Presenting

"Principles of the Relay Cure"
or the so-called
"Transfer Therapy"

ACT I

FIRST DOCTOR: What seems to be the trouble?

PATIENT: My foot.

FIRST DOCTOR: Your foot? In that case you'll go down to Clinic F.

PATIENT: Yes, but that's just it, I can't walk.

FIRST DOCTOR: Oh, really? Well then, they'll carry you.

ACT II

SECOND DOCTOR: What seems to be the trouble?

PATIENT: My foot.

SECOND DOCTOR: Which one?

PATIENT: The left one.

SECOND DOCTOR: Splendid. Orderly Junebug, carry this patient to Clinic LF.

ACT III

THIRD DOCTOR: What seems to be the trouble?

PATIENT: My left foot.

THIRD DOCTOR: Very good, but is it more of a nervous complaint or a physical pain?

PATIENT: Nervous.

THIRD DOCTOR: Wonderful. I'll have you transferred to the clinic for those with nervous disorders of the left foot, or Clinic NLF.

ACT IV

PATIENT: My head's starting to ache slightly.
FOURTH DOCTOR: Great. Now we'll finally be able to make a slight improvement in the statistics of the clinic for the mentally ill.

ACT V

FIFTH DOCTOR: That patient looks sad. Are you by any chance longing for another life?
PATIENT: Oh, yes, extremely.

EPILOGUE

(*An elegant carriage from the Rest Institute* ETERNITY-AETERNITAS *pulls up, and the Patient, now liberated from cares, but well stocked with several thousand diagnoses, drives off in the well-known direction.*)

CURTAIN
comes down forever

1947

THE LITTLE THEATRE OF *THE GREEN GOOSE*

Has the Honor of Presenting

"The Seven Sleeping Brothers"

FIRST BROTHER: (*Snores.*)
SECOND BROTHER: (*Snores.*)
THIRD BROTHER: (*Snores.*)
FOURTH BROTHER: (*Snores.*)
FIFTH BROTHER: (*Snores.*)
SIXTH BROTHER: (*Snores.*)
SEVENTH BROTHER: (*Snores horribly.*)

CURTAIN

1946

THE LITTLE THEATRE OF *THE GREEN GOOSE*

Has the Honor of Presenting

"Greedy Eve"

In which appear:
THE SNAKE, ADAM, and EVE

SNAKE: (*Gives Eve the apple on a tray.*) Take a bite and give it to Adam.
ADAM: (*Roars*) Give me a bite. Give me a bite.
EVE: (*Eats the whole apple.*)
SNAKE: (*Aghast*) What'll happen now?
ADAM: It doesn't look so good. The whole Bible's a total loss.

CURTAIN

1946

XII. "Greedy Eve" (Eve, the Snake, and Adam), from William Korff's production of plays from The Little Theatre of *The Green Goose*. (Photograph by Warren C. Levy.)

THE LITTLE THEATRE OF *THE GREEN GOOSE*

Has the Honor of Presenting

"Rain"

CHORUS OF PEOPLE WAITING FOR THE BUS: Oh, how boring it is to wait for the bus.

RAIN: (*Begins to pour.*)

CHORUS OF PEOPLE WAITING FOR THE BUS:
> Screw this rain.
> Screw this waiting.
> Screw this bus.

A MAN DRIVING BY IN HIS CAR: (*Gets out of his car in front of the line of people waiting.*) My car's very tiny. My car won't hold all of you. But there's one simple thing I can do: I can get out of my car; I can stand in line; I can wait and get soaked with you.

(*Stands last in line.*)

CURTAIN

1949

THE LITTLE THEATRE OF *THE GREEN GOOSE*

Has the Honor of Presenting

"Lord Hamilton's Night"

In which appear:
LORD HAMILTON
INNKEEPER
and GRANNY

Setting: An inn, "At the Sign of the Gold Owl and Multiplication Table." A windy night in early spring.

INNKEEPER: Goddam. I wanted to close up now. Alas. Here comes that terrible rake Hamilton, with an unsteady gait, holding a Dutch lantern above his head to light his way. We'll have to open up, Granny.

INNKEEPER'S GRANNY: (*Opens up.*)

LORD HAMILTON: (*Entering*) Good evening, ghosts. Give me something to drink. Life is a pun, and a pun is nonsense with a double meaning. So I'd like a double whiskey.

INNKEEPER'S GRANNY: (*Pours him a drink.*) Here it is, milord.

LORD HAMILTON: (*Pulls out a pistol and shoots pure, innocent Granny dead.*)

INNKEEPER'S GRANNY: By Jove!
(*Dies.*)

INNKEEPER: I notice that your lordship has taken the liberty of murdering my beloved Granny as a prank. Isn't that too much?

LORD HAMILTON: (*Observing with interest the cloud of smoke above the muzzle of his pistol.*) I don't know. That's up to you. Add grandmother to the bill.

INNKEEPER: (*Adds her to the bill.*)
Wind. Terror.

CURTAIN

1947

THE LITTLE THEATRE OF *THE GREEN GOOSE*

Has the Honor of Presenting

A Meteorological Drama
entitled
"Family Happiness"
or
"Watch out for Expletives"

In which appear:
DADDY
MUMMY
GRANDMA
TINY TOT
THUNDER AND LIGHTNING
and PORPHIRION THE DONKEY

SCENE: A quiet little apolitical, domestic fireside after supper.

GRANDMA: It's so cozy here! (*Adjusts her glasses and darns everything over and over again.*)

MUMMY: (*Looking at Daddy*) Together at last! (*Cries from happiness.*)

TINY TOT: (*Plays with his plush toy dwarf.*)

(*Pause; silence; happiness.*)

DADDY: (*Suddenly*) No, I'm rotting in this bourgeois household! I've had enough! I'm made for better things! I feel I have unlimited potentialities! Hold me back! (*Looking at Grandma and Tiny Tot*) Thunder and lightning! Blast it all!

THUNDER AND LIGHTNING: (*Blasts it all and totally does away with the problem of a quiet little apolitical, domestic fireside after supper.*)

PORPHIRION THE DONKEY: Gracious me, and it all seemed to be getting off to such a nice start!

CURTAIN

1947

THE LITTLE THEATRE OF *THE GREEN GOOSE*

Has the Honor of Presenting

"The End of the World"

GOD: Rrrrrrr. I proclaim the end of the world. Rrrrrrr.

(The whole cosmic contraption starts to come apart.)

BUREAUCRAT: Rrrrrrr. That's very fine. Rrrrrrr. But where is the relevant document in this case, duly stamped and bearing the number assigned to it up there, which should have been entered in our correspondence file?

(It turns out that there was such a document, but that it got lost, so although the end of the world really does take place in actual fact, officially it doesn't count for anything.)

CURTAIN
falls optimistically

1947

241

IV

The Bim-Bom Troupe and the
Afanasjeff Family Circus

THE BIM-BOM TROUPE

Three Plays from
Joy in Earnest (1956)

Translated by Daniel Gerould from Jerzy Afanasjew, *Sezon kolorowych chmur: Gdańskie teatry eksperymentalne* (Gdynia: Wydawnictwo Morskie, 1968).

"Snouts"

(An Antimilitarist Picture)

by JERZY AFANASJEW
and the BIM-BOM TROUPE

Cast:

POLITICIAN FOR A CERTAIN POWER—T. Wojtych
CHORUS OF NAZIS—J. Futa
                 B. Kobiela
                 J. Karwowski
                 T. Kowalik
                 O. Wasilewski

Time: two minutes

(The second curtain opens. At the back of the stage a flat backdrop showing three huge heads in Prussian helmets with spikes. Horrific white eyes peering out from under the painted helmets. The faces are skulls. The mouths are gigantic, man-sized. Enter onstage, from the right side, a little man dressed in black. He is the Politician for a Certain Power. Tail coat, patent-leather shoes, white cuffs—why, even white gloves. Instead of a face, a sneering empty strip of white cardboard. A paper face. Worse, the absence of a face. On his grotesque head . . . a top hat like a black pot. How very small the politician seems compared to those huge heads looming in the background. He comes over to the middle of the stage, with all the airs of a politician bows to the audience, pulls out a white baton from the inside pocket of his tail coat with a graceful flourish, raises his hands and . . . turns in the direction of the huge heads. Across his shoulders ÜBERROOSTER *is written in Gothic script. He begins to conduct. And now the mouths of the huge heads start to move. Singing can be heard coming out of the heads—resounding, ever mounting. As they sing, the mammoth open mouths on the backdrop create fathomless abysses. Heili-heilo-heila, heili-heilo-heila, heili-heilo-heila, ha, ha, ha, ha, ha, ha, ha! Louder*

and louder. Nearer and nearer! The singing reaches full strength. The Politician for a Certain Power bows to the public. Without paying any attention to where he is going, he steps backward to the rear. And that is when he falls into one of the snout mouths on the backdrop as they are opening in song. The snout mouth devours him with relish. It swallows him to the accompaniment of a fascist march which it is singing. To the accompaniment of this Nazi fracas, the joyful tramp of hobnail boots, fortissimo. Darkness.)

"Faust"

by JERZY AFANASJEW
and the BIM-BOM TROUPE

Cast:

ACTOR WITH THE GREAT THEATRE—J. Afanasjew
POSTER HANGER—M. Kochanowski

Time: two minutes, thirty seconds

(*Enter the Poster Hanger on the proscenium in front of the curtain. Gray workman's overalls; bucket with paste, brush, roll of posters under his arm. He wanders slowly across from the left to the right of the proscenium. A circle of light escorts him. He draws near the left side of the proscenium. There is a small signboard for sticking up posters waiting for him there. The Poster Hanger puts down his bucket, smears the signboard with paste, sticks up a poster with the lettering "Faust." He picks up his bucket and goes back the same way he came. The light remains on the poster. The Great Waltz from the opera* Faust, *played on two pianos, slowly cuts in. The curtain opens.*)

The stage represents the theatre as though seen from the back. Upstage another curtain opening. In front of it, the prompter's box. The Actor with the Great Theatre stands with his back to us, facing an audience further upstage. He is dressed in the classic costume—white ruff, lace cuffs, silk cape, ring—and is making broad, striking gestures for the spectators. The Actor begins his Great Soliloquy. The Greatest Soliloquy in the World, about the preservation of one's youth. His soliloquy is full of fascination and satanism. His movements the Movements of an Actor with the Great Theatre. The Greatest Theatre in the World!

The Actor has finished. Great Applause from the Great Audience flows through megaphones. The Actor with the Great Theatre steps back to the rear, beyond the dividing line of the curtain, which is opening and closing upstage to the bravos. When the curtain opens every now and

then, the Actor strikes the official pose as Faust, bowing deeply and expansively. When the curtain is closed again, the Actor "becomes a private person"; his figure shows fatigue; he wipes the sweat off with a handkerchief. There, the curtain upstage opens for the last time! And it closes. Now the stage is lighted by a dim, dirty, workaday light. The Actor with the Great Theatre becomes little, pathetic, hunched over. He takes off one of his beautiful shoes and dumps a stone out of it which was hurting him during his Great Soliloquy. Tired, he wipes his forehead again with a dirty handkerchief kept hidden in his sleeve. He looks in all his pockets for his glasses, and having found a weird little pair of spectacles, he now plans to come down from the stage. Therefore he turns facing us, puts the glasses on his nose, and lo and behold, suddenly . . . he notices the audience, the real audience, our audience, which has been spying on him from behind! Shocked, throwing up his hands in a gesture of amazement, he speaks to us, to the audience, in a puzzled tone of voice, as though he couldn't explain to himself why people are still sitting in their seats and the curtain still hasn't come down.
ACTOR WITH THE GREAT THEATRE: . . . Intermission . . .
(*Then, quickly, he shuffles out.*)

INTERMISSION

"The Professor"

by SŁAWOMIR MROŻEK

Cast:

STUDENT—E. Krzemiński
PROFESSOR—T. Wojtych
DIRECTOR OF THE SCHOOL—ROOSTER—W. Bielicki
VOICES I, II, III, IV—The Company

Time: nine minutes

(The Student appears in front of the curtain on the proscenium. Blue uniform, white stockings, a slingshot in his hand.)

STUDENT: It was mathematics class. It was autumn. Rain was falling. The fires hadn't been lighted in the stoves yet. None of us had done our homework. The Professor announced, "Each student will have his turn at the blackboard and do three problems." Logarithms. Discriminants. Polynomials. Rain. And there was only one last resort. Our old ruse. We all knew about it. And that very day we decided to use it. I can still see the Professor coming into the classroom, looking very small and old-fashioned . . . "Professor, sir, don't you remember?" I was the one who had discovered that the Professor loved to talk about the city of his youth. The city the Professor was in only once. The city of Vienna.

As soon as we had discovered his secret, the Professor couldn't defend himself anymore. Absolutely terrified of mathematics, we would cynically get the Professor excited. "Professor, sir, tell us about the Burg! Professor, sir, tell us about the Bahnhof! Professor, sir!" Until he gave in and started to tell us all about it, growing so enthusiastic that his glasses began to gleam. And meanwhile we—feeling relieved—pitched pennies, threw spitballs, and carved funny sayings on the wooden benches with a penknife. Such as "Cicero's bust is in our class / But your Vienna is a pain in the

249

. . ." All right, our standards weren't too high. So that's what always happened. Until one day . . . He came into the classroom more hunched over than usual. The fires hadn't been lighted in the stoves yet. The windows were all fogged over. Logarithms, discriminants, polynomials . . . An odor of chalk and ink. Rain was falling . . .

(The curtain goes up. The stage represents a classroom in a lycée for boys. The outlines of several school benches and the Professor's desk are visible, drawn on white boards against the background of a hanging black backdrop upstage. The students sit two by two on several benches further upstage. They are dressed identically—uniforms with high collars, knickers, long white socks, and black gaiters. Over their heads, against the black background of the backdrop, something like a little cloud, which has made its way into the classroom; it is partly covered with tulle and partly serves as a school blackboard with a log written on it: $(x + y) = A \, e \, (+ c)$. *The Professor stands behind the lectern on his desk. Shapeless gray pants that are too long for him, gray hair, threadbare old frock coat, old-fashioned flowing tie. A globe at his feet. In the rear, upstage behind him, the door to the corridor. The Professor keeps shuffling his textbooks and exercise books back and forth . . . He speaks half-angrily, grumbling.)*

PROFESSOR: Vienna, Vienna! Well, now, Vienna!

CHORUS OF VOICES: Pfessor, sir . . . !

VOICE I: Please, Professor, sirrr! Tell us!

CHORUS OF VOICES: Pleeeease! Tell us!

VOICE II: What it was like in the Praterrr! . . .

CHORUS OF VOICES: . . . In the Praterrr! . . .

VOICE III: In the Schonnbrunnnn! . . .

CHORUS OF VOICES: . . . Brunnnn! . . .

(The Professor shakes his head impatiently.)

VOICE IV: *(From the corner, in a high-pitched treble)* And the Wurcle!!

CHORUS OF VOICES: *(Imploringly)* Pfessor, SIR! . . .

(The Professor shakes his head, then repeats more gently)

PROFESSOR: . . . Vienna . . . *(He looks out the window; lost in thought, he repeats once more)* Vienna . . .

(A coach passes by outside; the sound of horses' hooves can be heard clattering against the wet asphalt. The effect fades away. The Professor goes on talking, more to himself than to anyone else.)

PROFESSOR: Oh, yes. Who would have thought then . . . Going to the Kronprinz by hackney coach, the electric trolley ringing its bell, the cobblestones glistening . . . Huge black umbrellas, umbrellas like this . . . (*He demonstrates with his hands, as though he were showing what a big fish he had caught.*) . . . What am I saying? Bigger . . . Like this, I'd swear! The rain on the hood of the cab: pit, pit, pit, pit, pit . . . Just a minute. Or like this: pit, pat, pit, pit, pat, pit . . .

(*Voice I, the student on the last bench, to a classmate in a stage whisper*)

VOICE I: We haven't heard that one yet! . . .

PROFESSOR: . . . Vienna . . . Now here's the Kaiser Platz and the two-wheeled cabs, the hackney coaches, the rickety old buggies, the elegant carriages, and here and there an automobile: beep-beeeep, look, everybody! Up above, a violet-colored mist; lower down, the gas lanterns, the yellow spheres, and the reflected gleam from the wet pavement. And the din. Oh, yes! The din! Whoa! Hey! Just where do you think you're going, old boy? No getting through here. No getting through? Keep on, keep on, can't you see I'm going to the Burgtheater too?—To the Burgtheater?—Yaaa, that's right, to the Burgtheater! To the Burgtheater . . . A throng crowding at the doors. (*He twirls his nonexistent mustache.*) The ladies are making their entrance. Drops of rain on their furs, long trains trailing behind their gowns. And the gas hisses—flunkies in livery bow down to us. And the jangling of spurs on marble staircases. Plumes of ostrich feathers swirl in the mirrors. A final moment in the foyer for adjusting one's cravat . . . (*He adjusts his cravat.*) . . . Just two more steps and we're in our loge.

VOICE I: (*Listening with rapt attention*) In our loge!

PROFESSOR: Of course: I was twenty years old then! (*The Professor, who until this moment has been sitting down, now stands up, holds out his arms in front of him, half-closes his eyes, and remains silent for a moment.*) . . . Three flights higher! The parterres and the galleries! The alabaster foreheads of ladies against the dark red hangings. And torsos of white, black fields of frock coats—the glitter of watch chains and opera glasses. A lively uproar, fans rapidly moving, earrings aquiver, precious

necklaces blazing up and dying out . . . We sit down . . .
(*He sits down.*) . . . The program. (*He pushes a school exercise
book in front of him.*) Cuffs to be checked . . . (*He adjusts his
sleeves ostentatiously.*) . . . Someone peers through a lorgnon
. . . (*He suddenly leaps up in a burst of enthusiasm and starts ges-
ticulating.*) All the silver jewelry, coruscation, cascades of light
from the lamp caryatids, sparks, flashes, fireworks, billions of
glances, the mirrors and everything all together—good Lord,
it was like a solid mountain of light! At the very summit a
vast chandelier of crystal, with at least one hundred candles!
The whole theatre was like a star . . .

VOICE II: (*Carried away*) . . . Like a star? . . .

PROFESSOR: (*Embarrassed*) Naturally. And in front of the stage
itself there was the pit for the orchestra. (*The students, listening more and more attentively, rest their chins in their hands, and
lean their heads forward to hear better.*) From my loge you could
see wonderfully. All the different instruments were there—
the tympani and the strings, violas, drums . . . We should be
able to hear something soon now . . . First the violins, then
the French horns. Good Lord . . . They're starting to tune
up. There! (*He imitates the different voices of the instruments as
they sound before the beginning of a concert.*) . . . Such variety.
Like this . . . (*Listening intently, he puts his finger to his lips.*)
. . . Sssh . . . As though a bird were singing. (*He whistles.*)
A little brook . . . A tiny grove . . . (*And then, in the animated
classroom, he begins to mimic the percussion by drumming loudly on
the lectern.*) The drums beat a thunderous warning!! Hahaaa!
(*He guffaws triumphantly, stirred by the percussion; then suddenly,
quite transported, he speaks in a low tone.*) All of a sudden I take
a look . . . I see the conductor! As though the lights had
been delicately blown out. Dusk falls. The murmur of voices
dies down. Suddenly lighted from below, the curtain becomes a bright claret-colored rectangle which draws all eyes.
Right in front of the footlights there rises up the silhouette
of the conductor. And an odor of dust, a blending of warm
perfumes. With a rustle of pages he thumbs through the
score for a brief moment. He raises his hand, he gives the
signal . . . And so the overture begins. (*He starts to hum. He
hums more and more boldly. He begins to conduct. More and more*

energetically, unconstrainedly. At first the students nod their heads in time with the music; then they enter into the parts for the leading voices. Murmurando. Then more and more distinctly they mimic the various instruments. Crescendo. By degrees the Professor enters completely into his role as a real conductor directing a real orchestra. Finally, with the fortissimo, he starts yelling, in the height of ecstasy, without stopping conducting but outshouting the orchestra.) Look, the first tremors shake the curtain. Gradually . . . it's starting to go up . . . The heavy plush becomes detached from the rows of footlights. Soon the performance will begin! And more and more loudly, fully, boldly, now—the stage can be seen!!! And on the stage . . .

DIRECTOR OF THE SCHOOL: *(He appears in the doorway.)* Professor! *(Everything comes to a stop. Dazed, the Professor still does not come back to reality. He remains rooted to the spot with his hands raised.)* Come with me to my office immediately!

(The Professor partially regains consciousness, awkwardly gathers up the exercise books, texts, and pencils. His hands tremble. Looking straight ahead of him, he climbs down from his dais and passes through the proscenium. He follows the Director, who turns around and goes out first. At this moment a small cockscomb, like a rooster's, can be seen on the Director's head. The students follow the Professor out with their eyes during his entire passage across the proscenium. After the Professor has left, they remain seated for a moment, which is held for rather a long time, with their heads twisted on their shoulders, looking at the door. Finally one of them gets up and speaks loudly, almost dispassionately, with a delicate mixture of objectivity, respect, and admiration.)

STUDENT: What a performance!!

CURTAIN

Selection from
Good Evening, Clown

Selections from "The World
Is Not Such a Bad Place . . ."

Translated by Daniel Gerould.

Good Evening, Clown (1962)

by JERZY AFANASJEW
and the AFANASJEFF FAMILY CIRCUS

Commedia dell' arte
or
"Theatre in the Theatre"

The following are members of the theatre:
THE FIRST HARLEQUIN
PULCINELLA
THE FALSE COLUMBINE
PANTALONE
THE BEAUTIFUL ISABEL

The pantomime is based on three separate "stage strips," three tracks of action. Stage A (the proscenium and the passageway) is the real stage, on which the actors in the street-fair show do their acting and present the play to the people. Stage B simulates the backstage area. Stage C represents "the theatre from the rear," the shadows of the actors seen as though from backstage against the curtain. The spectator has a chance to take a peek at the backstage life of a street-fair theatre. The actor going from the backstage area (stage B) to the proscenium disappears behind the curtain of stage C, we see his shadow, and he appears on the proscenium A. In this way the stage space in front of the spectator watching the play from one location takes on what appears to be rotatory motion. We watch the actor from the rear, from the front, and this amounts to a kind of coefficient of the properties of . . . rotation. The play consists of solo performances—pantomime dramas: lyric, comic, and

This selection is approximately the first third of the show, with one omission.
Translated from Jerzy Afanasjew, *Sezon kolorowych chmur: Gdańskie teatry eksperymentalne* (Gdynia: Wydawnictwo Morskie, 1968).

tragic. Running out from the stage is the "flower way," a passageway connecting the stage with the auditorium, used in the
Japanese theatre KOKUSAI.

PART ONE OF THE WONDER SHOW

*(The lights go out slowly. The Theatre Doorkeeper comes out in front of
the closed curtain—he is an Old Japanese with a little silver bell in his
hand. He heads for the "flower passageway," lighted by leaflike net-
works of little bulbs, which sticks out into the hall where the auditorium
is. A misshapen figure, with a tremendous hump under his red kimono,
he limps with one of his thin black legs. On his face, the grotesquerie of
a classic Japanese mask. The Old Doorkeeper speaks a totally weird,
unrecognizable, improvised "language" from the Far East. From his
pantomime dance gestures we can guess that he is recounting what in a
moment it will be possible to see in the apse of the theatre. With pro-
tracted gestures he calls for quiet and concentration. The ringing of his*

XIII. The Afanasjeff Family Circus in *The Comedy of Masks*. The Gdańsk City
Carnival, 1961. (Photograph by J. Rydzewski.)

XIV. The Afanasjeff Family Circus in *Tralabomba*. Gdańsk, 1962. (Photograph by the Central Film Agency.)

bell during breaks in his singsong speech is a cry for concentration. With humble movements the Japanese extends an invitation, as it were, to watch the street-fair wonder show. He goes out hobbling.)

Lights on the Great Curtain. The street along the passageway dims slowly.

(Distant revue music. The Lady Conductor comes out in front of the curtain. Diminutive cylindrical tail coat made of red satin, legs in dark tights, crooked slippers, baton, ludicrous glasses on her nose. She turns around, directs the invisible street-fair orchestra, which apparently is submerged in the shadows of the curtain. The music, obedient to her frenetic gestures, grows in intensity. The Lady Conductor goes out.)

The curtain rises.

(The stage represents the setting of classic commedia dell' arte. Upstage a street-fair theatre still veiled by a curtain; a triangle of brightly col-

XV. The Afanasjeff Family Circus in *Good Evening, Clown.* Gdańsk, 1962. (Photograph by Z. Grabowiecki.)

ored lights covers its top. On the theatre booth, festive wreaths. Two upright pianos stripped down to the bare strings, one on each side. In front of them, funny little trees—artificial rubber trees in silver flowerpots. To the right, an unstitched armchair; in front of it, a drum; on the drum, a shoe. On top of the upright piano, a bunch of cymbals. In front of the entrance to the "green garden" of the theatre, among brooms of paper trees, stands "rich" Polichinelle. A character frozen in the unmoving gesture of a porcelain figure on a rococo clock. Polichinelle's hands, black as shade, embrace the immaterial light lying before him. His obese white stomach glistens in this light. Polichinelle's face is

an impassive mask with sly round eyes through which for centuries he
has been looking immobilely at the world's soul. The mask of a face old
as the hills, wreathed in the sinister moss of a dirty beard. Hair black,
luxuriant, like a Gypsy's; a diplomat's top hat bought at an auction;
marked by a dark shadow, his mouth open for a scream. Now here
comes Harlequin, entering with tiny little steps. Perhaps from a trip,
since he has a tattered suitcase in his hand, a dignified top hat on his
bright locks, and a long dark scarf trails around his neck. He puts
down his carryall, and having taken out a feather duster made of
rooster feathers, he dusts the sounding boards of the upright pianos, the
miserable paper trees, the porcelain-bright Polichinelle. He pulls a little
key out of his suitcase, and having inserted it between the unfortunate
Polichinelle's shoulders, he carefully winds up his boss, all the while
making improper faces full of weary effort. The sound of Polichinelle's
spring being wound up is heard from hidden loudspeakers. And lo and
behold, Polichinelle begins to move. Like a wooden puppet's, his funny
head wobbles in an unsightly fashion. A strange mechanism makes the
hands of the street-fair statue move. With the step of an inanimate object
he moves forward, closes his huge mouth; with the sleepy movement of
someone just awakened, he stretches his clownish bones and extends his
precious hand to Harlequin. Running through the whole gamut of lighting effects, the spotlights of the street-fair theatre brighten up the
grayness of the sleeping stage. As though the lid of night had been taken
off! Behold the Dawn of the Performance! Behold . . . the Dawn of
Stage Life! The stage sparkles with bright color and shiny glass. Raising his hands comically, Polichinelle sings his greeting to the people in
the musical modulation of Gregorian chant.)*

POLICHINELLE: (*Shaking Harlequin's hand*)

Good evening, . . . Clown! (*He approaches the "flower passageway," sings plaintively and every now and then whistles imperiously,
making it evident that Harlequin is to clear off the stage! Harlequin
trembles with fear like a delicate hothouse plant.*) . . . I am Pulcinella, or Punch. The Director of this theatre. Once I was a
famous clown; I clowned for kings—yes, kings. Now that ar-
thritis has turned me absolutely inside out, I only direct this
here (*sarcastically*) . . . *lousy* . . . business. Because the
theatre is . . . like a girl, Ladies and Gentlemen! It constantly makes demands on us for new caresses and kisses.
Oooh! Just imagine, Dear Friends, that this stage that you see

before you is her head (*points*), right here! Her eyes are just here, . . . her mouth over here. (*Polichinelle addressing people on the right and left side of the auditorium*) You're sitting on her bosom, and you . . . (*To someone sitting in one of the rows farther back*) . . . Hey, Mister! Just where did you sit down . . . my dear Sir? Whaat? (*Threatening playfully with his finger*) My, my, my . . . Every evening we see your tears, or your merriment, because as a matter of fact, even though a good many of you are . . . (*discreetly*) . . . "pilferers." What unites us is a common love of the theatre: for You, it's the Theatre of Money Making; for Us, it's the Theatre of Playing Roles for You . . . with Us as beggars. So it would seem to follow from that . . . that you're not the ones who come to the theatre to amuse yourselves, but just the absolute opposite!! So I beg you: *don't spoil our fun;* go on stealing; keep up the pilfering; be inhuman to your fellow man, or otherwise you'll spoil . . . our fun! . . . If you didn't exist with your absolutely *marvelous* flaws, just what would we have to do, we poor . . . Clowns? But as it is . . . we complement each other marvelously (*to himself*), . . . like the nut and the bolt, like the lady and the gentleman. (*Harlequin appears, gives the "director" a washbasin with a wet shirt. Polichinelle goes on singing while he's wringing out the shirt disgustedly.*) Really and truly, looking at you people out there takes a lot out of a person. In all the theatres all over the world actors are wringing the sweat out of their own shirts in their attempts, somehow or other, to amuse you, fatsoes rolling in money and sitting pretty. Thus, in inaugurating our evening tonight and wishing us all mutual fun, I say to you . . . (*Punch bows to someone in the audience.*) . . . Good . . . Evening, c-l-o-w-n! (*Laughing mockingly, he takes a large bowl of Cologne water and a holy-water sprinkler out of Harlequin's hands. Walking up and down the "flower passageway" and giggling, he consecrates the street-fair audience with hairdresser's water. Finally Polichinelle sits down in the director's chair. His belly shakes with laughter.*)

(*From behind the trees a trumpet flourish is sounded. And a bugle call! A bizarre little cabaret theatre opens its doors; with a rollicking gait, like the Capitoline geese, out comes a fantastic street-fair orchestra.*)

Who isn't there? A beggars' orchestra made up of not too honest profes-
sions. A beggars' Mafia perhaps? Or thieves who stole a theatre out of
nostalgia? Or a nativity play? Or charades? Flimsy wigs, artificial
noses, goatees, philistine glasses, top hats shiny as chamber pots, long
pants; only one of them has garters hanging like a watch chain by his
side. Lighted by the "flower passageway," they go out among the
populace, play on drums, blow on trumpets, and the lights flash all the
colors of the neon signs in Place Pigalle. They blow horns, fray the
nerves of the string basses, raise up fanfares from all four corners.
Waddling like geese, they stop in front of the pseudo trees, where they
begin to play a truly insane brand of Dixieland.)

(Astride a misshapen mare, the Black Pianist rides in—in Harlequin's
arms, lashing him with a whip. Tiny pearls of light flash neons of
musical rhythm. The Black Pianist showers the human horse with blows
when the latter, maltreated mercilessly, falls imploringly on his knees;
Harlequin's white fur coat against the background of the stage; the
Black Pianist beats him in time with the music. Harlequin covers his
face. He twists about ridiculously like a fish out of water. The riding
whip beats out the rhythm on Harlequin—the music of laughter in the
hearts of the populace seeking to be amused. Exit the Black Pianist.)

(Onstage the beaten Harlequin. "Laugh, all of you," the music cries
out. It quiets down. Harlequin gets up. Coughing, he wipes his mouth.
Out of the loudspeakers, whistles and cheers from the auditorium. Har-
lequin waits; the hubbub dies down. Time to begin the juggler's pan-
tomime. He draws near the audience. He makes movements as though
juggling with balls of air. What's happened? Has he really forgotten
what he's supposed to do? Has he gone crazy? Polichinelle watches.
While he's juggling, between gestures, Harlequin begins talking to him-
self; he addresses the audience in a singsong kind of language. Has the
audience really upset him? Has he really got angry, honey? Polichinelle
watches, more and more astounded. This wasn't what was planned for
the performance. In the abstract language of birds of paradise, Har-
lequin tells about his youth. He recalls his great creations! Youth! He
played Hamlet! At the Great Theatre! And here is another role! He
shouts it out in a voice made raspy by old age. He bore the captured
flag triumphantly. His step younger and younger. Springier. Time goes
backward. He sees the public from the period of his youth. He cries out.

*He greets them in a great voice. He thinks: Look! Admire me once
again! I am the way I was before! I'll even sing. Comically, as though
he were about to fly to pieces in a moment, he sings. Perhaps once it was
an aria; now it's hoarse dissonance. He grows silent, even though he
keeps his mouth open all the time. His throat has cracked. With disbelief
he touches his hand; he helplessly attempts to say something in explanation. Time knows no mercy. Harlequin won't sing any more! Frightened, opening his mouth like a fish, he backs out through the curtain of
the street-fair theatre.*

[An act by Harlequin's wife has been omitted.—Ed.]

*(Small stage of the theatre. Backstage. We see the theatre from the rear.
An oval mirror reflects the light and a cheap flower. A ladder; on it, a
carnival head. An empty beer case, bottles, a candle. Upstage, a pink
curtain; on it, the shadow of the Black Pianist beating Harlequin.
Sharply etched shadow of the riding whip comes down slowly on Harlequin. From the other side of the curtain, distant applause, music.
Harlequin in a ridiculous pantomime of weeping. Shuffling, Polichinelle comes running in with a salami and a cigar. Getting edgy, he
peeps through the curtain: isn't it time for Harlequin's exit? Harlequin
weeps. Polichinelle takes the cigar out of his mouth. He gives it to
Harlequin. Harlequin-Clown kisses his hand. Time for Clown-
Harlequin to go on. Polichinelle opens the curtain. The Clown
straightens out his clothes and disappears. Whistles greet him from the
tape recorders.)*

Darkness

"The World Is Not Such a Bad Place . . ." (1968)

by JERZY AFANASJEW

Owing to the fact that visual artists created our theatre, a brightly colored breeze from painting permeated the matter of the theatrical art which we produced. The images in Bim-Bom were canvases which we wished to paint; they were a three-dimensional country from a painter's utopia where visual artists often wander with their thoughts. On the pathway of each of our conceptions there always existed at the beginning a forest of shapes and colors.

Chagall interested us more than Brecht, Utrillo rather than Piscator. *Joy in Earnest* had something like a film script, a conscious organization of movement, sound, and image. Both film close-ups and long shots were played in the window of the stage. Film, and therefore Movement, were the working spotlight of our conceptions. Of course, in the montage of successive images—and also in the montage of external movements—there did not exist the mechanical exaggeration that often dominates ballet or mechanical theatres. The actor was left the flexibility of improvisation; he was allowed to create various colors.

The script of the performance, with its specifications of place and of temporal dimension, determined the architecture of the sculpture of this temporal-spatial show. In a picture created by a painter there exists a conscious line for the eye to follow as it looks. These disquieting stimuli are the motor force for vision's

Translated from Jerzy Afanasjew, "Świat nie jest taki zły . . . ," in *Teatry studenckie w Polsce*, ed. Jerzy Koenig (Warsaw: WAiF, 1968).

leap from form to form, from color to color. Likewise, in Bim-
Bom, a theatre of visual artists, the spectator's fantasy was
guided by the use of all available devices of light and music in
order to condense the most possible into each scenic moment.

The conventional transitions used in the language of film
also had their counterparts in our theatre. Film fade-outs, in-
dicating the end of scenes, were effected by a gradual dimming
of the lights; film dissolves, marking the passage of time, were
achieved by the intersection of planes of light.

The stage was extended toward the rear by opening successive curtains; successive images presented different planes, a
different time, and even a different scale. The proscenium, on
the other hand, was the place for talking with the audience—
the private territory of the theatre where time as it existed in
the auditorium was in operation. We made use of an artificial
horizon, lighting from below, and all possible sound effects.

[Several pages are omitted.]

We wanted to create a circus as sad as the face under the
skin, and at the same time to create a show full of movement,
gags, speed, the pulsation of the world's neon lights, the vibra-
tions of machinery, the accelerated mime of the world seen
with increased speed, a show of lightning-fast smiles and the
grimaces of the day, a show of people, the hum of their conversations, a day whose doings, reduplicated many thousands of
times, make up life. And at the same time silence, pantomime—a mirror, a kind of reflection of life in the water,
where no voice can be heard, but opening mouths are seen
when the time for observation comes.

The world too is a circus under the dome of the sky. Time
with his ruthless whip is its director. Clowns appear in it and
create art; prestidigitators appear in it and some turn out to be
philosophers; there are great sages—who are nothing but tight-
rope walkers; and trained horses often call to mind human beings.

The circus is at the same time the opening exhibit of the
world's variety. It is something fleeting, a kind of reflection, a
gleam in the eye, a bit of rushing shadow, a torn piece of news-

paper read as it flies before one's eyes. An improvisation. Every
novelty is to some extent circus for mortal man.

Instead of churches we have museums. Instead of by an-
achronistic prayers, man is liberated by a movie show. Isn't it
possible that sometime in the future, in the era of robots, museums of modern art (in which a sunbeam will begin to be admired) will be built on the highest heights, and bells will call the
faithful? Isn't it possible that the actor, the clown, will become a
more and more necessary magician for the "African tribe" of
the mechanized? We are governed by television, the theatre,
the newspaper. It is only an illusion that we govern them.

The circus. Unbridled potentiality for intersecting planes of
thought. For breaking with the rules of the classic model pat-
terned after *Sèvres*. Classic beauty shall have to put up with
such innovation. The landscape of a dump is just as good a setting as a palace. Rather than a sword, let's have a broom. It is
not the *arc de triomphe* of a suave theatre of ideas with the
gracious perspective of the Champs Elysées, but something
misshapen, a mongrel, a bastard, a stone chimera from Notre
Dame, which is an angel for poets. For Happy Drunks. For
Lovers. For Artists in jeans. For the Saints of Jazz.

The circus. That's where you can dance Bach on the high
wire, play Chopin on a piano aflame with live flames. The mon-
ster organ of our offices, the typewriter, plays Liszt.

The great operatic overture to the opera *The Factory Seam-
stresses* is played on sewing machines; a tenor mute as a post
thrills the audience by means of a golden speaker planted in his
throat. What does he need a voice for, if it can be dubbed? A
cripple without legs jumps about like a flea. What does he need
legs for if the film can make use of trick shots?

The circus. Some street Picasso in an art student's torn pants
cut up the Mona Lisa and put her back together again as a
marvelously smiling giraffe.

There are no straight lines in nature. There are crooked,
wavy, closed lines. The eyes of nature pulsate uneasily. A clown
is as changeable in his moods as nature is. Abstract in his ir-
regularities. A clown climbs up the ladder of his years. He
works his way up! Death with a scythe awaits him under the

dome. The higher he goes, the more wonderful a light shines on the clown. And on this ladder he writes his poetry to the world and darns his socks. And despite the fact that he sees above him that face without eyes or lips, he says from his height to the audience: "The world is not such a bad place, as long as apple trees blossom." And with a broad gesture he sows seeds on the stage so that peaceful grain and peaceful apple trees can grow. Of course it is all fantasy. But how difficult it is to free one's own hand. How difficult it is to paint a face, to scrape corroded paint off a painting, to squeeze it back into a tube, to weigh it. How difficult it is to do this without spoiling the painting.

[A page is omitted.]

Our "Circus" is not the true circus. It is an étude on circus themes; it is our poetic homage to the art of mimes and comics, an art that we, as young people, have not yet known. The art of gesture and gag. The theatre of which we are disciples is clearly distinct from the question of literature and film, without at the same time keeping us from having our say in all these disciplines individually. A theatre of the kind that our "Circus" represents compels us to take up and study purely visual matters. Drama becomes the composition of faces . . . hands . . . the sculpture of expression.

[Two paragraphs are omitted.]

Literature has devoured the street-fair show, where the actor was also the author. Nowadays the manuscript of one great tragedy reproduced in a hundred thousand copies, translated into all the languages of the world, makes thousands of actors in thousands of theatres experience the same emotions written by one single individual. Instances of original and unique plays scarcely exist. The landscape of the interior world is becoming standardized. In legitimate theatres as well as in movie theatres plays are "shown." Now the actor has only the possibility of interpreting someone else's emotions . . . The actor has become only an ACTOR. The ordering of our lives, the conveniences of contemporary city-dwelling, with a thousand nickel-plated tubes, television, film, make artists turn into petty bourgeois.

They submit passively without realizing that technology is killing their own poetics. The circus has remained a physical theatre. A trained horse will always be a trained horse, and that last careless step will always threaten the dancer on the high wire. It's not true that people are changing. At most, people are only growing up. They will always have fear or laughter in their eyes. Our aim is to make people laugh. By gesture, facial expression, music. So that "Circus" can be an experience for all: the child, the workman, the soldier, and the finicky intellectual and artist. We go about our work keeping in mind the paintings of Breughel the Elder, the silent film, classic literature and music hall, Chaplin, Eisenstein, Pudovkin, and Grock, cabaret and the Proletkult.

Unlike the Wrocław Pantomime Theatre, which made popular visual ballet-like staging, our "Circus" made use of gags. The comic gag, the ludicrousness of the situation, creates what we call the comic. Thus our gag was not only a visual gag—because that would have transferred the meaning of the comic mimodrama into the sphere of artistic ballet-like impressions which would have been closer to the languid and refined *commedia erudita* than to our *commedia dell' arte*. Just as letters create words, so comic gags, strung together appropriately by mime, create comedy.

In literature (Chesterton, Shaw, Twain, Hašek, Čapek) gags make up the ludicrous. Buster Keaton, Chaplin, Grock, Popov are excellent actors, gag painters. If there are various styles in literary language, it is likewise possible to create various styles in pantomime. In pantomime the word does not create; the actor does. The pantomime actor is a swindler of geometry. He is a liar of space. He is a "pure" actor. On his dance depends whether he will succeed in conjuring up before us a nonexistent garden of shapes, in sculpturing and coloring the empty air of the stage. The mime is at the same time the montage maker of time. He sets back or puts into motion stage time, outside whose window the landscape of the mime's storytelling passes by.

V

Tadeusz Różewicz

Birth Rate

The Biography of a Play for the Theatre (1968)

by TADEUSZ RÓŻEWICZ

Today, October 31, 1966, I am on the verge of giving up. I have no desire anymore or the necessary energy; I don't believe in the need of bringing this play to life.

For several weeks now work on this theatre piece has been nothing but rage and frustration. The quantity of notes, clippings, sketches, and scenes, the number of individual elements for the piece grows without any end in sight. But today I faced the greatest obstacle. It's not a question of difficulties of a technical nature; it's something fundamental: I feel that "the times," "the spirit of the times" (I believe in that famous phantom which for us dramatic poets is as real, as stubborn and vengeful as "the ghost of Hamlet's father") . . . and so I feel that "the spirit of the times" now demands serious drama (perhaps tragedy), not comedy. All my ideas of a comic nature suddenly appeared sinful to me. The very act of writing comedy became an act of betrayal and a waste of time. Today I spent long, painful hours in the company of this work of mine—which for many years now has been living and growing within me, in my imagination. The last day of October, 1966. Cold, overcast. Tomorrow is All Saints' Day; Wednesday is All Souls'

Translated by Daniel Gerould from Tadeusz Różewicz, "Przyrost Naturalny," *Dialog*, No. 4 (April, 1968), 97–101. An earlier version of this translation appeared in *Performing Arts Journal*, I, No. 2 (Fall, 1976), © 1976 by Daniel Gerould.

Day—November. And I, an inhabitant of the greatest cemetery in the history of mankind, I am going to keep on writing a "comedy" called *Birth Rate*. Yesterday evening I wrote out the title again in black letters. I explain to myself that I am a "literary man," and therefore I am entitled to write not only serious drama, but also comedies and humorous sketches.

Forms must have a certain amount of free space around them if they are to exist and have the possibility of developing. It can be silence. In my play *Birth Rate* the problem is how to handle a living, growing mass of mankind which, due to lack of space, destroys all forms and cannot be "bottled up." In Act III the walls burst and a torrent of people pour through the cracks. The very process of bursting, the crumbling of the walls, is the "action." Whereas voices and words have nothing to do with the action.

I think that this is the first time since I started writing plays for the theatre that I have felt such an overpowering need to talk with the director, designer, composer, actors . . . with the whole theatre. But I am (here and now) alone. I feel the necessity of immediate contact with those people while I'm in the process of writing. I could actually begin the rehearsals for the piece right now. I'd gladly forego the full literary text of the play for a scenario. But I'm alone and I'm compelled to write a literary work, to describe what would be easier to *transmit* in direct contact with living people. I do not have my "own" theatre or director. Perhaps in a few years a director will turn up quite by chance who will want to work on my play, and I will be invited to the "world premiere." I have been putting off writing this play for a very long time. I began it in 1958 at almost the same time as *The Card File*. Actually I didn't "put it off," but I couldn't bring myself to set down and describe what already existed in my imagination—in a changeable, but real shape. Which kept growing. I couldn't make up my mind to pick up my fountain-pen/pruning-shears, to start lopping off images and ideas and get down to the sad task of describing the piece (sad and a bit tiresome). Discouraged by the knowledge that it would be preferable to improvise it all with a theatre group, I repeatedly broke off all attempts at writing it down. Only when I clearly realized that I was exclusively condemned to writing things down, did I set about writing this play. (I still don't know whether to limit myself solely to the literary text of the play, or to describe the "history" of the piece, to give its biography.)

In the earliest version, the play was to take place (happen) in a conventionalized train compartment or streetcar into which people keep crowding. It was to be an interior arranged like a train compartment. When the curtain rises, the compartment is empty. A young man enters the compartment; he sits down in a relaxed fashion; he can even stretch out on one of the seats. Next a young woman enters the compartment. They strike up a conversation, which turns into a flirtation and mutual attraction. During the course of the play people keep crowding into the closed interior. Individually or in pairs. At first the forms of civilized behavior prevail. Forms in the broadest sense of the term. The space allows for the preservation of forms, or in other words, civilized (polite) relationships. But people constantly keep crowding in. Now there is no more room on the seats. People are sitting shoulder to shoulder. Still they keep coming in. Old men, women, and children. Sportsmen, pregnant women. People climb onto the racks intended for the baggage. They stand in the aisles. But they still offer apologies, still get indignant, still hold their children up high above their heads. Nonetheless, the forms are changing. Before our very eyes they undergo a frightening metamorphosis produced by lack of space. The ones sitting inside have as their chief goal trying to shut the door. A High Priest enters with a majestic step. He utters a series of platitudes, offers blessings, pats little children on the head; knocked to the floor and then thrown into a hanging baggage net close to the ceiling, he babbles on in an unctuous voice about the dignity of motherhood, the "rhythm method," and the sinfulness of contraceptive devices. Pregnant women tell about their troubles with their husbands, while others go to take the cure at spas, in despair at their infertility. All the while the pressure mounts from the inside, the walls start to buckle. The living mass is so tightly packed together that it begins to boil over. There are two or three explosions in close succession. Movement blends with shouting.

Finally everything comes to a standstill. Out of the mass the young people come forward in silence. They sit down beside one another and start to flirt and exert mutual attraction. In the stillness their voices suggest the billing and cooing of pigeons.

That was my vision of the play, based solely on movement, on the growth of a living mass. The dialogue was to occur only at certain moments and constitute particular phases of the process that was taking place within a closed space.

In the course of the years I collected clippings from newspapers, I assembled extracts from brochures and books, I carried on a correspondence with a specialist on demography, a schoolmate of mine from high school who became one of the world's leading authorities on the subject.

The development of this theatre piece of mine proceeded, as it were, on two levels. On the one hand, my imagination went on producing and accumulating new "images," while on the other hand the "documentation" grew as information kept piling up. In the course of the years since this idea first occurred to me, certain images have receded or quite simply vanished without a trace, since they had not been recorded in written form. In any case, the same thing happened to the clippings and notes, some of which disappeared, some of which are lying in mounds of papers, and only some of which have been preserved until today, until the moment of realization. Of course in the realm of the play (drama), the thing developed from image to image, but those images grew on a heap of notes and news items, on the journalistic and statistical manure from which the images extracted their nourishment (information).

If I had written down all those images and all that information, a book amounting to about 300 pages of manuscript would have resulted. What struck me most of all was the inaccuracy of all the statistical data. And so for years on end there coexisted within me images and statistical data. One of the articles bore the title: "5,000 Infants Born Every Hour." The article appeared several years ago in the British journal *Forward* and was based on data in the United Nations *Demographic Yearbook*. Of course, in translating this data for "theatrical" use, I sketched out the following images: Babes lie on tiered wagons arranged in rows like rolls in a bakery. Nurses push the carriages or go around in circles with a load of children, but the circling around goes faster and faster. This image of the (so to speak) conveyer belt grew out of the image of a production line, a conveyer belt in a mine, or certain paintings depicting heaven and hell as imagined by artists of the fifteenth and sixteenth centuries—where angels and devils transport whole armfuls of souls, saved or damned, to their appointed places.

Another image that I wanted to include was a cellar in which there were women-vessels. I imagined it as a scientist's laboratory, vaulted like a cellar, where women-vessels stand in rows in the shape of amphoras, jugs . . . The scientist would go from vessel to vessel, look into them . . . His tour was to be interspersed with soliloquy and dialogue. The women—living beings—were to be speaking vessels. For example, one of these "Vessels" says to the Scientist-Hermit:

> strike me
> with your stick
> touch me
> plant your branch
> in my anthill
> and life will gush forth

However, I had got that numerical data concerning the birth rate permanently under my skin. The scene in the "chastity belt" workshop, the scene in the "cell," and the scene in the "hermitage" serve only to establish the atmosphere for the explosion of the "population" bomb, which is the central and decisive scene in the piece.

The conversation between the scientist (a pseudo schizophrenic) and the pseudo nurse takes place in isolation from the external world. Nevertheless, there is a feeling of apprehension that behind the walls of the "bunker" another world is growing, bubbling, and multiplying, and this feeling penetrates with telling impact into the isolated "bunker."

Questions of celibacy, virginity, the pill, the rhythm method—all of this must somehow be reckoned with in the piece. The scope of my readings was wide, and at the moment it would be difficult to mention all the items that I "absorbed" in the course of gathering material. Thus there are quotations from the writings of Saint Jerome which were to be used in the conversations between the hermit and the women (vessels of sin); there are popular pamphlets published by the Planned Parenthood Association; there are also technical handbooks, memoirs, marriage manuals, etc., etc. One of the first drafts of *Birth Rate* started with the "Ballad about the Vessel." Naturally it was on the subject of woman (vessel of sin). The notes from the Church Fathers come from this time too. These notes were arranged in a certain order which was finally to take the form of the "Ballad about the Vessel":

> how long have we borne this treasure
> in our clay vessels
> (I have no oil)
> take a hand mill and grind the flour
> lay bare your shame
> reveal your legs
> plunge through those rivers
>
> the belly is god
> in the thighs his might (the devil's)
> and his strength in the navel
>
> sad to tell
> how many virgins fall each day
> how many nests become the dwelling place
> of that proud foe
> and how many rocks are hollowed by the snake
> who then abides in their crevices . . .

(The image of a snake/satan who hollows out rock/virgins and lives in their crevices acquired an ambiguous richness of meaning for me.) A crucial matter was the question of "warmth," that "warmth" without which there is no love. That warmth which is generated by bodies coming together and rubbing against one another. I was violently assailed by the image of a hermit (perhaps Robinson Crusoe—or some other castaway) who lights a fire by the circular movement of a wheel or with flint and tinder.

The question of "warmth," about which certain aesthetes (enemies of the human species) are given to saying that it is "cow-

like" warmth, was (and is) one of the chief problems of my play
Birth Rate. We see how it gets warmer and warmer in the closed
space. People produce warmth. This whole living mass is somehow warmed up.

January 11, 1967

> And besides, in life people do not constantly shoot each
> other, hang themselves, or make proposals of marriage. And
> they don't constantly talk cleverly. Most of the time they eat,
> drink, flirt, talk foolishly. So this is what needs to be shown
> on the stage too. A play should be written in which people
> come and go, eat dinner, talk about the weather, play whist.
> . . . Everything on the stage should be exactly as compli-
> cated and at the same time exactly as simple as in life. People
> eat dinner, they simply eat dinner, and at that very moment
> their happiness comes into being or their life falls to
> pieces . . .

I do not hesitate to use these remarks of Chekhov's for my
own purposes. I hope to have them justify my own "comedies" and "so-called comedies." Once more I'm overcome
by doubts. I cannot write in this "mode" any longer. The contemporary comic writer is a clown who wades in pools of blood,
in rivers of blood which inundate him from many parts of the
world. I do not intend to conceal the difficulties. For several
months I have not been able to arrive at the unique shape, the
true form of this play. I scratch my tongue and bang my legs
against jokes.

> The darkness outside the window
> the menacing darkness

Bizarre news out of China—reaching us here by means of
the radio. I put the play aside once again and went back to
reading newspapers and books. Finally . . . (but it's not important). I feel that I'm steering the thing in the wrong direction.
Or perhaps I am being steered and pushed in the wrong direction by the "thing"? When I lie in the dark with my eyes open, I
have the feeling (I feel) that this particular piece of writing is
like the fact of dying deprived of any meaning. Why does my
first idea—pure and sharp—start to be covered with a fool's cap

and bells? Cancerous tumors are growing on the organism of
the play. I am becoming just a tool in the course of the writing
. . . And I do not want that . . . A cursed dilemma.

January 13, 1967
    Yesterday I was not able to work out anything new for this
play. From morning on I escaped by reading the newspapers. I
read Chesterton (he has become horribly dated), I corrected
my abortive poetry, I read Porębski's *Cubism,* I wrote some letters, I went to "The Heather," I listened to the radio: the situation in China, the President's address to the American Congress, the war in Vietnam, the death of Zbigniew Cybulski. In
the evening I looked at illustrated magazines from 1966. I
watched Cobra on TV; I wished that I were with the people
downstairs in the "club room." I went back to listening to the
radio again. At midnight: a soliloquy. I reproach myself for
becoming addicted to writing poetry. I get up. I turn on the
light. I go back to writing the play. I look over my notes from
1966: a drama "without an ending." I don't want this play "to
end." The critics don't see anything. They don't see the basic
differences: the plays of ABCDMYZ and even the plays of
Witkacy and Gombrowicz have an "ending." My plays have no
ending. That is one of the fundamental differences. Persuaded—sometimes I let myself be persuaded—by theatre
managers or directors, I tacked on some kind of ending just to
keep the peace. For example, in *The Laocoon Group* and *Spa-
ghetti and Sword.* Another matter: a problem that keeps me
from sleeping. Time. Just what does this cursed time do in a
play? The themes of my plays do not develop through time, so
the action does not "develop" either. That is the problem! If a
play is to be written—and not some documentary montage,
newspaper reports, court records (dramatized?). Not political
treatises, sketches of manners and morals! Nor the Eichmann
affair, Pius XII, the Rosenbergs, Oppenheimer, Stalin, Chur-
chill. The latest trials, wars, international incidents, generals'
memoirs, letters . . . all that can always be counted on to interest theatre managers, critics, and audiences . . . but these are
secondary matters for the art of the drama. The new art of the
drama—after Witkacy and Beckett—must start from the prob-

lem of a new technique for writing plays, not a "sensational" topic . . . it's possible to show the impotence of Caesar, or of Rudolph Valentino, the Deputy in slippers on a hobby horse, Bormann playing the flute, a revolution in an insane asylum . . . it's possible to paste together the history of the murder in Dallas with a cheap "literary" commentary . . . it's possible to do many different things. But all that is barren journalistic labor. All that lugging the spectator into various true events which have nothing to do with the art of the drama. For me the problem is not the "beginning," "middle," and supposed "end" of a drama, but the duration of a certain situation. I divide theatre into two kinds, into "exterior theatre" (the most important thing in this theatre is the action, what happens on the stage, and this is classical theatre and even romantic theatre) which goes up to contemporary theatre, up to Dürrenmatt and Witkacy; in Beckett for the first time we are witnesses not only to the apparent action, but also to the disintegration of this action on the stage . . . in Beckett this disintegration is the action. To define this more exactly: the "exterior" theatre has already become a "historical" theatre, a theatre whose evolution has come to an end—I'm not talking about the interpretation of those texts by directors and critics. Thus I divide theatre into "exterior" theatre and "interior" theatre. To arrive at this "interior" theatre I have followed the traces and signs left by Dostoevsky, Chekhov, and Conrad . . . What happens in Chekhov's dramas is secondary; it is not the "plots" or their "denouements" that we always remember, but their "climate"; we feel, with all our senses, their atmosphere, the emptiness between events, the silence between words, the sense of expectation. In Chekhov, motionlessness, not motion, is the essence of the play (performance). A great deal has been written and said on the subject of that gun hanging on the wall in the first act . . . which must be fired in the last act . . . a number of superficial theories have been based on it, always citing Chekhov . . . So the gun must be fired in the last act? And what if it's not? They quote that statement, but why not quote less striking truths which Chekhov also enunciated? Less striking, but more important for his own plays and quite possibly for the art of the drama in our times as well. "Most of the time they eat, drink, flirt, talk foolishly . . . People eat dinner, they simply eat dinner, and at that very moment . . ."

How often between the words spoken by the "heroes" of his plays we find the phrase "a moment of silence." And how heavily these "moments of silence" weigh in Chekhov. For me, almost as much as all the words said in the drama itself. Moments of silence between words, between events . . . often build and push forward the "action" of the drama. What counts is what these "moments of silence" are filled with, what they are filled with by the "heroes" of his plays, by the author, and by the spectator-listeners. More than a hundred years have passed since Chekhov's birth. The "moments of silence" were filled with the life and expectations of his generation. In our plays and in our dramas the moments of silence are, and must be, filled with different thoughts, with different experiences, with different memories, with different hopes and different fears. In my plays the moments of silence are filled with the thoughts of an anonymous inhabitant of a big city, a nameless figure living in a metropolis, a faceless human being whose life has unfolded between the gigantic necropolis and the constantly growing polis. The poet and the polis? The poet and the necropolis?

In the final scene of *The Cherry Orchard,* Anna exclaims: "Farewell, old life." And Trofimov answers her: "Welcome, new life!" And here lies the meaning of Chekhov's creative spirit, his theatre, his comedies. And how about our "heroes"? Let's consider what the "heroes" of Beckett, Dürrenmatt, Hochhuth, Weiss, Mrożek, Pinter, and Albee say "Farewell" and "Welcome" to. And what do the "heroes" of Witkacy, Ionesco, and Gombrowicz say "Welcome" and "Farewell" to? And do the "heroes" of Sartre, Camus, and Genet have the courage to exclaim "with a pure heart," "Welcome, new life"?

In one of the favorite books of my "youth under the Nazi occupation"—in Conrad's *Lord Jim*—there is a scene which for me is "the heart of darkness" of that great epic about honor, betrayal, cowardice, and love.

"Anyhow, a dog there was, weaving himself in and out amongst people's legs in that mute, stealthy way native dogs have, and my companion stumbled over him. The dog leaps away without a sound; the man, raising his voice a little, said with a slow laugh, 'Look at that wretched cur,' and directly afterwards we became separated by a lot of people pushing in. I stood back for a moment against the wall while the stranger managed to get down the steps and disappeared. I saw Jim spin round. He made a step forward and barred my way. We were alone; he glared at me with an air of stubborn resolution. . . . The dog, in the very act of trying to sneak in at the door, sat down hurriedly to hunt for fleas.

" 'Did you speak to me?' asked Jim very low."

Despite the romantic gesture at the moment of death, despite the splendid battle, despite the tragic love affair, for me Jim's true drama took place in a rather shabby, tawdry setting filled with the hubbub of the courtroom . . . In a passageway. In a corridor. Someone yelled at a mangy dog, at a mangy stray dog which was really there . . . But Jim thought that it was said about him. " 'Did you speak to me?' asked Jim very low." For me this is the most tragic moment in Lord Jim's life. The whole drama of his life is contained in this episode. In it, in this scene there are elements of the "interior" theatre about which I have been thinking and talking.

Bibliography

GENERAL WORKS

Błoński, Jan. "Les Nouveaux Auteurs." Tr. Gilberte Crépy and Zygmunt Szymański. *Dialog*, Special French-Language Issue, VIII (June, 1963), 133–141.

Brockett, Oscar G., and Robert R. Findlay. *Century of Innovation: A History of European and American Theatre and Drama since 1870*. Englewood Cliffs, N.J.: Prentice-Hall, 1973.

Csató, Edward. *The Polish Theater*. Tr. Christina Cenkalska. Warsaw: Polonia Publishing House, 1963.

Czanerle, Maria. *Wycieczki w dwudziestolecie: O dramacie międzywojennym*. Warsaw: P.I.W., 1970.

Esslin, Martin. *The Theatre of the Absurd*. Rev. ed. Garden City, N.Y.: Doubleday, 1969.

Falkiewicz, Andrzej. "Problematyka 'Ślubu' Gombrowicza." *Dialog*, No. 2 (1959), 77–94.

Filler, Witold. *Na Lewym torze: Teatr Witolda Wandurskiego*. Warsaw: P.I.W., 1967.

——. "The Poet and the Theatre." *Le Théâtre en Pologne/The Theatre in Poland*, Nos. 10–11 (1967), 61–64.

Gerould, Daniel C. "The Non-Euclidean Drama: Modern Theatre in Poland." *First Stage*, (Winter, 1965–1966), 206–211.

Greń, Zygmunt. *Rok 1900: Szkice o dramacie zapomnianym*. Cracow: Wydawnictwo Literackie, 1968.

Grodzicki, August. "Un Aperçu historique." Tr. Gilberte Crépy and Zygmunt Szymański. *Dialog*, Special French-Language Issue, VIII (June, 1963), 125–132.

Grzymała-Siedlecki, Adam. *Na orbicie Melpomeny*. Warsaw: WAiF, 1966.

Hutnikiewicz, Artur. *Od czystej formy do literatury faktu*. Toruń: T.N.T., 1965.

Jastrzębski, Zdzisław. *Literatura pokolenia wojennego wobec dwudziestolecia*. Warsaw: P.I.W., 1969.

Karwacka, Helena. *Witold Wandurski*. Łódź: Wydawnictwo Łódzkie, 1968.

Kelera, Józef. *Takie były zabawy, spory w one lata: Szkice i felietony teatralne, 1968–1972*. Wrocław: Ossolineum, 1974.

Kłossowicz, Jan. "Avant-garde Drama in the Twenty-Year Inter-war Period." *Le Théâtre en Pologne/The Theatre in Poland*, Nos. 7–8 (1965), 33–38.

———. "From Romanticism to Avant-Garde." *Dialog*, Special English-Language Issue, 1970, pp. 115–128.

———. "Polscy ekspresjoniści." *Dialog*, No. 7 (1960), 112–125.

———. "Próby dramatyczne awangardy dwudziestolecia." *Dialog*, No. 3 (1960), 97–109.

———. "Profile teatralne." *Dialog*, No. 11 (1967), 125–133.

Kott, Jan. "Introduction: Face and Grimace." In Witold Gombrowicz, *The Marriage*. Tr. Louis Iribarne. New York: Grove Press, 1969.

———. *Theatre Notebook, 1947–1967*. Tr. Bolesław Taborski. Garden City, N.Y.: Doubleday, 1968.

Kridl, Manfred. *A Survey of Polish Literature and Culture*. Tr. Olga Sherer-Virski. New York: Columbia University Press, 1956.

Kudliński, Tadeusz. *Rodowód Polskiego Teatru*. Warsaw: Pax, 1972.

Lasota, Grzegorz. "Wandurski." *Dialog*, No. 9 (1958), 105–110.

Lau, Jerzy. *Teatr Artystów: "Cricot."* Cracow: Wydawnictwo Literackie, 1967.

Łempicka, Aniela. "Nowy teatr 'Wyzwolenia.' " *Dialog*, No. 6 (1969), 123–133.

Marczak-Oborski, Stanisław. "Artistic Trends in the Polish Theatre, 1918–1939." *Le Théâtre en Pologne/The Theatre in Poland*, Nos. 5–6 (1969), 3–9.

———. *Teatr czasu wojny: Polskie życie teatralne w latach II wojny światowej. 1939–1945*. Warsaw: P.I.W., 1967.

———. *Życie teatralne w latach, 1944–1964*. Warsaw: P.W.N., 1968.

Miłosz, Czesław. *The History of Polish Literature*. New York: Macmillan, 1969.

Natanson, Wojciech. *Stanisław Wyspiański*. Poznań: Wydawnictwo Poznańskie, 1969.

Pamiętnik Teatralny, Nos. 3–4 (1957). Special Wyspiański Issue.

Piwińska, Marta. "Przed 'Kartoteką' i 'Tangiem.' " *Dialog*, No. 11 (1967), 81–108.

Przybylska, Krystyna. "The Modern Polish Theatre." *Queens Slavic Papers*, I (1973), 68–79.

Ratajczak, Józef. "Co jest 'Skoro go nie ma?' " *Dialog*, No. 10 (1970), 79–94.

Reychman, Jan. *Peleryna, ciupaga i znak tajemny.* Cracow: Wydawnictwo Literackie, 1971.

Schiller, Leon. "The New Theatre in Poland: Stanisław Wyspiański." *The Mask*, II (1908–1910); rpt. New York: Benjamin Blom, 1966. Pp. 11–27, 57–75.

Segel, Harold B. "Poland." In *The Reader's Encyclopedia of World Drama.* Ed. John Gassner and Edward Quinn. New York: Crowell, 1969. Pp. 664–674.

Sivert, Tadeusz, and Roman Taborski, eds. *Polska Myśl Teatralna i Filmowa.* Warsaw: Państwowe Wydawnictwo Naukowe, 1971.

Skwarczyńska, Stefania. " 'Chocholi taniec' jako obraz-symbol w literaturze ostatniego trzydziestolecia." *Dialog*, No. 8 (1969), 99–119.

Sławińska, Irena, and Stefan Kruk, eds. *Myśl teatralna Młodej Polski.* Warsaw: WAiF, 1966.

Szydłowski, Roman. *The Theatre in Poland.* Warsaw: Interpress Publishers, 1972.

Taborski, Bolesław. "Gombrowicz" and "Poland." In Michael Anderson et al., *Crowell's Handbook of Contemporary Drama.* New York: Crowell, 1971. Pp. 186–188; 359–371.

Temkine, Raymonde. *Grotowski.* Tr. Alex Szogyi. New York: Avon, 1972.

Terlecki, Tymon. "Polish Drama and European Theatre." *Drama Critique*, X (Winter, 1967), 30–38.

——. "Polish Historical Antecedents of Surrealism in Drama." *Zagadnienia Rodzajów Literackich*, XVI, No. 2 (1973), 35–50.

Tulane Drama Review, XI (Spring, 1967). Eastern European Drama Issue.

Wodnar, Estera and Mieczysław, eds. *Polskie sceny robotnicze 1918–1939: Wybór dokumentów i relacji.* Warsaw: P.I.W., 1974.

Wróblewska, Teresa. "Kniaź Patiomkin: Antynomie rewolucji." *Dialog*, No. 3 (1968), 79–103.

——. "Post Scriptum do 'Romansu siedmiu braci śpiących w Chinach.' " *Dialog*, No. 4 (1968), 151–152.

Zabicki, Zbigniew. "Wandurski—człowiek 'Wielkiej reformy.' " *Dialog*, No. 7 (1969), 122–134.

Zaworska, Helena. *O nową sztukę: Polskie programy artystyczne lat 1917–1922.* Warsaw: P.I.W., 1963.

JERZY AFANASJEW

Afanasjew, Jerzy. *Sezon kolorowych chmur: Gdańskie teatry eksperymentalne.* Gdynia: Wydawnictwo Morskie, 1968.

——. "Świat nie jest taki zły . . ." In *Teatry studenckie w Polsce*. Ed. Jerzy Koenig. Warsaw: WAiF, 1968.

Gerould, Daniel. "Bim-Bom and the Afanasjew Family Circus." *The Drama Review*, XVIII (March, 1974), 99–103.

KONSTANTY ILDEFONS GAŁCZYŃSKI

Błoński, Jan. "Pozytywny ekscentryk, czyli o 'Zielonej gęsi.' " *Dialog*, No. 4 (1959), 99–106.

Drawicz, Andrzej. *Konstanty Ildefons Gałczyński*. Warsaw: Wiedza Powszechna, 1968.

Gerould, Dan. "From a Theatre Journal, Paris, Prague, Warsaw: European Influences." In *Breakout!* Ed. James Schevill. Chicago: Swallow, 1973. Pp. 227–231.

Wyka, Marta. *Gałczyński a wzory literackie*. Warsaw: P.I.W., 1970.

SŁAWOMIR MROŻEK

Drama at Calgary, III, No. 3 (1969). Special Mrożek Issue.

Galassi, Frank. "The Absurdist Vision of Sławomir Mrożek's *Striptease*." *The Polish Review*, XVII (Summer, 1972), 74–79.

Kott, Jan. "Mrożek's Family." *Encounter*, XXV (December, 1965), 54–58.

Taborski, Bolesław. "Mrożek." In Michael Anderson et al., *Crowell's Handbook of Contemporary Drama*. New York: Crowell, 1971. Pp. 319–321.

Tarn, Adam. "Plays." *Polish Perspectives*, VIII (October, 1965), 6–7, 10–11.

TADEUSZ RÓŻEWICZ

Fik, Marta. "Teatr Tadeusza Różewicza." *Pamiętnik Teatralny*, No. 1 (89) (1974), 3–16.

Łukasiewicz, Jacek. "The Poetry of Tadeusz Różewicz." *Polish Perspectives*, (August–September, 1967), 65–71.

Piwińska, Marta. "Różewicz, romantyzm, awangarda." *Dialog*, No. 7 (1969), 109–121.

Taborski, Bolesław. "Różewicz." In Michael Anderson et al., *Crowell's Handbook of Contemporary Drama*. New York: Crowell, 1971. Pp. 386–387.

Wyka, Kazimierz. "Problem zamiennika gatunkowego w pisarstwie Różewicza." *Teksty*, No. 1 (19) (1975), 53–71.

ANDRZEJ TRZEBIŃSKI

Bartelski, Lesław M. *Genealogia ocalonych: Szkice o latach 1939–1944*. Cracow: Wydawnictwo Literackie, 1969.

Jastrzębski, Zdzisław. *Bez wieńca i togi*. Warsaw: P.A.X., 1967.

Piwińska, Marta. "Witkacy w 'Laboratorium dramatu' Trzebińskiego." In *Studia o Stanisławie Ignacym Witkiewiczu*. Ed. Marian Głowiński and Janusz Sławiński. Wrocław: Ossolineum, 1972. Pp. 139–161.

STANISŁAW IGNACY WITKIEWICZ

Błoński, Jan. "Powrót Witkacego." *Dialog*, No. 9 (1963), p. 71–84.

——. "Teatr Witkiewicza: Forma formy." *Dialog*, No. 12 (1967), 69–83.

——. "U źródeł teatru Witkacego." *Dialog*, No. 5 (1970), 81–90.

——. "Wstęp." In Stanisław Ignacy Witkiewicz, *Wybór Dramatów*. Biblioteka Narodowa. Wrocław: Zakład Narodowy im. Ossolińskich, 1974.

Degler, Janusz. "Witkacego Podróż do Tropików." *Literatura Ludowa*, No. 3 (1974), 19–28.

——. *Witkacy w teatrze międzywojennym*. Warsaw: WAiF, 1973.

Dukore, Bernard F. "Spherical Tragedies and Comedies with Corpses: Witkacian Tragicomedy." *Modern Drama*, XVIII (September, 1975), 291–315.

Esslin, Martin. "The Search for the Metaphysical Dimension in Drama." In Stanisław Witkiewicz, *Tropical Madness*. New York: Winter House, 1972, Pp. 1–4.

Folejewski, Zbigniew. "The Theatre of Ruthless Metaphor: Polish Theatre between Marxism and Existentialism." *Comparative Drama*, III (Fall, 1969), 176–183.

Gerould, Daniel C. "A-Causality and the Strangeness of Existence in the Theatre of Witkiewicz." *Dada/Surrealism*, Special Film and Theatre Issue, 1973, pp. 36–41.

——. "Discovery of Witkiewicz." *Arts in Society*, VIII (Fall–Winter, 1971), 652–656.

——. "The Playwright as Child: The Witkiewicz Childhood Plays." *yale/ theatre*, V, No. 3 (1974), 6–9.

——. "Witkacy." In Stanisław Witkiewicz, *Tropical Madness*. New York: Winter House, 1972. Pp. 239–259.

——. "Witkacy on the American Stage." *Polish Perspectives*, XV (September, 1972), 72–82.

—— and C. S. Durer. Introduction. In Stanisław Ignacy Witkiewicz, *The Madman and the Nun*. Seattle: University of Washington Press, 1968. Pp. xxiii–liii.

Grabowski, Zbigniew. "S. I. Witkiewicz: A Polish Prophet of Doom." *The Polish Review*, XII (Winter, 1967), 39–49.

Iribarne, Louis. Introduction. In Stanisław Ignacy Witkiewicz, *Insatiability: A Novel in Two Parts*. Urbana: University of Illinois Press, 1976.

Kott, Jan. Foreword. In Stanisław Ignacy Witkiewicz, *The Madman and the Nun.* Tr. Bogdana Carpenter. Seattle: University of Washington Press, 1968. Pp. vii–xvii.

Kotarbiński, Tadeusz, and Jerzy Eugeniusz Płomieński, eds. *Stanisław Ignacy Witkiewicz: Człowiek i twórca. Księga pamiątkowa.* Warsaw: P.I.W., 1957.

Krzyżanowski, Jerzy R. "Witkiewicz's Anthroponomy." *Comparative Drama,* III (Fall, 1969), 193–198.

Micińska, Anna. Introduction. *622 upadki Bunga czyli Demoniczna kobieta.* Warsaw: P.I.W., 1972. Pp. 5–46.

——. "Na marginesie 'Narkotyków' i 'Niemytych Dusz' St. I. Witkiewicza." *Twórczość,* No. 11 (1974), 30–47.

Miciński, Bolesław. "Stanisław Ignacy Witkiewicz (Witkacy)—Plan Odczytu." In *Pisma.* Cracow: Znak, 1970. Pp. 197–200.

Miłosz, Czesław. "The Pill of Murti-Bing." In *The Captive Mind.* New York: Knopf, 1953. Pp. 3–24.

——. "S. I. Witkiewicz, a Polish Writer for Today." *Tri-Quarterly,* No. 9 (Spring, 1969), 143–154.

——. "Stanisław Ignacy Witkiewicz." In *The History of Polish Literature.* New York: Macmillan, 1969. Pp. 414–420.

Pamiętnik Teatralny, No. 3 (1969); Nos. 3–4 (1971), 466–527. Special Witkiewicz Issues.

The Polish Review, XVIII, Nos. 1–2 (1973). Special Witkiewicz Issue.

Pomian, Krzysztof. "Witkacy: Philosophy and Art." *Polish Perspectives,* XIII (September, 1970), 22–32.

Puzyna, Konstanty. "The Prism of the Absurd." *Polish Perspectives,* VI (June, 1963), 34–44.

——. "Witkacy." In Stanisław Ignacy Witkiewicz, *Dramaty.* Vol. I. 2d ed. Warsaw: P.I.W., 1972. Pp. 5–46.

Rudzińska, Kamila. *Artysta wobec kultury: Dwa typy autorefleksji literackiej: Ekspresjoniści 'Zdroju' i Witkacy.* Wrocław: Ossolineum, 1973.

Sokół, Lech. *Groteska w teatrze Stanisława Ignacego Witkiewicza.* Wrocław: Ossolineum, 1973.

——. "Witkacy in World Theatre, I: On European Stages." *Le Théâtre en Pologne/The Theatre in Poland,* No. 1 (January, 1974), 16–20.

——. "Witkacy in World Theatre, II: In America." *Le Théâtre en Pologne/The Theatre in Poland,* No. 2 (February, 1974), 26–29.

Studia o Stanisławie Ignacym Witkiewiczu. Ed. Marian Głowiński and Janusz Sławiński. Wrocław: Ossolineum, 1972.

Szpakowska, Małgorzata. "Filozofia społeczna Stanisława Ignacego Witkiewicza." *Twórczość,* No. 11 (1974), 48–71.

——. "Witkiewiczowska teoria kultury." *Dialog,* No. 10 (1968), 104–128.

Taborski, Bolesław. "Stanisław Ignacy Witkiewicz." In Michael Anderson et al., *Crowell's Handbook of Contemporary Drama*. New York: Crowell, 1971. Pp. 491–493.

Tarn, Adam. "Witkiewicz, Artaud and the Theatre of Cruelty." *Comparative Drama*, III (Fall, 1969), 162–168.

Le Théâtre en Pologne/The Theatre in Poland, No. 3 (1970). Special Witkiewicz Issue.

Wirth, Andrzej. "Brecht and Witkiewicz: Two Concepts of Revolution in Drama of the Twenties." *Comparative Drama*, III (Fall, 1969), 198–209.

Witkiewicz, Stanisław. *Listy do syna*. Ed. Bożena Danek-Wojnowska and Anna Micińska. Warsaw: P.I.W., 1969.

*Twentieth-Century Polish
Avant-Garde Drama*

Designed by R. E. Rosenbaum.
Composed by Vail-Ballou Press, Inc.,
in 10 point VIP Baskerville, 2 points leaded,
with display lines in Palatino.
Printed offset by Vail-Ballou Press
Warren's No. 66 text, 50 pound basis.
Bound by Vail-Ballou Press
in Joanna book cloth
and stamped in All Purpose foil.

Library of Congress Cataloging in Publication Data
(For library cataloging purposes only)

Main entry under title:
Twentieth-century Polish avant-garde drama.

  Bibliography: p.
  CONTENTS: Witkiewicz, S. I. The anonymous work: four acts of a rather
nasty nightmare.—Witkiewicz, S. I. A few words about the role of the actor in
the theatre of pure form.—Trzebinski, A. To pick up the rose. [etc.]
  1. Polish drama—20th century—Translations into English. 2. English
drama—Translations from Polish. 3. Experimental theater—Addresses, es-
says, lectures. I. Witkiewicz, Stanisław Ignacy, 1885–1939. II. Gerould,
Daniel Charles, 1928–
PG7445.E5T9   891.8'5'2708   76-13659
ISBN 0-8014-0952-7